"Brilliant! It made me (
and educated me all in o
be read by every woman.'

Tammy Rosales, Wife, Mother, Survivor, US

"This book is astounding. It is an INVALUABLE tool for any woman. What I especially like is that Anna writes about the early stages of the seduction as well as what happens once the woman is in the trap. This book is written from direct experience, and it shows. A MUST READ for anyone who is confused about why their relationship doesn't feel good, and for others who wonder if their loved one is in a bad relationship, but don't want to interfere. This lack of interference is just what the abuser relies on. Read and take note!!!!"

Elaine Palmer, MBA, PhD,
Mother of an Abused Woman, NZ

"I truly stumbled across this gem of a book and know that the completion of reading it was the start of my healing process. [It] has given me hope that I CAN and WILL heal...."

Brittany Baird, Survivor, US

"The last thing I expected was to be **uplifted** by a book on this subject, but I was. We can only imagine what Ms Moss went through because she doesn't tell us. Instead, she has sifted her experience to produce a map to keep us safe on the sometimes rocky road of relationships. A **valuable** work of **uncommon insight** and **great compassion**."

Smith Varner, Attorney, Survivor, US

"This information could save untold private suffering and public resources."

N C Jules, Security Executive, US

"An **easy-to-read** guide ... Behaviors and warning signs are described in all their guises and in detail. Resources are offered for **moving forward** to **reclaim the joy of living**. An **informative, satisfying** and **deeply helpful** book for thinking people."

Rita Davenport, Media Personality, US

"**Very thought-provoking and comprehensive.** Provides the reader with detailed behaviors that can be utilized to assess relationship dynamics. Appropriate for individuals assessing their personal relationships and professionals providing case management or therapeutic services."

Angela R Ausbrooks, PhD, LMSW, Texas State University, US

"**A hand up to the abused and a wake-up call to all.**"

Father of an Abused Woman, Name and Location Withheld

"The deception behind all abuse and control is ugly and yet it is ubiquitous. It happens every day. It must stop. Women need to educate themselves about this issue. This book is **ESSENTIAL** reading."

Jody Petersen, Silversmith, Survivor, US

"The warning signs of abuse revealed by an unflinching look back at a savage marriage. The dots she connects between early childhood experience and adult pathology should give us all pause. If every reader took this information to heart, we could waken to a better society in this lifetime."

Jayne Layne, MFA, Artist, Survivor, US

"A safety manual for thinking people. Not melodrama or soap opera, but real facts from real life. Logic and reason do not apply in the world of abuse—it IS like being on another planet. I wish this had been written long ago. It would have spared me. But it still gives solace and understanding, even now. A must read."

"**Gripping!** I wish I had had access to this information before my marriage. I needed to see the red flags in my life at that time and to understand what they meant. It would have saved the lives of my beloved pets. As an educator, I feel that this is a **must read** for all women today—especially in light of the increasing rate of abuse being reported in the news. It is time for all of us to take our heads out of the clouds and face this reality in our society. **5 stars.**"

"**Real**, insightful, compassionate, **powerful**, personal, moving, **inspiring**, practical, clear, **needed**."

"Anna writes **knowingly** and **brilliantly** about **what it is like** to be in a relationship with an abusive male... Thus she is able to draw on an almost **pure experience** of this living hell, while giving a **crisp perspective** of ways to extricate oneself from the maze. Would that all women in these circumstances could be such '**a force to be reckoned with**'."

THE BIG BOOK

of

RELATIONSHIP

RED FLAGS

ANNA MOSS

SAXONY HILL PRESS

Cover design: KC Graphics

Book design: Elle

Photographs: Getty Images

2013 edition: Dian Jones, editor

ISBN 978-0615908427

We hope you enjoy this book from Saxony Hill Press. Our goal is to provide high-quality, thought-provoking books for women who think and do.

Dedication

To those who want to love and be loved with clean hearts.

For those I lost or nearly lost in the great battle: Joey, Tuxedo, Rowdy, Teddy, Mischa, Mila, Elizabeth, Cossette, Little Man, Buddy, Hootie, Pasha, Kishon, Echo and Sarah (as well as the horses in his "care": Tux, Rahja, Missy and Khosabi).

"Your gravest enemy will hide in the last place you would ever look."

Julius Caesar

Introduction

*I*t didn't hit me when I walked in and took a seat in the waiting room. It hit me when the Director of Client Services came to get me. Her smile was warm, but her ice-blue eyes had already seen right through me. She knew. *I have barely been married a year and I'm about to talk to a social worker at a women's shelter.*

Carol led me to her book-lined office, pointed to a chair and asked what she could do for me. *Maybe you could just take me out back and shoot me.*

I gave her a two-minute summary of my deteriorating marriage to give her the background for the real reason I was there—to ask my BIG question:

1

Me: "It's quite awful, so I am wondering—how I can I tell if my husband is bipolar?"

Her: "Does he treat other people the way he treats you?"

Me: "Oh, no!"

Her: "Does he mistreat you in front of others or when you're alone?"

Me: "When we're alone."

Her: [leaning forward] "He's not bipolar, he's abusive."

Me: [speechless]

She expanded upon her point while I sat there in shock. Then, she handed me a book and suggested I read it in private as my husband would be provoked by its implications.

Her: "Would you like to see the facilities?"

Me: "Um. Okay." *Does she think I'm going to leave my husband and come here?? OMG. What have I done??*

We walked through the comfortable and secure two-story building, finishing the tour back in the reception area. She told me to call her if I had any other questions and disappeared up the stairs. I walked out and drove back to the house in stunned silence. It was two days before I was able to be alone so I could begin to read the book. It was the beginning of an incredible journey, a tipping point in my marriage and a turning point in my life.

The Counterfeit of Love

The things you hear a lot when people react to a story about an abused woman go like this:

- "<u>Oh, she was probably asking for it</u>." DECODING: The notions of someone acting without decency, reason or compassion in a primary relationship have not been examined. A relationship engineered through hypocrisy, deceit, double standards, manipulation and withholding is beyond their experience.

- "<u>What the hell is wrong with her</u>?" DECODING: If a woman is being mistreated, it's because her partner is trying to correct or compensate for her deficiencies. Some might say she should be grateful he is trying to work with her instead of throwing her out.

- "<u>I wouldn't take that crap!</u>" DECODING: Completely absent from comprehension is the toll that abuse takes on the mind and body. The immobilizations of battle fatigue, depression, fear and trauma are unrecognized or unknown.

- "<u>Well, why doesn't she just leave</u>?" DECODING: The many and sizable obstacles most women face in exiting are unknown. The circumstances of having no way to exit and nowhere to go are inconceivable.

These reactions are typical, they give credence to the excuses that flow from an abuser's lips (and 10 years ago, I may have said or thought some of the same things). These attitudes express *relationship illiteracy*—a lack of knowledge that lowers standards and perpetuates abuse.

Now that you've heard from outsiders ("the uninitiated"), people who have not been touched by relationship abuse, I want you to hear from an insider, from someone who lived through it:

- "That would never happen to me." DECODING: Abuse was outside her frame of reference, she assumed she was an adequate judge of character although she had no knowledge whatsoever of the warning signs of a charismatic con. If she ever thought of it, she thought it would happen to another kind of woman. She did not consider herself a prey item for a predator.

- "I never saw it coming." DECODING: She thought she knew who and what he was. After a few flourishes of the traits she needed to see, she took the rest at face value. She didn't know enough to see the early deceits for what they were. Even when he began to manipulate her, she did not recognize it as such, understand what he was doing or where it would lead. When he told her the things he was doing were for the good of the relationship, she believed him.

- "I cannot believe what this has done to my life." DECODING: Her lack of knowledge led to prolonged immobilization, loss and suffering. She sustained damage to every aspect of her life. Until she got enough truth to realize what she was involved in or until she shut down, the abuse penetrated her at a deep level. It delivered massive damage to her subconscious, her seat of power, which she would need to recover. It also wiped her out financially.

Like it or not, interpersonal abuse is part of the social matrix in which we live. If we wish to avoid it, we need to open our eyes. If we wish to stop it, we need to think a new thought.

Inadequate Information

Many of us were raised with instruction about how the world *ought to be*, not how the world *really is*. As children we could not know we were not being told the truth about some things, we simply internalized our experiences as the way the world was and the way we were.

For the most part, our caretakers did not fail us or lie to us; chances are, they didn't know either or couldn't see the forest for the trees. (Although there are caretakers who do fail their children and you will learn about that later.) We accepted what we were taught and internalized it with adequate result—until we were targeted by a charismatic con artist. We didn't know it at the time, but we were becoming prey for a predator. We thought we were falling in love, but we were being taken down. If we had been warned about this, our lives would have been different—more peaceful, productive, better. This book is the warning I wish I'd had.

Important Premises

Please note:

- The "doer" of interpersonal abuse is referred to by several terms (with slight variations in meaning by context): *abuser, charismatic or intimate con artist, pathological, perpetrator, predator, psychopath, toxic partner.*

- The advanced perpetrator is referred to as a *master abuser* and *super predator.* He succeeds in maintaining an effective persona that allows him to operate as a sub-criminal moving through society undetected—he fools everyone. He has refined his con and the apparatus that supports it to a high degree. This allows him to target and gain access to highly desirable prey items.

- The "receiver" of interpersonal abuse is referred to by several terms (also with slight variations in meaning by context) as *prey, target* and *victim.*

- The descriptors "high functioning" and "low functioning" refer to the victim's access to her highest potential. Abuse, neglect, violence and trauma inhibit the flowering of the soul and blunt the ability to tap higher potential.

- The male gender is used to refer to the perpetrator *only* because this is the statistical norm (the reported ratio of male to female perpetrators is about ~ 9:1). I believe there are far more victims of both sexes than have been reported and documented.

- This book is anti-abuse. *Nothing* herein should be construed to express anti-love, anti-male or anti-marriage sentiments. I am well aware of female predators (they will be addressed in upcoming works).

Amen!

- Difficult and dangerous relationships are not the same thing, there are crucial distinctions that every thinking woman needs to know.

- The two sides of the human equation in a toxic relationship possess vastly different potentials for future health and happiness.

- Violence is *not* limited to physical savagery and its wounds are not always immediate, obvious or physical.

- Abuse by definition is only a one-time occurrence when it is recognized in the moment and the victim exits the relationship or situation. There are key distinctions to know about conflict and abuse, about staying in and leaving a difficult relationship.

- Abusive behavior is understood to be an established pattern of force in which one person's will is visited upon another person (or animal) against their will and to their detriment. It occurs along a spectrum of intensity and visibility, from the disturbing to the deadly.

Contents

Part Three: Psychopathic Dynamics of Subjugation

Part Four: Masks and Personas of the Charismatic Con

Part Five: Spiritual Dynamics of the Abyss

Part Six: Mind Games for Soul Destruction

Part Seven: Choices at the Threshold

Part One: Weaponized Behaviors for the War

"Secrecy and silence are the perpetrator's first line of defense. If secrecy fails, the perpetrator attacks the credibility of his victim. If he cannot silence her absolutely he tries to make sure no one listens."

Judith Herman, MD
TRAUMA AND RECOVERY

Mark & Nikki

By their first anniversary, the wheels were coming off. Mark put Nikki through a whirlwind courtship after a chance meeting in the upscale coastal town where they both lived. Contrary to her normal reserve, Nikki fell head over heels and let Mark sweep her off her feet. They embarked on an intense relationship and were married within six months.

The wedding plans fell to Nikki, who wanted to do it herself, even though it would be at the cost of scaling back her fledgling business. This was her gift to Mark, who was too busy with his surgical practice to get involved. All of this was unspoken and understood by both. The arrangements didn't just take Nikki away from her work, they took her away from Mark, and that was when the little dissensions began. Mark would gripe about the time it took her to work on the wedding, but he never offered to help or hire a planner.

Nikki's stress level went up and up and up. She felt things coming to a head and dreaded having a disagreement or letting Mark down before the wedding. Things did come to a head but instead of an upset, they lead to an unexpected and magnanimous gesture by Mark. Knowing that Nikki was fretting about the momentum she was losing with her own business, Mark stepped in and suggested she take a year off so she could relax ("It's your turn now") and enjoy the first year of marriage ("I might do the same thing").

He swore he would make good on his earlier promises so they could do some serious traveling. He promised to relieve her of her financial burdens so that she could feel safe and never have to fear 'the wolf at the door." He promised to support her because he wanted her to know what it was like to be taken care of. He promised

11

that he'd make sure she never regretted taking the year off. Nothing could have been less expected for Nikki. She realized she was wondering if Mark would lose his temper and call off the wedding. His superman strategy disarmed her and made her feel ashamed for doubting him.

Nikki had been self supporting since her junior year of college. She had never been dependent on any man since she had left her family home to go to college. The idea of being taken care of by her husband had never occurred to her. She rolled the concept around in her mind for days wondering how it would work and what it would feel like.

Mark began to cajole her to give him her word that she would accept his offer so they could get a good, solid start on a long life together, the life they had both waited for. Mark had been married before, Nikki had not. They wanted to get this right. Mark applied pressure, but he did it in ways that melted Nikki's heart. Right before the wedding, she agreed.

Mark maintained high humor through the rest of the wedding activities. Nikki marveled at him. When they were pronounced man and wife, as he leaned down for the traditional kiss, he gave her a look that made the hair on the back of her neck stand up. She shuddered and shut her eyes.

During the honeymoon, Nikki saw the first dark mood and received the first verbal zingers. Taken aback, she chalked them up to fatigue. In the course of their month-long tour of the Mediterranean she felt something in Mark ebbing and something else rising. They stayed in cheap motels, split single entrees in the evening and spent most of their waking hours walking at high speed through little towns. When she'd suggest they stop somewhere to eat or rest, he'd look her up and down and tell her she didn't need either.

It was not at all what she'd envisioned. Something was roiling in her husband that had never presented itself to her before, but she couldn't name it. He seemed to be propelled by some kind of unseen force. Wherever they went, he moved at high speed and never had anything to say about where they were or what they were seeing—it was as if they were having entirely separate experiences.

His hostility and unavailability settled on her like a cold headwind, draining her, making her feel less and less able to go on. When they were out on the road, Mark drove the tin can rental car hard at high speed giving no attention to its effect on his passenger, his new wife. Nikki held on in silence, watching and wondering, but not comprehending.

Once they met another couple for dinner that Nikki has spoken to earlier at a museum. She was ecstatic at the prospect of a nice meal and normal conversation. She enjoyed herself and was relieved to see Mark doing the same, but back at the motel, she was stunned by his critique of her behavior as inappropriate and selfish.

Several times during their island hopping, they got separated in crowds and it crossed Nikki's mind that she had been abandoned. Mark's behavior kept her on edge and made her feel so threatened she couldn't even process her feelings, much less try to express them to him.

Sometimes, he was the Mark she loved, but sometimes he was not; she did not like and could not respond to the other one. She wanted to talk with him, but except when he wanted sex, he was evasive and on the move.

By the final days of their trip the honeymoon had become joyless for her. The succession of cheap motels, insufficient food and a missing husband left her feeling panicked, insecure and afraid to show either emotion. Something inside told her to keep her fears to herself. When they checked into their last flea-bag motel, Nikki retreated to the bathroom, took a lukewarm shower while roaches scurried across the tiles and cried.

Back at home, the other Mark continued to show up without provocation. Nikki began to feel helpless because she could not see what it was that was summoning his evil twin. He began to make snide remarks to or about her under his breath as he left the room. He taunted her about not having enough of her own money. He begrudgingly provided the funds she needed to cover her expenses but never without requiring explanations. He seemed to enjoy it when his inquisitions brought her to tears. After several months without any talk of travel, Nikki had had enough of being at his mercy and decided to pick up where she'd left off with her business.

She was unprepared for Mark's reaction. They had their first big disagreement in which he called her names, accused her of deceiving him and using him. His verbal assault was so over the top, it rendered her speechless. It was if nothing that been agreed before had ever happened.

14

The context in which her present circumstances evolved was dismissed as if it was figment of her imagination. His tirade, his twisted accounts of events and most of all his seething anger so rocked her, that all she could do was sit there and take it.

For the next week, she tiptoed lightly to keep from provoking him but came no closer to understanding what was going on with him.

One day, he blew up about something and chased her down to the basement. He stood over her and blew, then stormed up the stairs bellowing that he didn't want to ever see her face again in his house. He slammed the door behind him and stomped up to the third floor. She stayed in the basement overnight, where she had heat, but no food. She curled up in a ball on the airbed and slept with her cats and dogs for the first time in months.

Mark and Nikki never talked about anything of substance anymore. They talked about the news, the weather, the house, but nothing of love or the future. Nikki was so sick at heart, she could not eat or sleep. Every waking thought chased ideas blindly for understanding and keys to fixing.

Mark's inexplicable rampages became part of life. Nikki was paying in spades for quitting work and not buying a car. ("I've got three nice cars, why would we need one more?"). Some of his explosions happened outdoors and she wondered what the neighbors could hear. She also wondered what they'd seen in the past and what they knew.

Over the following months, she became a prisoner in his home. She complied out of exhaustion and fear. She did not know what to do or where to go. She had no way to communicate with the outside world except through email when he turned the internet on, which was usually a few minutes in the morning and a few minutes in the evening— the same times she was tasked with fixing his meals. He kept everything under lock and key.

Anything that she wanted to do was mocked, most of her attempts to go out where blocked ("We can do that together" and "You don't need to do that."). She was not allowed to see people or have a social life, and by the time it got to this point, she was so worn down she didn't try to fight it because she didn't know how. She didn't know anyone within two thousand miles. Her family and friends did not know what was happening to her because she was too ashamed to tell them and because Mark made sure her letters never got posted and their letters never got delivered. When phone calls were made or received, he stayed in the room.

With great trepidation, Nikki decided to separate from Mark and go stay with friends in another town. She made her plans in piecemeal, and only told Mark when everything was arranged. He received the news in sullen silence.

The day after, the old Mark was back. It pulled at her but she resisted and stuck to her plan to go away for a while. Mark was undaunted and for the first time in their marriage, came home with a bouquet of flowers. She smiled even though she felt like crying.

A year before, Nikki had been a happy, independent woman. Now she was living with a man she did not know, did not like, did not trust, could not communicate with and was afraid of.

The next Sunday, on the way back from a rare outing, a drive along the coast, Mark said he wanted to take a back road and see how his new car handled the curves. They climbed the west side of the coastal hills as the sun began its slide down a flaming sky. They got to the top, Mark took a few turns on side roads and pulled up to a lone picnic table on a ledge with a panoramic view. He got out and walked to the edge. Nikki followed him. He put his arm across her shoulder, something he had not done in months. She tensed. He looked down and kicked the ground as if he was trying to find words, but he said nothing.

He stepped over the guard rail and started down the steep path summoning Nikki to follow. She did, slipping and sliding but relieved he was in a good mood. They came to another ledge with another spectacular view. He turned to her as she came up beside him and smiled. Standing with her hands in her pockets, she smiled back. He put his hand at the back of her neck and caressed it, then in a fluid motion, grasped her forearm and flung her headfirst over the edge. She didn't make a sound except for a gasp. She fell for several long seconds before hitting the rocks below with a thud. Some of her hair covered her face, the rest of it splayed out around her head like a shampoo ad.

He leaned forward and regarded her broken body, waiting until he saw the trickle of blood flow from her broken skull. He turned on his heel, jogged up the path, slid behind the wheel and in an elevated mood drove off.

| 1 |

A Relationship Road Map

Some of the sights and sounds you're bound to see on a trip through the treacherous terrain of a relationship with a toxic partner include:

- Unrelenting demands placed upon you
- The loss or destruction of something you value so that he can show up (hero-like) to save the day
- His saying one thing, but doing another (often the exact opposite)
- His engaging in multiple inscrutable, illogical behaviors that confuse and destabilize you
- Created crises and unnecessary chaos
- Application of increasing control and pressure through the steady removal of your resources
- The charming of others to deflect future suspicion when he has delivered his coup dè grace on you
- Supplanting your goals, opinions and plans with his own
- Keeping you isolated and intimidated
- Promises (small and large) made to compel your compliance, although few or none are kept (or even remembered)

- Dismantling of your support network (family, friends, co-workers, business associates) behind your back
- Acting normal to assert his harmlessness and plant seeds about your "problems"
- Playing on your emotions to get or keep you ensnared in the relationship
- His responding to challenges from you with brutality or "hurt feelings"

When all else fails, it is not uncommon for an abuser to assault or murder his partner and then exit the scene of the crime (to include moving to a new location where he can start all over again).

Human Evil

Stanford Psychology Professor Emeritus Philip Zimbardo, PhD wrote,

"Evil is the exercise of power to intentionally harm, hurt, destroy. This includes the commission of crimes against humanity."

The success of human evil in the form of a charismatic con artist or intimate predator rides on three things: access, damage, detection.

Evil tells lies to get its foot in the door. These go undetected even when they are of mind-boggling magnitude. It knows how to get in. No one suspects, so no one sees it coming. The cons of predatory evil are *unbelievable* to the uninitiated. They are dismissed if they are noticed at all because they are so unreal. (And evil counts on this.) The lies are unreal only because they are yet outside the context of personal knowledge.

Those of us who have been touched by evil, when we dare to look back to try to understand, have learned what happened. We wanted to understand what happened so that we will know what to look for, so that there will not be a next time.

Evil defies natural responses because it comes from another *jurisdiction*. Lives and fortunes are lost every day because someone is trying to deal with evil using logical thinking or intuitive ideas. (And evil counts on this.) Logic and intuition are no defense against evil because it is illogical and counter-intuitive. It is also insane.

Human evil succeeds where it can move about unrecognized; it moves about unrecognized where its prey is *uninformed*. (And above all else, evil counts on this.)

Evil in Relationship

Evil does not respect authority or tolerate resistance. Two of the hallmarks of an abusive relationship are that, after the gloves have come off, the woman has become so subject to the toxic partner that she has been conditioned not to defend herself in any way. These conditions are hallmarks of soul destruction. This is what ongoing abuse does to the core self at the soul level—it "gets into" her so that she begins to think she does not deserve to live.

> "...many of these women have been beaten so much that their fear mechanism is dulled to the point that they take in stride risks that others would consider extraordinary ... being struck and forced not to resist is a particularly damaging form of abuse because it trains out of

the victim the instinctive reaction to protect the self. To override that most natural and central instinct, a person must come to believe he or she is not worth protecting. Being beaten by a loved one sets up a conflict between two instincts that should never compete: the instinct to stay in a secure environment and the instinct to flee a dangerous environment."

Gavin de Becker
THE GIFT OF FEAR

The charismatic con artist uses romance, rushing and isolation with strategically placed and timed promises to keep his victim immobilized. As this sequence plays out, her natural expectations keep being blunted because the promises she's been given are not kept. It's like being slapped over and over—pretty soon, she gets the message and gives up.

This is the basis of abusive conditioning. The mind (heart and spirit) are assaulted to the point that the will is sapped and victim gives in. The predator does not want his prey at full strength, so he does what he needs to do to weaken her.

In the animal model, the predator may "play" with the prey for a while, but it cannot begin to feed until the prey has died or stopped moving. I hope you see the parallel here.

The problem of intimate predation is beyond the government's ability to fix; further, it is not the government's responsibility, it is ours. The most meaningful solutions come from the individual and spread—they always have and they always will. The many forms of interpersonal violence have spread like wildfire, so can the solutions.

The con of an intimate predator is sublime and mesmerizing, until you see through it, then it is horrifying. The consequences are also diverse and formidable. The emotional plundering inherent in a dangerous relationship depletes the victim. When she becomes restive, she is fed apologies, more promises and weasel words, both subtle and blatant. These penetrate her subconscious, corrupt her thinking and weaken her grasp of who she is and what is possible for her. At the same time, her other relationships, assets and purposes are strained, damaged, removed.

Two Types of Predators

There are two broad categories of pathological partners: the *emotionally disturbed* and the *pathologically disturbed*. This book focuses on the latter because he figures most prominently in the most severe forms of intimate aggression.

He is the most dangerous predator on the face of the earth, responsible for more suffering and waste than any other human phenomenon. Sandra Brown, MA identifies the three major characteristics of personality pathology. They express an individual's *inability* to:

- sustain positive change
- develop to emotional or spiritual depth
- cultivate insight about their effect on others

These are hallmarks you can rely on, but it is important to understand that the most pathological traits of predators do not appear pathological at the start. That is why specialized knowledge is needed to supplement the intuition of what Gavin de Becker calls the "wild brain."

Pathology camouflage is how and why predators succeed. They are masters of disguise. They are cunning and diabolical in ways that most of us have never imagined, let alone experienced. Their prowess is not to be taken lightly for it is behind the suffering of millions of humans and animals every year.

Two Kinds of Prey

There is another broad distinction that applies to the human equation of a toxic relationship. The two kinds of women preyed upon can be described as *targets* and *victims*.

Targets are accomplished, independent, high-functioning females whose romantic histories do not include multiple dangerous liaisons. They are the desired prey of more sophisticated charismatic con artist; they are also the desired prey of super predators. Victims tend to be unaccomplished, dependent, low-functioning females whose romantic histories show patterns of abuse in relationship. They are the regular prey of opportunistic, unsophisticated predators.

The tragedy of abuse is that it begins in the home. It is most often perpetrated by adult caregivers, including the parents. When a child grows up with abuse, neglect and violence, the usual result is a life sentence of the same, as either perpetrator or victim.

The thing that targets and victims have in common is *relationship illiteracy*—they do not know the warning signs of abuse and they do not have a self image adequate enough to propel them out of a relationship at the first sign of pathology. The target "takes it" because she thinks she can handle it or rise above it. The victim "takes it" because it is all she knows.

Yes! I could have figured it out!!!

We are all shaped by what we grow up with, our earliest influences are the most profound and unless we take steps to repair any damage done, we are destined to express both the good and the bad that formed us.

Victim prey grew up with abuse—she witnessed it, experienced it or both. She perpetuates it in her life (and her children's lives) because it's all she knows. These are ways her victim status shows up:

- All of her intimate relationships become abusive.
- She is unaware of the extent to which negative influences from her childhood are affecting her, so she does not inquire into them.
- She is naive, undiscerning and frequently exercises poor judgments about her circumstances and the people in her life.
- Her relationship pattern consists of taking refuge in-between destructive relationships.
- She spends her time at the shelter talking about the drama of her abusive relationship with animation, but without comprehension of the fundamentals behind the behaviors on both sides of the equation.
- She has not learned how to "connect the dots."
- She is upset by the abuse she's experienced, but she doesn't seek to understand the principles of abuse so she can avoid it in the future.
- She seeks immediate relief, but she doesn't seek long-term remedy.

- The men she gets involved with are bullies, charmers, punks.

- Alcohol, drugs and criminality often figure in her partner's life, and sometimes in hers.

- Lack of discipline and moral lassitude are factors in her day-to-day life.

This kind of woman goes from one pathological man to another; she often uses public assistance in between relationships. Some victims fight their way out of this lifestyle, but most don't. Like their abusers, a certain amount of denial is at work in their psyches, which keeps them from getting uncomfortable enough with their situations to seek real and lasting positive change. Tragically, their children take on the habits and behaviors they live with and grow up to be the next generation of abusers and victims.

Target prey has not experienced abuse before. She does not know what it is from personal experience and so, she does not recognize it when it is happening to her. Because abuse is painful and strange, she is motivated to end it so that she does not experience it again. These are evidences of target status:

- None of her previous intimate relationships have been abusive.

- She is in deep shock, but wants to understand what has happened (what she has fallen for), so that there is not a repeat performance.

- She uses her time at the shelter to rest, study and prepare for what she needs to know and do to get back on her feet and move forward with her life.

- She has generally healthy habits and participates in as many therapeutic options as possible (individual and group therapy, job training, life strategies, relocation, etc.).

- She is highly motivated to learn how to avoid ever falling prey to another abusive individual.
- The abuser that targeted her is a charismatic con artist of considerable ability, often successful in his public or professional pursuits. This type of predator has abundant resources which give him many advantages in his nefarious pursuits.
- Alcohol, drugs and criminality do not figure in her relationships.
- She is competent, effective and focused in her day-to-day life.

In her book, WOMEN WHO LOVE PSYCHOPATHS, Sandra Brown, MA reported more than 20 "super traits" she found in targets. Compiling this research led Brown to consider what too much empathy can mean in a relationship. Her findings were that highly empathic women tolerated circumstances way out of their comfort zone. This made their over-supply of empathy an on-going risk factor because it is an innate characteristic. Brown also found that highly empathic women were highly relational and had high-bonding capabilities.

This makes the extraordinary nature of the seduction in a charismatic con all the more compelling. It feels like a key fitting into a lock—a lock that opens a door to experience that has not yet been opened in their life.

Brown also found that one of the trait sets targets and abusers share are those that have to do with engagement. Targets have the drive to do, the ability to manage multiple roles, a taste for adventure or luxury and zest for life. Abusers want excitation, control, gratification

27

and power. When her traits and his traits are "pointed towards each other" it creates a synergistic attraction that is irresistible for both of them. This contributes to the extraordinary passion of a charismatic con and its irresistibility.

Dangerous Liaisons

The experience of a pathological relationship can include aspects of brainwashing, fraud, imprisonment, battery, rape, sadism, torture, theft and sometimes murder. In this landscape, the difference between knowing and not knowing can mean the difference between living and dying.

When a person goes through a horrific experience, they often emerge from it like someone crawling out from under the rubble of their home after it's been leveled by a landslide or tornado. They're dazed, confused, injured and overwhelmed. They may have broken bones; they may also have more grievous injuries that don't show, like a broken heart. There may be little or nothing left of their possessions or their life force.

In each life affected by abuse, there are many things at stake; some material, some immaterial. These are things you do not realize are at risk until it's too late. For some of these losses, there is no insurance. Whatever you lose will register internally and the loss will eventually manifest in some way.

One of the antidotes to prolonged misery is to identify damage and tend wounds as much as possible. The saying, *"Nature hates a vacuum"* is relevant to the aftermath of a pathological relationship. Too often, the traumatized victim is unable to protect herself from negative influences. Like recovery after a serious illness or injury, the woman healing from abuse also passes through a period of lowered emotional and spiritual immunity.

It is crucial to place fortifying and supportive influences in her life right away. It is also crucial that she distance herself from people who do not understand what she has been through because they will be unable to be sympathetic and supportive. She has a lot of healing to do and their callousness will not aid her return to wholeness. There are many undesirable things that can beset someone weathering a great personal calamity. The woman recovering from relationship violence is not out of danger just because she has escaped from her abuser. This is what awaits her if she does not mount mental and spiritual self-defense.

Worry	Insecurity
Fear	Tinnitus
Self-doubt	Anxiety
Stress	Accelerated aging
Brain fog	Numbing
Headaches	Dyspepsia
Ulcers	Sadness
Poverty	Despair
Pain	Nervousness

In his landmark book, ANATOMY OF AN ILLNESS, Norman Cousins shared his personal discovery about the powerful role that belief plays in recovery. He wrote,

"The will to live is not a theoretical abstraction, but a physiologic reality with therapeutic characteristics. Never underestimate the capacity of the human mind to regenerate."

For the woman who has endured a dangerous relationship, her total involvement is the all-important factor in the success of her recovery. The more she wants to buck the odds by healing, the greater her chances of doing just that. Such life force in the face of great pain is a visceral confidence that is picked up by the body and translated into higher immunity.

Life force may be the least understood power on earth. In the 18th century, William James wrote,

> "human beings tend to live small, far inside self-imposed limitations."

Healing is a time to be vigilant in guarding against subsequent wounding from heightened emotional, financial and spiritual vulnerability. Being vigilant does not mean rushing; it means being careful and exercising discernment.

| 2 |

The Facts

Predators go where their prey is—no exceptions. A certain kind of woman is highly sought after by the type of man that abuses women. He seeks her out for a number of reasons; key among them are particular qualities that make the process easier and more enjoyable for him. In general, women who are targets (ideal prey) are sought because they are:

- Compassionate, forgiving, idealistic, cooperative, willing, understanding
- Busy, vibrant, loyal, intelligent, principled, accomplished
- Overextended, immobilized, compromised
- Lacking adequate self-image and boundary setting

Who?

The type of man who searches for this kind of woman comes from all walks of life. You cannot discern him by how he looks, where he lives or what he does for a living. You can discern him only by being able to see and

31

understand the signs of his hidden agenda. Handsome men, privileged men and professional men can abuse hideously because of their assets and attributes.

> "Approximately 1/3 of the men counseled for battering are professional men who are well respected in their jobs and in their communities. These have included doctors, lawyers, ministers and executives."
>
> David Adams
> "Identifying the Assaultive Husband in Court"
> BOSTON BAR JOURNAL

He is "other," he is different from other men. He is charming, compelling, disarming, romantic and focused. His voice melts you. His attentions take your breath away. He speaks with a knowing and an intensity that stirs you. He talks of a life you've only dreamed of—until now. And now, he wants that life with you. He knows your nature and circumstances will work together to enable him to lure you into his trap while he constructs the situation he wants. This situation is complex, and it will take some time to put it all together. But he is willing to take the time and invest a lot of energy into it because he knows it will pay off for him.

Your family and friends are glad for you and seem to be impressed when they meet him. But months or years later, when it's all over, a few of them are bound to say they felt something wasn't quite right—that he seemed too good to be true, he was a little too smooth, and the like. But they didn't want to spoil anything, so they held their tongues. Would you have been able to receive their critical concerns then? Probably not, because you were already falling under his spell and already stepping into his trap without even realizing it.

What?

Being healthy, successful and well-adjusted is no guarantee you won't experience ups and downs in relationships; but difficulty is one thing and abuse is quite another.

Relationship red flags warn of behaviors that mask intent. The type of man who leaves a trail of red flags in his wake uses many devices to achieve his goals: distraction, language, personality, money, technology—alcohol, drugs and time, among others. If you become involved with such a man, you will encounter signs along the way. The more trusting you are and the more cunning he is, the less likely you'll recognize what you're seeing. Why? Because he is so unlike you that his hidden nature would be incomprehensible to you.

Which I definately said!

When you see multiple red flags, you are dealing with a man who is not only unhealthy, but also dangerous; and this changes the rules—ALL the rules. To proceed, you must understand the implications—ALL the implications.

Once you learn to discern these signs, you will know when you have reason to slow down, step back and take a critical look. Slowing down is not easy to do, because it interrupts the magic of what is unfolding between you and this man. It screams against everything in your DNA. Slowing down goes against what you as a woman are wired to do: create, forbear, nurture and love.

Know this: taking a step back will not damage a real relationship—quite the contrary. A healthy man will respect such a request, because he cares about you and wants what's best for you. An unhealthy man will begin to reveal his agenda, because he cares only about himself and getting his needs met.

If you have the strength of will to learn to recognize and respond to red flags for what they are—and when you are falling in love, it is almost unbearable—you will spare yourself a world of hurt. You will save your children, your animals, your friendships, your career, your reputation, your home, your bank account, your hopes, your dreams, your life. You will also spare your loved ones the agony of watching your life torn to shreds.

When?

When you find yourself in a landscape littered with red flags, you are standing on heavy ground. Though the man who has brought you there is charming, dashing and mesmerizing, part of what you feel is be a primal response to danger.

There can be a fine line between danger and excitement, and it's easy to mistake one for the other.

When you see red flags:

- Do not underestimate the risk you take once you're in the relationship. Getting involved is easy. Getting out is not. Be aware of justifying your behavior or his if it could compromise your self- reliance or your safety.
- Do not overestimate your ability to negotiate what lies ahead because you are experienced. Age, logic,

money and intuition will not save you from the ravages of a close encounter with a pathological abuser.

- Do not assume you are immune to its effects and consequences just because you recognize a red flag. Everything you have and everything you are could be at stake.

The *number* and *nature* of red flags are indicators of the *severity of abuse* to come. When you see an abundance of red flags in behaviors and/or circumstances, you are flirting with disaster. The man (or woman) to whom they pertain is more than challenging or difficult, he (or she) is dangerous. Although this type of person does not exist in great numbers, they have many victims and wreak devastation and havoc beyond imagination.

Why?

Clinicians and researchers in the field hold varying opinions on which circumstances most influence the development of psychopathy. The possibilities are:

- Heredity ᴡ ʙᴏʙ ʏᴇs
- Early childhood trauma ʏᴇs - ʙᴏʙ
- Family violence ?
- Extreme substance abuse ɴᴏ
- Traumatic head injury ɴᴏ

Most believe that abusers are made, not born. Another way of saying this is that, except for substance abuse and head injury, psychopathy is something that children get from their parents—a kind of generationally-transmitted mental illness. The abuse (which includes neglect) of babies and children by their parents is at the heart of much psychopathy. These abused children

35

develop as damaged souls and grow up to inflict pain and suffering wherever they go. There are exceptions, but they are rare; and exceptions don't disprove the rule.

When babies, toddlers and young children are chronically mistreated it doesn't just damage them emotionally, it interferes with the normal development of their brain—the frontal lobe and sometimes the temporal lobe. It's impossible to break the cycle of violence when the perpetrator is brain-damaged. This is also the reason some criminals exhibit 100 percent rate of recidivism—they are not resisting the treatment and training they've received, they are hopelessly abusive because they are irreparably brain-damaged. *interesting*

The window for saving children in violent households is only open until they reach five years of age. Several opinions exist about the reasons that certain adult pathologies are so entrenched and resistant to change. One comes from the work of Bruce Perry, MD, PhD, who is regarded as the international authority on brain development in early childhood. He has pioneered both neuroscience and clinical research into the effect of abuse and trauma on the developing human brain.

Dr Perry's work shows that the type of man who mistreats women was mistreated during the first five years of his life. As a child, he experienced or witnessed enough neglect or trauma that it affected the development of his brain. More specifically, the part of his brain governing the emotions of respect, compassion and empathy did not get wired right. The resultant damage to his brain dimmed some of his emotional capacities. As an adult, this man does not have normal awareness of or feel normal emotions about other people. Functionally, this condition is referred to as *without conscience.* This type of brain damage cannot be fixed later in life by drugs, surgery or therapy. This is a terrible waste, but it is not your fault or responsibility.

Where?

Red flags exist in all kinds of relationships— professional and personal, public and private. The red flags described in this book occurred in the context of a marriage. But everyday they occur in other contexts, and the same rules apply, although to different extents due to different contexts. Abuse is no respecter of persons. It infects those who live in mansions and trailers, those who work in courtrooms and schoolrooms, those who speak from pulpits and podiums. Abuse occurs in boardrooms and bedrooms.

In whatever context red flags appear, they indicate the complete or partial absence of conscience and soul, a gross imbalance of power and all else that follows from these circumstances. There are many acts that, committed against a neighbor or employee, would be illegal and actionable; yet if committed against a spouse are allowed by law.

Friends, neighbors, co-workers, clergy, educators are all in positions to observe red flags around the target of abuse. These are a few telling signs:

- She begins to wear clothing to cover wounds. She wears long sleeves and turtlenecks in warm weather.

- She withdraws from normal activities and relationships. She quits doing what she used to do.
- She begins to act and even look different. Her entire demeanor changes. She becomes listless or unnaturally cheery, like a Stepford wife.

The abuse of a woman by her husband is perhaps the most complex and emotionally charged form of violence in the world. It is a betrayal so cruel and overwhelming because it is inflicted on the trusting by the trusted.

In many instances, while the woman is terrorized by her husband, she is marginalized by the community. About half of all abused women reach out to someone in their church before seeking help elsewhere. It is not uncommon for uninformed clergy to tell these women to go home, pray for strength and submit to their husbands. Some of these women are later killed; others descend into near total desolation.

Other red flags show up as financial losses. The wife is kept from working, her attempts to work are sabotaged, her resources are exhausted; family and friends may step up to help or be blocked by the toxic partner; public funds are spent on legal, medical and social assistance that may not be adequate.

To a large extent, workers in education, ministry, law enforcement and the judiciary remain uninformed about the true nature of physical abuse against women (children and animals). They are tragically uninformed about the full spectrum of nonphysical violence. It should be noted that the rates of family violence and domestic abuse in law enforcement and military households are *twice* those of civilian households.

A retired colonel said the following to psychologist and author Dave Grossman:

> "Most of the people in our society are sheep. They are kind, gentle, productive creatures who can only hurt one another by accident. Then there are the wolves, and the wolves feed on the sheep without mercy. Then there are sheepdogs and I'm a sheepdog. I live to protect the flock and confront the wolf."

Do you believe there are predators out there who will attack and maim without mercy? You better believe it. There is evil and there are sick people who are not only capable of these deeds but adept at them. The moment you deny or discard that information, you become prey and it's only a matter of time until your number comes up.

| 3 |

The Force

This is the big one. This is the core of abuse and violence. It's what drives an abuser and makes his engine hum. *Control* is the name of the game. It's what he lives for. It's what he *has* to do. It's what he can't help but do. It's his *nature*. Every lie he tells, every question he asks, every story he makes up, every holy law he invokes, every look he gives you, every reason he uses, every excuse he offers, every manipulation he orchestrates, every demand he makes, every posture he assumes—each and every one is employed to control your heart, mind, spirit and body.

His pathology drives him. His quality of life depends upon his ability to find ways to gratify himself, which he does by asserting control over other people and situations, but most especially over you. Some of the behaviors he uses are subtle; he deploys these like they're insignificant or he's performing them as a service to you. Other behaviors are blatant; he institutes these like he's laying down the law.

The controller lives by another code, he is in a class of people that could be described as "other" and it is not a class you want to be in. With such a person, there is no hope of ever leveling the playing field in a relationship. You can continue to make excuses for him, he can continue to make excuses for himself, but nothing will change because he does not possess the organic capacity to participate in a healthy and safe relationship.

The Leash

Control is the leash and it comes in many wrappers—it can be light and feathery, slithering and slimy, or sharp and unyielding. It can be achieved with roses and whispers, with innuendo and ultimatums or the back of a hand and the turn of a key. All of its methods, soft or strong, are encroaching and unrelenting. Every inch of ground a pathological gains is kept. He is a control-seeking machine, which is why his woman would be wasting her breath to try to negotiate with him, point out his unfairness or appeal to his compassion.

In the beginning, control feels like the silky soft caress of attention and devotion from the most wonderful man in the world. He's there for you. He's almost too good to be true. Everything he does reassures and resonates. You have never felt so loved or so safe. He pays keen attention to what you do, where you go, what you say, how you feel. *Studying me while I put on my make-up.*

When you become aware of his attention to the details of your life you're charmed, even touched. No one has ever shown such exquisite concern. The thought may float through your mind that he's too good to be true, and

41 *no, annoyed.*

the romance is like something out of a great movie or novel. It has made the quality of your daily life transcendent.

He seems to be able to read your mind. He anticipates your needs. You don't even need to ask, because there he is. In the name of love, he steps in to assist with his greater experience, brawn or bank account. And this is how a social predator begins to get in and get control over your lifestyle, routines, thoughts and emotions.

If you notice how he observes you, it would be comforting, not alarming; he dotes and adores, or he watches from a distance. But, after a while, he moves in, not to deepen the relationship but to test your boundaries, this will enlarge his taking control of your life bit-by-bit informed by what he's learned from watching you.

Unless you understand what he is doing, it will just feel like you are getting closer and closer. If at any time in the beginning you comment on or question the changes taking place, you'll find he has soothing reasons for everything, and so you go along and go deeper into the trance of becoming prey for a predator. For however many shining weeks or months it goes like this, you bask in the warmth of the glow of love. It feels good. It feels right. Then, the caress turns into a squeeze, and it increases until the constriction becomes undeniable. Then everything begins to feel like something else, but you're not sure what and you don't know why. You realize his attention has become stronger and more forceful.

By this time, you might be married to or living with him. You might also have become financially involved with or weakened by him—or both. You wonder if you're being too sensitive. You wonder if what you're feeling is somewhat *suffocated*. You tell yourself he's the most wonderful man you've ever known, and this other stuff is just all in your head.

A little more time goes by, and he seems to be taking more of an overlord position in the relationship and you wonder if he's taking the "head of the household" thing a bit too far—things that should be simple are getting complicated, non-events are becoming incidents, things that should be allowed are being prevented, helpfulness has turned into hindering and warmth into hostility. You find yourself feeling confused and maybe a bit threatened.

A trip to the grocery store to get ingredients for the evening meal turns into a mock trial. After your "trial" you are sentenced to your room for your supreme carelessness in failing to procure the necessary items on the previous trip. No spontaneous meal planning is allowed, no deviation from planned menus. Even though the store is a few miles away, the trip is declared extravagant, and you are declared *too stupid to live*. At times you think to yourself, *This is ridiculous.*

If you say anything later, when he has cooled off, he douses your concerns with tender words and eases up for a while. You give yourself a good talking to and get over it. You do not want to ruin what seemed to be the best thing you've ever had. You will yourself to relax and trust so that the man you fell for and the relationship you began will reappear. It doesn't and he won't. It begins again—and you realize it is not just in your head.

Something is happening, but you don't know what. Is he doing these things out of love or something else? You argue with yourself and feel foolish. When you talk to him, you hope something is accomplished, but nothing changes. It's like you can't get traction. You begin to feel like a non-entity. In the beginning you were cherished, now you are getting trashed.

Things begin to get a little thick. You could say he's taking over your reality. You seem to encounter opposition at every turn, especially over anything you want to do on your own or away from him. The simplest things are obstructed. You ask, you explain, you argue. You lose every argument because there is no level playing field, and the rules are unknown. It seems you must ask permission for everything.

Something is in motion, but you don't know what. This is not what you thought it was. You begin to feel defeated and exhausted in ways you can't explain—yet. Then by and by, you find yourself going along with the preference he's stated and the routines he's arranged, because he tells you that they're all for the relationship. If you resist the changes he wants to make, he assures you he knows best, the changes are for your own good. He even says that if you loved him you'd defer to his wishes. If this doesn't work, he asks you to just trust him. If you still have trouble bowing to his will, which involves pain and sacrifice, he finds ways to force you—and they will be vicious. You find yourself wondering if he will raise his hand to you. You tell yourself you will get through this, and the relationship will be the better for it.

Once he has achieved adequate control over you, the real show begins. He wields control with a wry smile and brute force. You don't have a moment to yourself. Your days are filled with endless mind-numbing chores, errands, minutiae and the ever-important caretaking of him; all done under his demanding and watchful eye.

And always, an incomprehensible and unpredictable hostility lurks under the surface threatening to attack if you don't comply—the tennis ball left on the stair, the jammed seat belt, the slick concrete floor, the broken garage door, the back country. There are a hundred ways he could do you in without raising any eyebrows.

Over time, unrelenting abuse takes its toll. Once lovely, capable and independent, you now second-guess yourself and edit your words carefully just to get through another hour. The danger here is not just his taking over your practical life, but his taking over your mental life—he is "getting into" you, or trying to. He does it like a wolf sucking the marrow out of a bone.

Repetition affects brain function. Consistent control and domination changes thought patterns in ways that are not unlike hypnosis, but that work like sabotage. The abuser's messages plant false and limiting beliefs in your conscious mind. With time, your subconscious accepts what it is fed and you fall under not just physical and financial control, but mental control, too.

If he lets you take a phone call, he stands nearby and starts giving you the "wind-it-up" signal after just a few minutes. You comply to keep the peace.

If he lets you use the computer, he appears every 15 minutes asking if you're done yet or telling you "that's enough." You comply because you're too tired to argue or too vulnerable to risk the consequences of resisting.

If you want to leave the house, see family or friends, use the car or have some money, you will have to make a case and then you will have to ask. You either go through the drill or you forgo the outing.

You dread and resent his control, but you have been manipulated into compromised circumstances. He seems to take some kind of perverse pleasure in making you lay out your needs, requests and plans for his consideration. It feels like a form of cognitive rape. He finds ways to deny most of your requests. He tells you what you need and don't need. He says he is taking care of you, even though he is treating you like a child slave.

You rein yourself in. You ask for less and less. The walls start closing in. In addition to the petty controls he institutes over your daily life, the straightjacket he wraps around your head thwarts every natural inclination you have to flee. You stifle every scream of protest because you realize you are not safe and you are dealing with a person who is unpredictable. You struggle. He watches.

Over time, the urge to flee and resist wanes, your strength ebbs. You no longer feel worthy, capable or deserving of the sweetness of life. No matter how lovely the day, there is a shadow over everything. You're kept on a chain, and it's never explained.

> *When a man loves you, he wants you to be free. When he can't love, he wants you on a leash.*

Language of Deception

Once the pathological establishes sufficient control over his target, he takes the game to the next level. He places his weapons and ammunition so that they are all pointed at her most acute vulnerabilities. His weapons of control are used to inflict overall damage as well as to deliver targeted wounds. She does not have any idea that this is coming. She is plenty occupied with trying to understand him and sort out his strange behaviors so that normalcy can return.

This is one of the cruel ironies of falling into the hands of an abuser. Even though you let him into your life because he seemed to honor what you cherished, that is where he aims the assaults of the next level of the game. Why? Because he has objectified you. He requires all of your time and attention. All of it. Anything else that crosses *yes!* your mind is to be eliminated. He is bringing you to heel. For example, if you are devoted to your parents, he belittles and criticizes them. He blames you for the space

He belittled anyone in my life!

they take up in your emotional life and any time you give them. He interferes with communications so that neither of you know what is going on with the other. Bit by bit, he isolates you from them (and everyone else that matters to you). He then denies, minimizes and punishes you for the upsetting effects all of this has on you.

Although you do not know he's withholding correspondence and information from you, you can learn how to tell when he is lying. The following are universal signs of deception transmitted through body language:

- His heart races
- His nose, brow or ears flush
- His pupils contract
- He touches his nose or ear with his middle or index finger
- He maintains almost constant (predatory) eye contact or he won't make eye contact at all
- He puts an object between himself and his victim during a deceptive conversation

Deception is the foundation of abuse, so it is crucial that you grasp its fundamentals (listed below) as well as its influences and consequences.

Lying requires a liar and a believer—it's a cooperative act, albeit an unfair one because the most accomplished liars go unexposed the longest. In lying, the liar gets what he wants as soon as someone believes the lie, takes the bait, buys it, etc., because when they do that, they enter into a tacit agreement with him, that is, they take the first step toward "going along." Here are some cues to lying behaviors:

- Liars use shielding phrases. They deflect suspicion by dropping qualifiers into their speech such as "to tell you the truth...", "in all sincerity...", "let me be blunt..." and "honestly...."

- Liars often immobilize their upper body while telling a lie.

- Liars either avoid eye contact or stare predatorily.

- Liars use a fake (cortical) smile which involves the mouth, but not the eyes.

- Liars shake their head or shrug while using affirmative words in a lie.

- Liars blink more often than normal while lying.

- Liars position their bodies and especially their feet towards an exit.

- Liars place themselves behind an object during a conversation in which they are telling a big lie.

- Liars often drop their voice while lying and keep it lowered for some time.

- Liars display anger typically with a sneer, which communicates contempt.

- And when they think they've gotten away with it, they smile (duping).

"Lying is like breathing to the psychopath. When caught in a lie and challenged, they make up new lies, and don't care if they're found out... Lying, deceiving and manipulation are innate talents for psychopaths...When caught in a lie or challenged with the truth, they are seldom perplexed or embarrassed—they simply change their stories or attempt to rework the facts so that they appear to be consistent with the lie. The results are a series of contradictory statements and a thoroughly confused listener.

[handwritten note: I noticed this with Bob.]

[handwritten note: So interesting. This is exactly how Bob responded!]

"They exhibit a cluster of distinctive personality traits, the most significant of which is an utter lack of conscience. They also have huge egos, short tempers and an appetite for excitement— a dangerous mix..."

Robert Hare, PhD
PSYCHOPATHS AMONG US

The Weaponized Behaviors of Interpersonal Abuse

Like physical illness, by the time symptoms are present, the disease is progressed. An abuser employs many behaviors to wear down his target.

✓BELITTLING   ✓BLAMING
✓CRITICIZING   ✓DEFINING
✓DENYING   ✓ISOLATING
✓LYING   ✓MINIMIZING

These behaviors permeate every abusive relationship to some degree. They are deployed according to the depravity of the perpetrator. A toxic partner uses biting humor, punishes his woman with the silent treatment, insults her in front of others, unleashes an obscene verbal assault before she leaves for an important meeting, reveals an affair before leaving on a business trip and so on.

yes
yes

or
Every time
I had guest over
for lunch or dinner
he started in on

me

50

| 4 |

Red Flag #1
BELITTLING

The pathological uses belittling to test boundaries. It starts out as offhand comments that hang in the air and sting the skin. When they first come out of his mouth, they're a shock. Belittling may be delivered with humor, which can change to sarcasm. It will have little or no basis in fact. It is a destabilizing weapon.

Either way, it is a shock to the system. No matter how mature and balanced you are, belittling from the one you love will begin to destabilize you and shift the balance of power in the relationship. Is he being mean or disrespectful, or are you being too sensitive? It's hard to know. The things he says are so unlike anything he's said to you before you don't know what to make of them. You try to write them off, but somehow you can't. As it happens more often, and with more sharpness, you feel bewildered, disabled and even frightened by the content of his messages and the look on his face.

He gets in your face when your opinions differ from his.

He gives you the silent treatment if you disagree with him.

He rolls his eyes in response to your political views.

He repeats something you've done or said in a crude way.

He patronizes your efforts or accomplishments.

He sulks when you mention your friends.

and criticizes them

He lies in wait for any opportunity to afflict you. He does this with such jejune abandon that you feel embarrassed for him and nervous around him.

You start second-guessing yourself and feeling like an imbecilic child. You feel inhibited about accomplishments and capabilities you once valued. This is the beginning of the internal destructions. Like a recombinant retrovirus, his poison begins to get you criticizing yourself like he does—cruelly and relentlessly. You begin to see your life through his eyes and feel lessened by it. You begin to wonder if he might be right.

"Go do your little work."

"You use a computer because you don't know how to communicate."

As you feel less and less worthy, you resolve to improve. You change some of your activities in hopes of stemming the tide of insults and put-downs. You let go of one activity, and then another and another. No matter what you adjust or let go of, he is unsatisfied and continues his belittling unabated. Over time, you watch as your life is devalued and taken apart. This is how it goes. He belittles everything in your life except himself.

Abuse destroys. Behaviors used against you work on two principles (which can later be powerful levers for healing):

- Abuse attacks your belief in your personal competency, your ability to take care of yourself.
- It also attacks your belief in the preservation of your personal dignity, your worthiness as a human being.

Abuse wears on the body, too. You feel inexplicable agitation, frailty, nervousness. You feel you're about to explode or scream, or both. You are besieged with headaches, muscular stiffness and joint pain, even if you've never been visited by these maladies before. Your body is holding far more tension than you know. The insidious nature of belittling supplants your beliefs about your competency and worthiness with his judgments to the contrary. Through repetition, those false beliefs become embedded in your brain, incorporated into your subconscious programming (your belief system about yourself and the world) and then they start showing up in your daily life.

> These things you give up are pieces of your life, but they're just targets to him, and it's open season on you now.

| 5 |

Red Flag #2
BLAMING

At first, when things don't go his way, the predator laughs. He rises above annoyances and irritating circumstances whether he's caused them or not. He does it with such panache that it impresses everyone who sees it. He plays the part of a man who can handle the unexpected and the unsatisfactory. His easy competence transforms one situation after another.

You see him handle situations with aplomb—for a while. Later, you see he is unwilling to deal with any inconvenience; the smallest things set him off. As things progress, you see he is unwilling to accept accountability for being set off. From then on, in most other regards, anything that is the matter is someone else's fault, and you never know what is going to set him off. In time, you find that, like a child, he blames you for his own behavior.

[handwritten margin note: wow! This is so right on.]

54

"If you would just be nice, I wouldn't have to get mad…"

"If you would just show me some affection…"

You realize he has set up his life so he is accountable to no one. This is because he has a big problem with any authority other than his own. If he hits any bumps in the road, he uses blame, charm, deceit or money to get what he wants. He blames you, he criticizes you, he defines you. The story of his life he tells you is a version that serves him then; it is loosely based on fact. He tells you how until he met you, he was happy. Now, he blames you for his unhappiness:

"It's all your fault."

"If you knew how to be a wife, this wouldn't be happening."

"You should be grateful."

"Other women would kill to be with me."

"Face it, you just can't do anything right."

When contradictions arise between reality and his story, he avoids accountability by exiting the scene or pointing the finger.

You find he rewrites history to suit his purposes, one of which is to maintain his blamelessness.

You hear him talk about something you saw, too, but it differs from what you saw.

You see he says and does whatever he needs to at the moment to achieve his purposes. In his mind, the ends justify the means.

You realize he's done this all along with you, and he will always do this with you. If you speak up about his, he blames you for it. He is not to be questioned. People learn by trial-and-error, it's how we're made. Blaming is a ruthless behavior that not only hampers learning but undermines confidence and blackens perspective. When turned on a young child, it is ugly and cruel. In violent relationships, perpetrators use blame to turn learning or new experiences into set-ups for future attack.

Instead of being able to learn your way around a new town for example, if you miss a turn or need to look at a map, you are blamed for being careless, stupid, wasting gas and time.

If you overcook or undercook a dish, you are blamed for ruining his meal, wasting utilities and food.

> "My parents are really well intended, but I think their way of dealing with things is denial and guilt. Nobody wanted to talk about it, and all I did was blame myself."
>
> Teri Hatcher on her sexual abuse as a child

Being blamed unfairly tends to lead to worry and dread, which consume vast amounts of mental energy. The energetic demands of living with a monster can cause rushes of heightened activity and sensitivity followed by crashing lows, adrenal exhaustion, mental fatigue and insomnia.

One adult blaming another for their own behavior is what children do.

| 6 |

Red Flag #3
CRITICIZING

At first, the criticisms are gentle. He offers them as a friend, in the spirit of concern and support (he still has the mask on). Then, his tone becomes condescending or imperious, and he delivers his critiques as if he's bowing down from his throne to whisper in her ear how disappointed he is in who and what she turned out to be, but because he's a great man (delusions of grandeur), he's putting up with her in the hopes she'll take his cues (dream woman). And he hopes she appreciates the chance he's giving her.

You are confounded and wounded, but you still trust him and care what he thinks, so you lay his words to heart. From his continual monitoring, he knows all of your vulnerabilities—which is where he begins to apply pressure through criticism. He knows that what he can't accomplish through control and deceit he can get done through the wearing-down process of unrelenting targeted criticism. His tone of voice becomes menacing, and his critical comments come more often.

He will criticize you for what you do and for what he does. The latter is an example of denial. He criticizes you (or others) for things he does. For example, observe how he responds to other drivers and see if he blows up when they make the types of maneuvers that he often does. If he is a rageaholic, he will accuse you of being disagreeable or inciting confrontations when he is the one who provokes them. It's normal to become dazed and worn by the cruelty and unreality of accusations and criticisms. It's also frustrating to know you cannot prevent them or respond to them. You always feel like you've just been had after one of his tirades. It's like death by a thousand cuts. As he sees you bleeding from the wounds he's inflicted, he offers self-serving words in hushed tones to help you deal with the awful truth about your many, debilitating defects.

"I'm just telling you this for your own good …"

"I thought you'd want to know …"

"I'm not trying to be mean, but … "

"I can't live with someone who …"

Implicit in his criticism is his expectation that you accept what he tells you as truth and incorporate it into your behavior and values. He sees this as your duty to him. If he perceives any difficulty or resistance on your part, he might add that he is much more sensitive than you and deserves your compliance.

His criticisms are ruthless attacks and incomprehensible demands all in one. As they become more inhumane, he claims his feelings are being hurt. As they become more unreasonable, he claims his hopes are being dashed. As they become more irresolvable, he uses them as fodder for yet more criticism.

Over time, his criticisms become louder and more threatening. Eventually, they are delivered in full-blown, full-volume, obscenity-laced character assassinations and white-hot rages. They suck all the oxygen out of the room and never fail to leave you aghast at what's been said and what he looks like while he's raging. He stoops ever lower. His criticism strikes like a rattlesnake. There is just enough warning to fill you with dread, but not enough to let you escape. From sun-up to sun-down, you are envenomated about:

The clothes you wear

Your choice of books, movies, music, foods

Your areas of interest or expertise

Your level of education

The way you talk, walk, cook, make love

The way you spend your time or money

The way you discipline your children or animals

Your political opinion, sense of humor

Your faith, family, friendships

All of your accomplishments, characteristics and all of your body parts are subject to his critical eye and all come up short. He seems to take special pleasure in bringing up any losses or mistakes from your past and rubbing your nose in them. Any and every misstep you've ever confided in him is used against you over and over. His criticisms range from the impersonal to the intimate. There is no past wound of yours that he won't tear open and abrade to make you bleed.

As your confidence and sense of self give way, you begin to feel ashamed of yourself and wonder why he ever wanted to be with you. You also wonder why no one else ever pointed out any of these crushing character deficiencies to you. All the criticism goes one-way: from him to you. In his eyes, you and you alone need critical correction. With enough time, he can take you apart with his words.

Studies show that most people over-criticize themselves to some extent. Continual criticism from your intimate partner in addition to self criticism is dispiriting. It inhibits the mind's natural rejuvenating actions of imagination and relaxation.

In an effort to avert criticism, you can find yourself running in a wheel like a hamster. Your days are spent on the hopeless quest to avert criticism by walking on eggshells and trying too hard. You find yourself making mistakes that are not typical as you struggle to function under the weight of his criticism. All of these reactions are natural, all are draining, but none are sustainable. With pathological criticism emanating from an abuser, no matter what you do, you're wrong.

Your natural response of self-defense may also be thwarted, in which case your brain records the implicit message that you're not worth defending. This is one of the most damning effects of abuse. It seeps into your cells and poisons the truth of who you are. The more isolated you are, the more quickly this can happen.

There are three broad types of criticism:

- Constructive criticism is best used as a signpost of what isn't working and needs to be adjusted, it allows forward movement.

- Destructive criticism halts progress and erects a failure mechanism in your mind that feeds on frustration, emptiness, loneliness, resentment, aggression, insecurity and uncertainty—all of which exist in abundance in the abusive relationship.

- Excessive criticism also inhibits the full expression of your personality. As you shut down and withdraw, your partner retaliates with yet more criticism as he stretches your nerves taut as a violin string.

Criticism cuts like a knife, but without leaving a mark on you, even though you've been run through.

| 7 |

Red Flag #4
DEFINING

He has definite ideas about what a woman should be. He speaks with passion about the feminine ideal.

The pathological tells his woman how many of these attributes he sees in her and how great it is for him to be with such a woman. In this way, he is giving his victim her marching orders (implanting his program). What is going on here is objectification.

When the predator finds the type of woman he seeks, he goes about his business of forming her into his dream woman. This has nothing to do with cherishing her or loving her or honoring her. It is about pouring his ideas into her head so that she will do his bidding and mirror him, as if she were a part of him.

At first, this feels validating and you appreciate it. He's acknowledging and respecting who and what you are, and what you've done with your life. It feels like he gets you. And it feels like this is the man you've been waiting for. What's going on here is that he's enrolling you in his program by telling you how to be and what to think. During the defining stage, you might also get your first deep look at his insatiability.

He's your man and you want to please him so you take note. Here and there, you try to do more to please him. But, it's not enough. Each attempt takes you further away from your true self and further out of your comfort zone. He receives your efforts with some acknowledgment and asks for more. And more—more than feels fair or right—more than can allow the relationship to prosper.

You find he assumes he has the right to define you. He misses no opportunity to tell you how you are to be. He dictates your behavior down to the smallest detail. Whatever you do, it's not enough for him. You find yourself trying to conjure up things to do to get him off your back for a while.

He tells you who and what you are.

He tells you what to do and what not to do.

He tells you what to think and what to say.

He tells you what you need and what you're going to get.

He does this with complete abandon, because he has no awareness of his own behavior and believes that it is his right to define you.

In THE VERBALLY ABUSIVE MAN, CAN HE CHANGE? Patricia Evans, PhD describes this situation as you providing the body in which your abuser intends to build his *dream woman*. The net effect is that you are his creation and you, therefore, exist to please and serve him. This is your sole purpose. In his eyes, the real you no longer exists or matters. You have been objectified. He is reminded of the real you when you express yourself. This is why self-expression gets you in trouble. Your real self gets in the way of his agenda, and he has little tolerance for this.

He presides over you and your relationship as a self-appointed judge; defining your personhood, making judgments, delivering sentences and expecting them to be carried out. He serves as the arbiter of your conduct, tastes and thought. Once charged, you are to police yourself by integrating and enforcing his judgments. He passes sentence on you with sweeping condemnations, and he expects you to believe him. You resist his judgments at first, but they get to you. You begin to feel cornered, conquered and condemned.

"See her? That's how a good woman treats her man. See? She's all over him. Why can't you be like that?"

"Here take this supplement. It's for women with low libido...poor memory..."

He says he cares about what you think and feel, but his actions show you otherwise. He asks you to alter yourself in certain ways and praises you for it even if the alteration isn't you at all. In the beginning, he cajoles you. Later, he demands. You feel like you're being emptied out and remade. The more you resist, the worse it gets.

Defining and objectifying you assaults your inner being. By doing this, he is free to take his behavior to the next level without missing a beat.

His like and dislikes are your marching orders ... into Hell.

| 8 |

Red Flag #5
DENYING

He has fashioned the architecture of his life—and with no small amount of effort—to give a pleasant and convincing impression of normalcy. It is artifice. The pathological knows he must appear acceptable. He judges things by appearance and assumes others do the same thing (superficiality). Based on such shallow criteria, his own PR promulgates the fiction that life is good and he is great (narcissism). Yet, denial is his knee-jerk reaction to any objection or external suggestion that something is amiss.

In the pathological, denial signals a lack of:

- Self-awareness
- Honesty
- Integrity
- Empathy

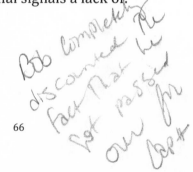

- Conscience

If you or anyone else points out a problem with his behavior, he denies it. If you insist, he asserts male privilege or some status point to quash your assertion. He is unable to receive any communication that counters his ego or his agenda. He denies you, and he denies himself. The surface of his life is a fiction. In public, he plays the role of good citizen, loving husband; in private, he torments you, but denies it:

"I haven't done anything wrong."

"You need to go to Wife School."

"I've bent over backwards to make you happy."

"You need to shape up and take better care of me."

"You do not know what you are talking about."

In his world, the material prevails over the immaterial. He is right and you are wrong. What he doesn't see doesn't matter; and he doesn't see anything about himself that doesn't serve him. His denial justifies and maintains his skewed sense of right and wrong and makes rational discussion futile. It's human nature to justify ourselves, but this degree of justification eclipses what is fair and honest. This is part of what it means to be involved with someone who does not have a conscience.

scary!

"I never said/did that."

"That's a damn lie."

"You get everything you want."

"You have to have everything your way."

"The problem is you have a personality defect."

"Your perception is wrong all the time."

When you've been mistreated, it's not long before your body begins to shut down. Since sex is important to him, this can lead to fiery confrontations. Nothing you say or do will get through to him. He is enraged that you're not available, but he does not begin to comprehend why. All he can think about is what he wants and what he needs to do to get what he wants. The more driven he is to get his needs met, which tends to happen with age, the more savagery he'll resort to.

Denial is a dangerous quality in general and one of the most dangerous of the toxic personality. It functions in the conscious mind. It shunts perception and stops every appeal to honesty, reason and fairness. The abuser is unwilling to consider the need for any change in his behavior, because he is unable to comprehend its fundamental evil. Being in a relationship with an abusive man often triggers denial in the object of his abuse. Her assaulted subconscious goes into denial for purposes of self preservation to keep her in the relationship with closed-loop, inner dialogues that go like this:

"It's not that bad."

"Maybe he'll stop _____."

"I'm not a quitter. I'm not going to give up on us."

"He might come to his senses and _____."

The problem is that none of these resolutions are possible with a partner who is so damaged (mentally ill or personality disordered). He does not have the organic capacity to change and sustain that growth. He is not capable of love or any other attributes required for a healthy relationship. Being battered by denial from your partner due to his unwillingness to take responsibility for his behavior and be accountable to you is destructive, even when you've grown used to it.

Your own denial deals two blows: the first is when you're not prepared to face reality or seize an opportunity to act; the second is when you realize this and shatter as a result. This is when you lapse into hoping "it" won't happen again. Wishful thinking is not a strategy, it's part of succumbing.

His denial is the refusal to admit responsibility for and cease all acts of cruelty. It is, therefore, one of the most hopeless attributes of the disturbed person. It prevents remedial communication and healing. The pathological's refusal to deal with problems other than by abuse or violence goes to the core of his defect: *moral insanity*. This was the term first applied to psychopathy as it emerged in the early 19th century.

Hopeless abusiveness is a painful reality, but when that's what your partner's condition adds up to, the truth is the only thing that will set you free. Everything else, especially making excuses for him, will keep you trapped, or worse.

> *Denial is the invisible foundation upon which he builds your prison and keeps the key.*

| 9 |

Red Flag #6
ISOLATING

It's natural for two people "in love" to want to be alone—especially in the beginning when passions run hot. True love is sublime, its counterfeit is also sublime. He doesn't have to tell her how much their time alone means to him, he shows her. He tells her how long he's looked for her and how she is all he wants, all he needs. The intoxication is mutual. The world can go away.

You don't perceive the doors he's closing at first. Isolation can lend drama to the forming of a romantic relationship, so it's not questioned or perceived as a red flag by the target. Isolation is critical to his success at weakening you and getting control of your life. The more alone you are, the better—for him. Like criticism, it starts off as one thing and turns into another.

He finds reasons not to go out.

He claims he never heard the phone ring.

Messages from your friends are misplaced or forgotten.

Cards from your family are lost in the mail.

Funds and permission to go see your loved ones are denied outright or delayed without cause.

When you begin to feel cut off and say so, he justifies it. He says it's the best thing for the relationship. He says you're all he needs and wants. You don't know how to counter that.

Isolation is almost always a factor in depression and physical maladies. Abusers could not do what they do if their women found ways to keep from being isolated.

Isolation is used in the penal system and in war, because it breaks people down psychologically.

Among other things, isolation means there is less to take your attention away from tending to him. In the weeks and months that follow, whatever matters most to you will be squeezed out of your life. He won't stop until you've been cut off from everyone and everything. He must have you all to himself. Further, he does not believe that you have any right to resist the isolation he imposes on you.

Isolation gives him freedom to do as he pleases with you; no one to hear, no one to interfere. The more isolated you become, the more control he has over you. The more isolated you are, the more dependent upon him you become—even if you have come to loathe him and have emotionally detached—and the more powerful he becomes in the relationships.

71

You cannot respond to him or anything else because of the emotional toll your losses are taking on you. It's like he's stabbing you with his left hand, groping you with his right and furious because you're not enjoying it.

Isolation breaks you down and keeps you confined. It keeps you from influences that could give you relief, broaden your perspective or renew your strength.

| 10 |

Red Flag #7
LYING

Liars distance themselves with language. They refer to something that "happened" as opposed to something they "did", they even describe their own behavior in the third person.

Liars use unnecessary formality. They refer to someone they know as "that man" or "that woman" and/or by their last name instead of their first, such as "Miss Lewinsky" instead of "Monica."

Liars use excessive detail. They offset lying with detail, sometimes to the point of overkill. Instead of describing something concisely, they go into great and unimportant detail.

Lying is the "love language" of the pathological, and he is a master of it. His speech is quick and smooth. His words are believed by you and others. He lies with abandon. He lies with his words, his deeds and his body.

One of the reasons he's an accomplished liar is because he has no conscience. He is doing whatever he needs to do to get what he wants. Another reason is that he knows the truth would radically change his ability to entrap you and your willingness to engage with him.

He mumbles to get out of direct answers.

He avoids your direct gaze. Sits in a position where he doesn't have to look

He uses charm or humor to derail inquiry.

He manufactures interruption to avoid exposure. at me.

He asserts his power by ignoring you.

He lies for all kinds of reasons, but mostly he lies to control you. When he goes into great detail, far more than is needed, he is lying. He tells you one thing one day and something else the next. When you tell him he's just given you two versions of the same thing, he lies some more by saying you are mistaken.

so true!

His lies are calculated to manipulate you into thinking the way he wants you to think and when you don't, the message is that there is something wrong with you. Remember, the abusive individual cannot tolerate authority or resistance—a different viewpoint can represent both of those.

Some abusers take great pleasure in the challenge (or outrage) of their partner's differing opinion. They go to work abolishing that opinion as well as anything they can find that guided you on your journey to it, such as your ability to do and your ability to think.

Some call this crazy-making. Some call it rewriting history. Physical therapist, survivor and author Sarah

Strudwick calls it his "putting your head in the washing machine."

He tells the lies, but you get hit with the backlash every time. The fact is that so much of what he says to you is untrue you cannot believe anything that comes out of his mouth anymore.

"You'd be lucky to be with me."

"I don't have a good enough memory to lie."

"I'm a generous, loving guy."

"You're being hyper-sensitive."

"I'm not a player."

Being fed a diet of lies starves the spirit and removes any semblance of justice from the relationship. It makes you want to shut him out or resist. You wonder if forbearance will somehow mitigate the lying. This is a vicious circle and a trap.

Consummate abusers are such inveterate liars, they believe their own falsehoods. Lying can be spoken in low tones in bed or bellowed in a speeding car.

His lying might be *projection*—putting his own actions onto you or *inversion*—telling the exact opposite of what is going on.

When you discover the magnitude of the lies he has told, and realize what they reveal about him, the relationship and face the catastrophic effects to your innermost being, it is almost beyond bearing.

If you do not know he is lying to you, and you learn of a mountain of lies all at once, your skin crawls, you feel nauseous, your mouth goes dry, your ears ring, you feel faint.

If you do know he is lying, or learn of his lies one at a time, your heart may race or your face flush. Later, when you reflect on the meaning of it all, you will feel foolish, stupid, gullible, shocked, disgusted, angry, hurt, horrified, humiliated—or you might already be numb.

When a man (or anyone) makes a big deal of telling you that he is honest or that he doesn't lie or goes to a lot of trouble to convince you or demonstrate his truthfulness, beware! This is the behavior of a liar.

> *Lying is cognitive rape. It poisons the heart and sickens the spirit.*

| 11 |

Red Flag #8
MINIMIZING

In the beginning, minimizing saves him some time and trouble. It lets him put things into neat little packages that can be thrown away or ignored.

If the pathological can't blame, deny, justify or obfuscate, he minimizes. This excuses him and puts the problem back in his victim's lap. He can serve it up with arrogance and conceit or with guilt and recrimination to achieve the desired effect: manipulation. There is nothing he can't minimize if it serves him.

Minimizing is an insidious and even sadistic behavior that, like denying and lying, works over time to weaken you and strengthen him. Day by day, it chips away at your personhood by making light of your experiences and disrespecting your needs. It also serves to call into question your emotional and mental faculties with the insinuation that you're off your rocker for being affected by the thing he's doing to you. Minimizing manifests as behaviors that all but scream at you to "shut up" or "go away."

One of the ways he minimizes is by refusing to consider or account for your interests or your side of an issue which, therefore, lessens his responsibility about something. He fails to reckon the emotional impact that his actions and demands have on you.

The man who destroys his woman succeeds in his brutalization, because the last straw was preceded by so much minimization that the woman lost her sense of self and value, which weakened her internal defenses, which further undermined her ability to resist or leave. When your needs, thoughts, feelings and responses are continually brushed aside and minimized, you can't help but begin to doubt yourself. When you realize that you're living in a war zone, and you can't trust yourself or rely on your own gut feeling, what do you do?

He gets you to quit your job or your business and then acts condescending, incredulous, even assaultive when you need funds.

He demands that you end a friendship, for no reason, and threatens to end it if you don't comply on his timeline.

He insists that you give up an animal you love and ignores or reacts with disgust at your suffering afterwards.

He walks away in the middle of a conversation—as if you're not there. The failure to resolve the issue is your fault.

He urges you to give up a project or plans that matter to you and then scoffs at your difficulty in doing so.

✓ *He delays a response to a request and then refuses to take accountability for the consequences of the delay he has caused.*

If he's an accomplished minimizer you may not even realize what he's doing. It may be so logically presented or subtly done, that the ultimate self-negation it delivers to you gets through undetected. He could be responsible for numerous losses you've suffered, but he won't acknowledge any of them because:

- Accountability for error is not in his repertoire
- Your pain does not matter to him
- He has no capacity for empathy
- His actions against you do not register
- He is in denial about who and what he is

In verbal exchanges during which you try to explain your feelings, he tells you to "get over it" or "get over yourself." His detachment and his inability to be compassionate, honest, loving and respectful makes you feel like you're trying to have a relationship with a stranger.

> *He minimizes you because he's not big enough to honor your experience.*

Part Two:
Intensifying Techniques for the Contest of Wills

"Pain is the price you pay for resisting life."

Philip McGraw, PhD

Keith & Karen

Karen was hospitalized for 14 days after surgery to repair a shattered pelvis. A young athletic woman, she was not the typical broken-hip patient—not at all. She was not elderly and she did not suffer from osteoporosis.

She'd fallen when she missed the top step of the basement stairs, lost her balance due to the heavy load of laundry she was carrying and fell backward. The tall stack of folded bath towels flew out in all directions as she went into a back-roll which opened up almost into a cartwheel before her body slammed to a stop with a sickening thud on the thick rug over the concrete floor. Her careening descent was cushioned here and there by the thick towels as they got swept down with her. She fell with such force it knocked the breath out of her and dazed her. She drifted in and out of consciousness as she lay sprawled at the foot of the stairs. Some parts hurt and other parts were going numb, she could hardly breathe, moving was unthinkable. She resisted the temptation to lift her head to try to look at her body.

Keith saw her there in a splayed heap three hours later when he came home from work. He viewed her from the top of the stairs, but did not come down.

She lay there long enough to become completely chilled by the cold from the concrete coming through the rug. She lay there waiting for Keith to summon help. *Why doesn't he come down here? Why won't he call an ambulance? Is he going to let me die here?* This scene came to mind but without gathering enough anger and incredulity to form the question. She eventually passed out. She awoke in the hospital and spent the following nine days in a fog of pain killers. Her ordeal at the foot of the stairs faded from her heart and the images were swept from her mind.

Before and after work Keith made a ritual performance of visiting Karen. He flirted with the young nurses while playing his part of the concerned and dutiful husband with perfect pitch. Unbeknownst to Keith, Karen had been 10 weeks pregnant when she fell down the stairs. The fall had cost her the baby. When the doctors informed Keith of this fact at her bedside, she saw him cry for the first time.

She had been trying to get pregnant for over a year, but had just about given up. Her body ached and her heart was squeezed with grief, but she couldn't cry, at least not yet. She had always been somewhat reserved, but in two years of marriage, which were playing out in ways unexpected and unwanted, many of her emotions were becoming less available. She had a dim awareness of this and that it was because it took more and more energy just to get through each day and hold her head up.

Karen left the hospital in a wheelchair which was to be her mobility for several weeks. When Keith rolled her into the house, she was surprised to see fresh flowers on the kitchen table. *The fanfare continues...* She was pleased to see the house wasn't in shambles—but she could see the effects of her absence. She could also see that Keith had made an effort to give her a nice homecoming, but somehow she couldn't quite warm to it.

Medicated and weary, Karen decided not to fight the pain, so she opted to go to straight to bed. She drifted off into the sleepless unconsciousness of pharmaceuticals. She did not hear Keith come home from work hours later. She was slowly coming up from unconsciousness and forming the thought of how dry her mouth was when she felt searing pain from the weight of him on top of her. She felt his fingers parting her, then him forcing himself into her. He clapped one hand over her mouth to muffle her and, like a jackhammer, pounded away. Afterwards, he flipped over, grunted and conked out. She lay there feeling as though the upper and lower half of her body had parted company. Unable to move, she was captive until morning when the home-care nurse arrived. Her pelvis screamed in soundless agony for days. This time, Keith's trespass was clear in her mind and undeniable.

The next day, Karen called her mom and asked her to come visit and help out around the house. She needed her help, but most of all, she wanted her company. *Mom, I need you so much.* Her mom arrived and immediately Karen felt bolstered by her presence in the house. She thought it would keep Keith on his best behavior. She thought wrong. One night, Karen couldn't help but cry out during one of his nighttime assaults. Her mother rushed to their locked bedroom door and stood there unable to help as the sounds of her broken daughter being ravaged came through.

The frequent nighttime assaults impeded Karen's recovery re-breaking bones, popping stitches and re-bruising skin. She ran out of ideas with which to concoct the stories she told the doctors. They never looked inside her or even asked if she was having sex. *They have no clue. No clue. Because they are sane and Keith is not. A sane man would not do this to his wife.* Pain medication became a daily staple by necessity. Karen hated taking drugs, but the pain was too much. She refused to tell her doctors what Keith was doing to her and swore her mother to secrecy promising to leave Keith as soon as she was able. Her mother went along for fear of worsening the predicament.

Somehow, the acute phase of pain passed and her recuperation progressed. Once the pain subsided, Karen was able to relax and enjoy her mom. They laughed and cried and talked of many things, except Keith. *This will all soon be history.* Karen began to regain her strength, she began to stand and walk although with a bit of a gimp. Feeling no small amount of reluctance, her mother returned home, her only comfort, Karen's promise that she was going to leave Keith as soon as she was on her feet. *Because that's what it will take to get away from him.*

Keith's continual savagery in the bedroom drove a stake into the heart of the marriage. Karen never brought up what the forced sex did to her because she realized it would not matter to him. *He does not care about me.* She vacillated between resignation and frustration.

Her body had changed in the months she was laid up. She'd lost muscle tone and stamina, even her equilibrium was affected. She wanted to be active again, but she wasn't pain-free and she had the distinct sense that something structural not might hold if she tried to do too much. For once in her adult life, she exercised her better judgment about taking things slow. *"Twenty-five and all used up."*

A year later, she was walking several miles a day, feeling good about herself and holding up better under Keith's rapacious sexual demands. The following winter, she conceived again and took extra care of herself to protect the baby. This put a hitch in her plans, but bought her more time to plan her exit. To her great relief, Keith controlled himself during the last trimester of the pregnancy. He did this by working evenings and weekends, which he said helped him cope with her unavailability. Karen suspected he was not at a work, but with another woman or other women, and did not care. *I hope he catches the clap and his pecker falls off.*

After their baby girl was born, she asked the doctor to talk to Keith about the time her body needed to heal. She thought this would be enough to shame him into a little self control. It wasn't.

During the first three months of her daughter's life, she was raped almost every night. She could hardly walk and bending over to pick up the baby was agony. She was so angry he would do this to her yet again—it made everything so hard. Her mind reeled. *Why is your release more important than my health? Why can't you be considerate of me? What if I get an infection? Is this what other men do to their wives right after childbirth?* It was during these weeks of having her bruised, torn tissues invaded that she decided to leave him and take the baby, even though she was not recovered from her various injuries and did not have much money set aside. If he tried to stop her, she'd report him. She planned it and played it out in her mind for months, and then she got pregnant again.

Her body changed more after giving birth to their son. Keith began to smack her on the butt or grab her breasts and tease her about her fuller figure. She was doing the best she could to get back into shape, but she was worn down by physical pain and a vague mental anguish that she never took the time to explore. The demands of two babies in two years overshadowed everything. Keith was not around much, which was a blessing but also a burden.

She loved her children, but hated her life. She was desperate to get away from him but didn't know how to go about it—she hadn't worked since they'd married and now she had two infants. He was an attorney, his brother was an attorney, his father was attorney; they would bury her and take her children. She could only imagine what their lives would be like in the custody of their father.

The following summer, as she sat on the back deck with her children, a different course of action occurred to her. Since she couldn't leave him now, she would re-dedicate herself to rebuilding her body so that she could stand up to him. She knew that if she could cut him off sexually, that would be it, he would let her go.

Over the next year, she exercised daily. It was all uphill at first, but she got some momentum going and began to feel her body changing. Strength began to flow into her arms and legs and core. She continued to wear loose clothing so that the changes wouldn't be visible, but Keith felt them at night. She continued her quest until she felt strong enough to be able to repel him. It wasn't long before she had her chance, and when she tried with all her might to resist him, he put his elbow into her stomach until it touched her spine, then jabbed his knee into her repaired hip, and the matter was settled. He knew her Achilles heels, and he was not going to be denied. She was sore and bruised for weeks, but where it didn't show. She wondered if some of his viciousness would flow into her and help get stronger.

Sometimes she wondered what the neighbors would think if they knew what was going on between the "happy young couple." She couldn't bring herself to tell her mom. Her parents had not been thrilled about her marrying Keith. They'd said she was too young, and there was something about him they didn't trust. She knew it wasn't their problem. As her granny had said, "You've made your bed, now lie in it." So she did.

With each passing day she felt more isolated and adrift. One night in the bathroom after the usual ordeal in bed, another idea came to her. She implemented it the next day: she cut back on her food intake until six months later, she was consuming only a few hundred calories a day. Keith didn't seem to notice for weeks. She got off the hook a few times with not feeling well, but he didn't like taking *"not tonight, I'm not feeling well"* for an answer. As her body began to shrink, she hit upon the idea of taking laxatives to speed the process. The first few times he took her after this, her bowels opened up and she made a mess in the bed. He recoiled. *Victory.*

After a few other messes, she removed herself from the bedroom without his objection. She installed herself in the den where she could sleep alone on the sofa. And this was how she kept him off her. It solved the problem. *At last.* She slept in peace as her body shrunk. She kept at her plan until she could no longer care for her children, at which point, her mom came back to help.

While she was still thinking clearly, she rewrote her will and recorded Keith's abuse with the request that her children go to her parents, not Keith. She attached copious documentation to support her request. Her mom and a court clerk witnessed her signature on various documents and filed them. Later, she got her mom to write her own account of the things she had observed. Much later, when the lack of nutrition began to take its toll on her brain, she refused to go to the hospital and was grateful when neither Keith nor her mom insisted—each for their own reasons.

The following month, Karen died of heart failure. She departed this life at age 28, weighing 67 pounds, but she gained her and her children's freedom from abuse.

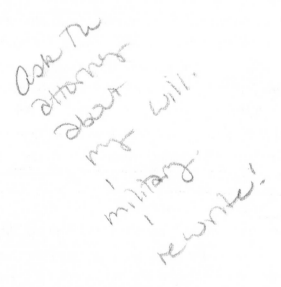

| 12 |

Fairy Tales

Many of us grew up with fairy tales that started out with "Once upon a time..." and ended with "happily ever after." This scenario was fed by media programming and social engineering throughout our lives—we believed this was how the world worked. Fairy tales swell childhood dreams and trigger fantasies, but they do not translate to real-life.

What do they teach us about relationships? Could it be they resonate with our hopes and dreams that our partner will be consistent, constructive, committed, faithful and truthful so we can move forward together? The caveat about fairy tales is that it's a wager on a future unlikely to end with happily ever after.

Once you understand the battle-plan of interpersonal abuse, you can begin to develop another mindset. When you start to see cues in behaviors and circumstances, you won't just feel uncomfortable or have a vague sense that something is a little off, you'll know what these cues mean and that knowledge will empower you. This mindset and the strength that comes from it is what will enable you to recognize a toxic person and make a conscious choice *before* you get caught in his trap.

Dangerous relationships are nothing new. The battle between awareness and unawareness, good and evil, experience and naiveté has played out between people (and nations) since our ancient ancestors first drew breath. Before digital media, this wisdom was taught to children in fairy tales which relayed sensitive aspects of the story in parable:

- "Little Red Riding Hood" warns of bloodthirsty wolves who pretend to be harmless, little old ladies in order to kill and devour whoever they can entice to come near them.
- "Cinderella" shows how members of one's own kin can betray out of jealousy. They deceive her by keeping her from the opportunities that are hers by right.
- "Snow White and the Seven Dwarfs" tells of another moral corruption. The vain and wicked stepmother, obsessed with destroying any other beauty, plays on the emotions of a gentle and unsuspecting soul.
- "Sleeping Beauty" depicts the elaborate manipulations of evil to destroy good. It seeks to destroy what it can never be or have by seeking satisfaction through usurpation.

These fairytales tell more than simple stories, they hold life lessons about all kinds of relationships. In other ancient tales, evil is depicted as a snake, a wolf, a giant or a hybrid. Today, a common personification of predatory evil is the abusive boyfriend or husband. Despite this level of incident, mass media misrepresents and underreports relationship violence in favor of sensational fare without much socially redeeming value. The tragic life histories of serial killers like Ted Bundy, Charles Manson, Jeffrey Dahmer, Gary Ridgeway, et al could be used as teachable moments to save lives, but they aren't. The media fails to inform consumers about the root causes of criminality and their chances of being victimized by it.

The issue of predatory evil in human society is a topic whose time has come. Many people have been touched by it, and many more are waking up to the reality and the costs of having predators loose in society. It is the beginning of a conversation that is long overdue and much needed.

While preventable personal battles roil, it's important to note that after the betrayals and ordeals, these fairytales end happily, good triumphs over evil and love prevails over hate. It doesn't often happen this way in real life, but it can—once you know the rules of the game. And sad to say, for the predators, it is a game, even though to you, it might be everything.

The Trance

The experience of a charismatic con that turns into an abusive relationship involves altered states or *trances*. Altered states are not uncommon in the course of daily life. You're subject to trance when you're getting your needs met:

- Hearing what you want to hear
- Getting confirmed in a belief
- Falling in love
- Receiving praise

Interesting

- Shopping for something you want

When you are in a trance state, you are more *suggestible*. (This is also true of being in fear, which is discussed later.)

The thing about the trance of getting taken by a predator is that it's *interactive*, which facilitates it becoming a *persistent* state. This is how it happens:

- It occurs under the radar—even though it's a powerful inner process, you're not conscious of it in the moment.
- If you aren't forearmed with information and you don't see it for it is.
- You are not able to snap yourself out of it, and so, you get subsumed by it.
- If the trance-inducing input abates enough that you do begin to come out of it, subconscious desire for the delight of it pulls you back in.

The desire for gratification is a powerful driver. It works on both sides and in different ways, of a toxic relationship.

So how do you know if a person in a trance? Here are some signs:

- changes in appearance – *rapid weight loss*
- changes in behavior   *carol saying*
- changes in personal morals   *'you were*
- changes in social values   *no   never this*
- taking inappropriate risks   *thin before'*
- risking the welfare of dependents   *marrying a psychopath*
- self-inflicted harm (not limited to physical)   *no*

Letting Bob control me.

Being in a trance happens when your perceptions are played with and your thoughts are manipulated in ways that harm you and benefit the manipulator. This altered state affects your entire outlook and warps your perspective in unproductive ways.

Bob telling me I have to look in the bank... ready to spend - of course you of

Promises are a central ingredient in the trance of a charismatic con. This is how dangerous relationships begin: with the promise of love, the promise to fulfill deep desires. The reason this is so effective is that promises attach to the core of your being and their irresistibility cut through your better judgment. Being set up to get what you want is primal stuff, which is why it works imperceptibly and powerfully. This principle applies to other kinds of cons (financial, political, professional, etc.). It's the same recipe just made with different spices.

The altered states that propel you into this experience get extra mileage from traits like naiveté, need for approval, loyalty, patience, compassion, persistence, love, self-sacrifice, eagerness to relate, forbearance, high willingness to trust, sense of responsibility and gullibility.

If you think about your greatest trials, you may see that some of them happened because you did not know enough about someone. What price did you wind up paying with your health, wealth or happiness because you didn't know the signs of deception and your own vulnerabilities? Has experience shown you that the ancient wisdom is true: you can be destroyed for lack of knowledge? Have you found that nothing can build you up or tear you down with more power than your primary relationships?

In the surreal land of abuse, the qualities of the perpetrator and the victim are like a key fitting into a lock.

The qualities that you have developed to nurture relationship are the lock into which key of the perpetrator fits. When this happens, you will soon find that you are utterly on your own. Intuition, fairness, logic, decency and reason do not apply. You are in a counter-intuitive world in which nothing is as it seems, truth is stranger than fiction and the stakes get higher every day.

Abuse is the counterfeit of love. It looks like one thing, but is in fact, the opposite of how it appears. It is executed with deliberation and can lead to utter devastation. The counterfeit can only be detected with *discernment*.

Every deception involves two parties: the deceiver and the deceived. As painful as this is to hear, every woman who gets deceived plays her part by falling for it. It's not hard to do. It happens thousands of times every day for lack of knowledge of the warning signs, which are hard to see and harder to believe.

Beliefs

One of the first steps in learning to respond to this scenario is to recognize *false beliefs* about yourself *and* your partner that allow you to be deceived. Your "belief filter" governs your perceptions and experiences. Chances are you hold many beliefs that are not based on fact but on erroneous perceptions pronounced upon you by others, which have no basis in fact. Your beliefs about your partner are likely a product of your interactions with him, your upbringing, your needs and his conditioning of you.

It's important for you to know that it does not matter to your brain where a belief comes from. Whatever your brain accepts as true is incorporated into your self-image and your circumstances. This sets up cause and effect outcomes in your life.

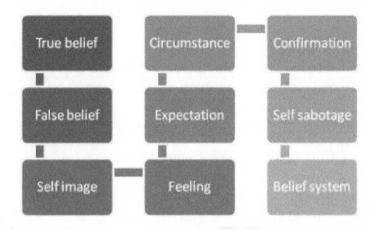

The effects of belief

An accepted belief that is false can be as powerful as outright sabotage because as thought, it causes you to work against yourself. Every experience is the effect of thought. The mental penetration or cognitive rape of the target's mind by her abuser is one of the most ghastly effects of abuse.

You believe that a man loves you because he wants to get married as soon as possible. You believe that a man loves you because he wants to take care of you. He could be rushing you and promising to support you for other reasons that you don't know enough to recognize or even suspect. In your belief and your trust, you mistake this for love—you fall for it. You go along and let yourself be deceived. Depending on how damaged the deceiver is, you could be inconvenienced or you could be incapacitated. *Rushing and financial control are two classic red flags.*

If you're struggling in a relationship right now and beginning to wonder if it might be abusive, here are some questions to ask yourself:

- Is your life better now than it was before? *So much worse*
- Are you personal standards rising or falling? *Falling*
- Do you have more or less peace of mind? *Less, much, much less*
- Health-wise, do you feel better or worse? *worse*
- Do you have more or less income and debt? *debt*
- Have any of your children started acting out? *Thank goodness no.*
- Has anything amiss happened to any of your animals? *yes!*
- Has your work been affected by your relationship? *What? work?*
- Are you losing touch with family or friends? *yes*
- Has any of your property disappeared or been damaged? *$ — yes!*

Getting clear about the difference between difficult relationships and dangerous ones will give you clarity and help you know where to draw your line in the sand. Part of mental maturity is the capability to commit and to go through the hard times with the one you love. However, this capability is abused and exploited when the one you love is not capable of doing likewise. It takes two.

Love That Hurts

As Oprah says, "Love shouldn't hurt."

I think it's safe to say she wasn't speaking about the pangs of development we experience in relationships that facilitate personal growth, she's talking about relationships that maim. This is what toxic individuals do, and if you can't face it emotionally, sometimes you can face it by looking at what is happening to your life. Abuse can happen without a man ever laying a hand on you. It can happen through criticism, isolation, impoverishment and mental cruelty.

There are many metaphors that can be used to describe principles of abuse in the context of predatory relationships; two of them are *communism* and *vampirism*.

Both of these are "sneak up on you" methods of mind control that induce altered states of consciousness. Communism uses propaganda, vampirism uses seduction or superhuman strength; both use deceit through lies and promises to accomplish their hidden agendas. People get taken in by the promises of equity and equality when they fall for communism and by the promises of love and immortality when they fall for vampirism. Of course, both take their prey by force and destroy them.

The learning curve here is significant, because the behaviors are counter-intuitive and the consequences are unimaginable. If you're in a relationship that's doing damage, and you have not yet been introduced to these concepts, it can be both painful and clarifying. When you're emotionally invested, it takes more time to make the needed mental adjustments than when you're not. This is one reason it's easier to avoid a dangerous liaison than it is to escape it. I assure you that the dividends to reap in all relationships and the internal rewards are worth every tear. Overcoming adversity is its own reward. Some of the greatest transformations and personal works have emerged when lives that were at the breaking point. Instead of breaking down, some individuals break through.

States of intense emotion—such as that of realizing your partner is hopelessly abusive—can plunge you into an emotionally-excited state that creates an opening between the physical and the spiritual. This opening is a portal through which both good and bad energy can flow. Once you reach this point, you have a fighting chance if you can master your emotions and thoughts:

- Keep focused on where you want to go
- Attend to your present circumstances
- Do not get derailed by annoyances, inconveniences and personal problems — *Stay focused, keep looking at the target.*
- Do not be seduced by gifts or promises
- Do not believe or rely on anything he says
- Do not worry about being ridiculed or misunderstood
- *Key* → Understand that you are at risk and he is the enemy
- Try to set some boundaries, but do not confront him
- Know and work around your own weaknesses
- Do not buy into his petty authority, but know when to go along with it in order to stay alive
- Never forget that no one can save you but yourself *- so true!*
- Apply the principle of mind over matter to help get through the darkest hours

Self-protection begins as soon as the scales fall from your eyes and you start to see the true meanings of previously inscrutable behaviors.

They have fallen — I see a light pointing in a direction on a completely different path.

Behind the Curtain

Once a woman has been emotionally enrolled, she has been entranced—put into a trance—by the experience of falling in love. When her partner is pathological more red flags begin to fly. As she becomes more involved, which follows sexual intimacy, the abuser begins to pull more tools out of his tool box. Of course, the entrapment happens under the radar. She does not realize what he is doing. She does not realize that moving towards deeper intimacy opens her to full-spectrum assault. She thinks she is getting into a relationship with a man who is just right for her, when in actuality she is experiencing the uplift of the first stage of a charismatic con. Her partner is playing a role.

During the courtship or pursuit, he will be irresistible, and things will get very compelling very fast. Predation requires disablement of the victim and speed. Predators have uncanny emotional acuity for assessing their prey and maneuvering them into vulnerability. When he is in top form, she is being put into a trance. Once the relationship has taken form and become exclusive (at least on her part), if she is with a pathological man, situational difficulties will begin to arise to scatter her force. This allows him to set up more situations that will create more difficulties for her later.

The cunning of older abusers can be mind-blowing when revealed. They tend to be masters of the game, meaning their deceits go undetected for a long time. They employ perfect pitch with every part of their con to keep their prey cooperative so that she moves ever further into the trap. The predator knows that intensifying techniques must not be applied too soon—that is, before the prey is entranced and entrapped. He sets the frequency, intensity, temperature and duration of his techniques for the desired effect. He deploys them, then he sits back and watches. For him, it's not a relationship, it's a game.

The intensifiers he uses sicken and devitalize you over time—like a virus. These techniques include behaviors that can be delivered in jest, in question, in anger and in inscrutable ways. For example, he first questions you for spending money on a necessity, like dog food. He then turns this into direct criticism or even insult that questions your intelligence, allegiance, priorities, etc. So, he could make a 'thing' out of your spending 30 dollars on dog food but later buy something extravagant and elective for himself. This is the kind of moral disconnect that leads to double standards and hypocrisy. When he doesn't try to hide them, it's because in his mind, the standards that apply to you don't apply to him, and vice versa. This is how the *other* operates.

This is how the mind of the pathological works and why it is impossible to make sense of his behavior. Yet, these types of incidents are common occurrences in pathological relationships and taken as a whole, they exert the deadliest stress—that of unfair and unbending difficulty. The infliction of these scenarios evidence additional attributes of the pathological namely, self-absorption, lack of self-awareness and failure to learn from their mistakes.

Unrelenting stress undermines confidence and saps will to the point that simple tasks and even conversation become difficult. Unfairness and double standards are at the heart of abuse. The insidious damage occurs at the subconscious level. The long-term effects of this experience can include:

- symptoms of PTSD *— I have been diagnosed with this.*
- hyper-vigilance
- flashbacks
- fear thoughts
- high startle reflex
- expecting the worst to happen

These are just some of the costs to be trapped in a pathological relationship, one in which the abuser must have the upper hand and does not tolerate resistance. This explains why he looks for a certain kind of woman on which to prey—a woman with a kind nature, a high willingness to cooperate, forbear and trust. He uses these qualities against her as he wrests away control over every aspect of her life, small and large.

The intensifiers most present in toxic relationships include:

DISTRACTION	DOUBLE STANDARDS
FOOD TAUNTS ?	HUMILIATION
MONEY	SEXUAL SADISM ?
SLEEP	TIME PRESSURE
WITHHOLDING	

One of the reasons an abuser gains intimate access in the first place is because he presents himself as appealing by *mirroring* to give you the impression that he really gets you. As he wins your heart, he also wins your trust. You begin to share your innermost thoughts, feelings and hopes never dreaming that these confidences will later be used against you. His reactions to your confidences and what you show him of your life never lead you to believe that you will later be attacked for being you. You don't open your life to him expecting that he will turn into a lunatic that fills your days with pain and suffering.

The amount of damage that can be done once the abuser is "in" your life is not to be underestimated. For those who have not observed what a pathological person can do, it is unbelievable. The amount of time and energy it takes to withstand such an invasion is also very considerable.

The abuser's techniques allow him to draw power from his prey while she is in an unguarded state—like a vampire sinking his teeth into the exposed jugular of a sleeping woman.

| 13 |

Red Flag #9
DISTRACTION

Distraction is about chaos and entertainment for purposes of deception and control.

In the beginning, the predator is easy going, engaged, agreeable, fun to be with. He works his charms and tells his stories so that his prey is mesmerized, so much so that she loses her balance. He makes sure that their time together is full to the brim, every activity is interesting and exciting, and the time they spend together gets more and more intoxicating.

The heightened qualities of the shared activities are just part of the delicious experience being prepared at the banquet of love. It often seems like a banquet. Many women describe the beginning of these relationships as the most intense romances they'd ever experienced.

Later, he arranges his distraction fix by inserting chaos into everyday life. Activities that could be done in a matter of minutes or hours are tampered with so that they require days or weeks to fix or sort out. The fixing may fall to her, which gives him the opportunity to proclaim her incompetence, or it gives him the opportunity to take over and inflict various forms of abuse along the way.

This chaos factor can be used with deliberation to abuse the partner and amuse the perpetrator, but it can also occur as a natural outgrowth of his advancing pathology, wherein his thinking really is disordered and the chaos is no longer contrived.

A little later on in the story, you realize something is off—it's not about being together, and it's not about pleasing you. It's about pleasing *him*. Period. It's about providing distraction for *him*—mental, sensual, social, emotional, etc. He feeds on it, and his appetite for it is endless. As time goes by, his attitude and behavior show you that when these activities do not appeal to you; this is of no concern to him. The abuser's demand that you "do something" to distract him expresses lack of compassion and lack of respect. The extreme need for distraction and excitation is a hallmark of psychopathy.

He expects all of your leisure or waking moments to be spent with him or doing something for him.

He interferes with any attempt you make to spend time alone, with friends or to pursue other interests.

He removes anything that takes your attention away from him.

You find he demands so much attention that you sometimes feel as if you are providing childcare instead of trying to be in a relationship. If you are committed to or dependent upon him, you see that this level of care is why you're there. You're not imagining it is extreme, you're experiencing that it is extreme.

Pascal spoke truth when he wrote,

> "man must know himself ... all human evil comes from a man's being unable to sit still in a room by himself."

Sitting still and being alone is unbearable for the pathological. He is not disposed to honest self-assessment, nor is he equipped to enjoy his own company. He must have someone or something to distract him from himself. Being alone and undistracted is not how he wants to spend his time. Like the energy vampire he truly is, he must have something to feed on.

You cannot sit in peace because he pumps you for ideas with which to occupy himself or entertain others; the latter of which, he does without hesitation, no matter how inappropriate.

He requires distraction in part because he does not think deeply on his own because he is shallow. He knows whatever he extracts from you could serve another purpose at a later time. Any thoughts or feelings you ever share with him are fair game to be examined, twisted and used against you in the future, in private or in public.

Over time, after private insults and public humiliation, you begin to have a hard time sharing your innermost feelings with him. Such withdrawal is only natural, but it creates a new problem. You now have to find a way to explain this retreat to him or try to camouflage it.

Over time, your part of daily conversations become shallow as you realize his have always been—but yours have become cursory for a different reason: self-preservation.

> You are to sacrifice yourself at the altar of his distraction needs.

| 14 |

Red Flag #10
DOUBLE STANDARDS

He openly operates with double standards because he fails to recognize them as such because he isn't thinking about his partner. He has one set of rules for his behavior and another set of rules for hers. He considers himself above or exempt from the status quo.

His denial, shallowness and narcissism combine to keep him from seeing what he is and what he is doing to his woman. (And remember, these are the same traits that drive him to seek distraction and entertainment through drugs, sex, alcohol, gambling, etc., so that he doesn't have to face himself.)

He alone is allowed to storm out of the house, slam the door, kick the dog, peel out of the driveway and so forth. If his partner raises her voice or wags her finger, she is called hysterical or overbearing.

His pathology prevents him from realizing how unfair it is to you to be treated with *less* consideration than other people, such as other family members. The double standards are asserted episodically or accrued over time because they are routine.

One of the dynamics at work below the surface is that the pathological partner *does not want you to have anything*. Part of his purpose is to remove the presence and usurp the position of anything you hold dear or could derive benefit from. He wants you to be focused on him. His thinking is so skewed, he fails to realize he is not giving you consideration.

He decides he doesn't want you to have something anymore and simply destroys it or removes it; this applies to inanimate objects, like cell phones, as well as living beings, like pets.

He has multiple cars, but won't let you drive one without requiring that you ask permission and have a good reason for your request.

He says things like, "My life is an open book," but deftly steers any conversation that could uncover evidence to the contrary away from him.

He goes through your coat pockets, your computer, your desk, your phone, your car, etc., but keeps all of his under lock and key. This isn't about trust as much as it's about control by monitoring.

He changes his plans in ways that impact you without discussion, but does not grant you the same privilege.

He has money and lavishes it on himself, but blocks you from working, puts you on a meager allowance, laughs at your lack and makes you account for every penny you spend.

He has time on his hands, but sees to it that you do not. He hovers and smothers, he needs this and that, he arranges the day so that you are continually "at task" and cannot have a moment to yourself.

There is no equitable or fair division of anything. When choices present themselves, he takes what he wants, leaving you with nothing or leftovers, but later complains that you always get your way.

When tasks are to be shared, you do all or most of the work, and he later complains that you don't do enough or do it long enough or well enough.

The purpose of all this is to block you from developing any fruitful alliances that would give you resources—social, financial or professional. He does not want you to get access to anything that would make it more difficult for him to keep you in his "vise." Emphasis on *anything*: he does not want you to have anything.

Gavin de Becker wrote in THE GIFT OF FEAR, that he believes a woman *consents* to abusive behavior when she doesn't leave after the first occurrence and lets it happen to her a second time. He says that if she is in a relationship where abuse occurs more than once, she is not a victim, but a volunteer. I take his point, but this position overlooks the reality of the financial trap (nothing to run with and nowhere to run to).

Social commentator and comedian Bill Hicks said,

"You think you are free? Try going someplace
with no money."

Anything that the abuser does allow you to do, he allows because it benefits him in some way. For example:

- exercise more so you can wear sexier clothing
- learn a language so you can translate for him on a trip
- study a particular cuisine so you can cook new dishes for him
- take a relationship improvement course so you can be a better partner

True to form, he pursues his own interests as he pleases and to the fullest extent his means allow. He places no restrictions on any of his pursuits, except perhaps to hide or misrepresent some of them from you.

He boasts about indulging other women in previous relationships while denying the isolation and poverty he keeps you in.

He tries to make you feel guilty for recoiling at his abuse. He says he would treat you better if you would just be nicer to him.

He complains about his needs not being met even though you give him consideration, make sacrifices and provide emotional support in the relationship.

He requires a great deal of attention—listening to him, agreeing with him, assuring him, ministering to him, doing for him, but it's never your turn. He doesn't give anything in return because he is not capable of giving of himself and because he has nothing of real value to give.

The daily indignities and punishments mean that you must alternate between rising above his behavior and giving up. Finding the mental and emotional strength for this becomes harder and harder with time.

You know you cannot safely express your deepest emotions, so you have to rise above them, too, and put on a poker face. You begin to feel incapable of accomplishment and undeserving of love. You come to accept the double standards as confirmation of your incompleteness as a person and your unfitness as a wife.

> The infliction of double standards removes all vestiges of decency and fairness—it is yet another form of interpersonal criminality.

| 15 |

Red Flag #11
FOOD TRIPS

Food is tied to sensual pleasures and body image. Unfortunately, many modern influences are unhealthy and unnatural: lips that look like clitorises, adult models who look like prepubescent girls, actresses with freakishly large or small body parts and so on.

Whatever the pathological prefers in this regard, he's sure to try to force on his partner. He monitors the food she eats, even to the point of tasting everything she puts in her mouth, such as a cup of coffee or a sandwich, even if she's made the same thing for him. He might do this during meal prep or at the table. He taunts her with food, especially if she is heavy. Like so many other unhealthy relationship dynamics, it's annoying, petty and pointless.

If you're a foodie entangled in one of these relationships, you find that he uses food to torment and control you. This can manifest in a number of ways. He expects you to adopt his eating habits or his recommendations for your food intake, whether they are to your liking or not. He objects to your favorite foods and forbids you to buy them *or* withholds them from you. He insists on meal schedules or cooking tasks that are difficult, impossible or unpleasant to follow. This takes away a primal, simple joy in life—eating or drinking what you want—and reinforces your designation as his property.

He comments on how you eat implying that there's something wrong with you; this positions him as your arbiter and overseer.

He criticizes the order in which you eat the foods on your plate.

He forbids you to eat except at mealtimes.

He knows little about food or nutrition yet tries to force his food and supplement choices on you.

He refuses to let you to take food supplements of your choice.

He forces you to eat more than you want to or shames you into eating less than you want.

He prevents you from buying certain foods because he doesn't like them or says they're too expensive.

The main purpose here is to make you self-conscious and inhibited—to give him power over you and to make you feel unworthy of having what you need or want. This is one of the universal wounds that all forms of abuse deliver to the soul: you are not worthy.

"You eat too slow/too fast."

You eat too much/not enough protein/carbohydrate/fat.

"You eat more/less than anyone I've ever known."

"You put too much/too little sugar/milk in your coffee."

"You don't need that."

He seeks to control your access to food. At home, he employs tactics like ridicule, insult or even threat.

He withholds access to funds so that you cannot exercise your own food choices, like going out to lunch with a friend, getting a latté or buying a bottle of wine.

He limits or withholds food from your children or your animals for no reason. When they cry for food, he gets mad and berates you for being incompetent or irresponsible.

When he does buy food for your dependents, he does so grudgingly and in the cheapest form possible. Whatever they were used to before, they will not continue to receive under his roof. He is indifferent to their welfare—except for how it could reflect on him, but he feeds on knowing that you are suffering over their deprivation.

He knows your clothing size but buys something too small and says that you could fit into it if you would eat less, exercise more and get in better shape.

As a result of whatever food controls he institutes, you find yourself struggling with any number of ailments, including, but not limited to premature aging, hair loss, insomnia, tremors, back pain, headaches, halitosis, dental disease, loss of appetite, loss of taste, indigestion, bloating, nausea, stomach ache, constipation, diarrhea, hunger.

Note: Extreme diets in general and fat-deficient diets in particular place many stresses on the body; some food regimens adversely affect brain chemistry. The correlation between chronically insufficient dietary fat intake and/or the consumption of excito-toxins with violent behavior has been clinically proven. Many ingredients in low fat and low sugar food-like products exert dangerous influences on brain chemistry among other adverse side effects. Whether someone is organically pathological or not, extreme diets can exacerbate hormone fluctuation, mood swings, explosive outbursts and other violent behaviors.

http://www.westonaprice.org/moderndiseases/hd.html
http://www.coconutoil.com/oiling_america.htm
http://efaeducation.nih.gov/sig/aggretion.html
http://www.efph.purdue.edu/media/speaker/joehibbelna bstract.pdf
http://www.florahealth.com/flora/home/USA/HealthExp erts/FloraArticle28.htm

What's eating him is anything that could comfort or nourish you.

| 16 |

Red Flag #12
HUMILIATION

What started out as humor in the beginning turns into something else once the woman is fully trapped. What was funny or playful has turned mean or hurtful; it is not fair or funny or true. What made her like him, now makes her uneasy with him. What brought them closer together, now drives them apart. What was once good for a mutual laugh has morphed to something that brings her to tears or rings in her ears for hours.

In the beginning, it was easy to laugh together. The way he treated you removed any self-consciousness and smoothed all the rough edges. It was a gift to feel so accepted and understood. It was like he "got" you, but then somehow, that changed. You could feel it changing, but you didn't how or why or what to do about it.

The easy laughter got sharp and before long he is laughing at you, amusing himself at your expense and quick to make light of it when you object. It starts out as little slips, but if you stay in the relationship for long, what you will see is that as things escalate, his mask begins to slip in public. Humiliation becomes one of his hobbies. He takes making fun of you into new territory where, without warning, you are demeaned, insulted, mocked and subjugated. It is shocking. You had no idea he had this sort of meanness in him. You wonder how he hid it and how you missed it.

He broadcasts your personal confidences and private opinions.

He makes fun of how you walk and laughs at how you talk or what you think.

He forces you to do things you don't want to in public and in private. It is punishing whether you comply or resist.

He calls you derogatory names at home and in front of other people.

He describes your interests and work as compensation for your personality defects.

He insults your family and friends and by association you with information that you cannot respond to.

He orders you out of his house and tells you to see if any of your old boyfriends will take you in.

Abuse as a behavior set is predictable, but the timing of the individual acts that comprise it are not. Once you've learned the secret language of a counterfeit relationship, you can predict what is going to transpire, but not when. Once you understand that behaviors have crossed the line and become abusive, you can begin to get a look at the big picture and what the future is going to look like if you stick around.

Humiliation can come at you out of the blue, or predictably, such as after a violent outburst. The latter is a common occurrence and shows how a pathological is not just cruel, but also contemptuous of the suffering he causes. Kicking someone when they are down or putting salt on the wound are two of his specialties.

In private, you are demeaned, diminished or treated like dirt. In public, you are mocked, ribbed or shamed. The hostility in these acts may not be apparent to others, but to you it is unmistakable. In the beginning, you're startled by it, embarrassed and horrified. It hasn't happened much yet, and it stings. It sits on you like a great weight, making you feel less and less and less over time. You go over the events of your humiliation trying to understand the how and why of it—in vain.

When there is no reason for his behavior, you don't have any solid ground to stand on—this is when the subconscious erosion begins. The terrible inner toll intimately known to every target of abuse:

- You start to second-guess yourself
- Your confidence wanes
- Your self-image sags
- You blame yourself as guilt surrounds you
- You begin to feel hopeless and inept
- You begin to see yourself in accord with his themes of humiliation

Humiliation can work its way into you and burn holes in your natural defenses. Even if you're able to get encouragement or help from outside influences, regular doses of humiliation can thwart the best remedial attempts. Under constant attack, you react less and less until you begin to feel less and less, because you are going numb. The bullets fly, and you no longer duck.

As far as he's concerned, nothing is off limits. Every day supplies new fodder for this weapon and you never know when he's going to reload and take aim.

> *He strengthens himself by stripping away your dignity—the invisible weakening that lasts and lasts.*

| 17 |

Red Flag #13
MONEY

Money is a medium of exchange, it is a fuel for getting things done, it is a tool for accomplishment, acquisition and enjoyment. Money opens doors.

Money allows you to take care of yourself, your family (two-legged and four-legged) and acquire or experience your desires. An abundance of money allows great comfort; a lack of money, great discomfort. So, of course money is a significant lever to most abusers, from the political megalomaniac to the charismatic con artist.

The abuser uses money to construct his persona, hunt for prey and lay his trap. Money almost always plays a key role in trapping the prey and preventing her escape. The abusive man looks for financial vulnerability he can exploit. A woman separated from or without her own money is easier to contain and control than a woman who has resources she can call on. Once the predator assesses the ease with which he can separate his prey from her resources, he goes to work putting his plan into action. Then, once the woman is well in hand, the games begin during which he exploits and worsens her vulnerabilities.

Of course, not all pathological men have money, so they use different techniques to use money to intensify control and suffering.

If He Is Rich

The abuser who has discretionary funds uses them throughout the relationship in a number of ways. In the beginning, he uses them to finesse his persona and up his game if needed, but most especially he uses his funds to lure. Once you're caught, he uses money to keep you trapped and force you to endure his depravities. When the relationship fails and you want to leave, you might be unable to do so if you have made decisions based on promises he didn't keep. If you have been talked into quitting your job—and this is part of the universal con of a pathological with money—you are bound to face high hurdles in getting away from him and regaining your independence.

He has used his socioeconomic position along with his knowledge of your circumstances to do two things:

- Influence you to form a false impression of who he is (soul mate, other half, great love, etc.)
- Manipulate you into a false sense of security about his support

He knows what he's doing and this deception is deliberate and devious on his part.

He tells you that you don't have to worry about money anymore because he's got more than he can spend.

He says that since he's well set, he wants you to relax and let him take care of things from now on because you've earned it.

He paints a lovely word picture about how life will be and you'll see it in your mind's eye, but that's the only place you'll see it because it will never come into being.

He presents you with an "unamended" pre-nuptial agreement (which is illegal in some states). This kind of pre-nup, also called a "whiteout pre-nup" gives you no consideration or legal standing, it reduces you to the rank of a houseguest.

He promises that someday he'll provide something that he knows you want or need very much, but he'll never do it. The promise is just a bait piece that he takes out of his tool box from time to time when other tools and techniques aren't working.

He promises to draft a will allowing you to live in his house if he predeceases you, but he won't carry through on it.

It's a fact, that the wealthier he is, the more insistent he'll be that you give up your livelihood. Even if you've always been independent, he knows just what to say to make depending on him palatable to you. The abuser's genius for knowing just what to say and how to say it to get what he wants is remarkable and unnerving.

"If you're with me, you don't have to work."

"You've done for others all your life. It's your turn now."

"I've worked all my life and I've waited years for someone to enjoy this with."

He asks you to trust him. He plays upon your dignity, independence and self-reliance. And most diabolically, he speaks to your dreams. He waits for you to catch the vision, accept his offer and let him into your life. Then, when it's too late, you see that your willingness to trust, to lean on him was all wrong and is now being used against you. Once you've stepped into the trap, you will become even more financially compromised. Once he's gotten you to quit working, he goes about disassembling your network and blocks all opportunities for you to rebuild yourself. Even if it is easily within his means to help you recoup a loss, he won't do it. From then on, he blames and ridicules you for being broke or compromised even though he engineered it.

[handwritten in margin: this is exactly what God did]

If He Is Not Rich

On the other hand, if he is financially compromised himself, he uses that to lure you into a false sense of need and caretaking. Even though he possesses an organic incapacity to feel compassion himself, he knows how to play on yours, and he does.

He gets you to take care of him for some reason, but then fails to get on his feet or start contributing to the household as promised.

He needs to borrow something from you, like a car, a cell phone, cash, your credit card, then abuses your trust by failing to safeguard it while in his possession.

He steals valuables from your house behind your back.

He tries to get you to put his name on some of your accounts or assets.

He asks you to invest in some business or project.

He uses your compassion for his children to get you to sacrifice yourself for them financially by paying for their childcare, clothes, medical care, tuition, car, etc.

The consequences of the money flag inevitably add up to loss. You may lose part of your net worth or be left destitute. The bottom line is that being the victim of a charismatic con can limit your ability to exit the relationship and to function in the world afterwards.

Lack of money can take away your dignity faster than just about any other circumstance. You can not only lose your standard of living, but lose your ability to put a roof over your head, food on the table and take care of your dependents and financial responsibilities. Lack of money taxes relationships, health and peace of mind. However a pathological plays the money card, what he seeks is power over you so that he can control your circumstances and destroy you. His success in these pursuits is predicated on your total resources. He uses your forbearance against you until he has used you up, at which point he will get rid of you one way or another.

This is how Claudia Moscovici describes the "idealize, devalue and discard" cycle of the pathological partner:

> "This process may take several years or only a few hours. It all depends on what the psychopath wants from you and whether or not

you present a challenge to him. If the psychopath wants the semblance of respectability–a screen behind which he can hide his perverse nature and appear harmless and normal–he may establish a long-term partnership with you or even marry you. If all he wants is to have some fun, it will be over within a couple of hours. If he wants the stimulation and diversion of an affair, he may stay with you for as long as you excite him. Despite the differences in timeline, what remains constant is this: eventually, sooner or later, you'll be discarded (or be led by the psychopath's bad behavior to discard him) as soon as you no longer serve his needs."

Over half of the homeless people living on the street are women—many of them are out there with their children and pets—after having fled a violent home. Getting you to give up your financial resources is a big red flag of bad things to come, especially if he has cajoled you into signing an agreement that would expose you to further loss if he doesn't keep his word.

Whether he has money or not, he really has nothing to give, and you will soon be forced to live like a refugee.

| 18 |

Red Flag #14
SEX

Many abusers are preoccupied with sex— actual and virtual. They use actual sex (including rape) as a tool for control and punishment. They use virtual sex (pornography) as a tool for distraction and gratification. In both contexts, the sex, like the abusive relationship, is counterfeit because it is a fraud and void of love.

A preoccupation with sex is a sign of arrested development. It comes as no surprise that many pathologicals exhibit this. Sex is the arena in which his warped ideas about women are revealed. He insists on total sexual receptivity or initiative. When she is not available or enthusiastic, she is condemned as being frigid or selfish. He flirts with other women or engages in other relationships but restricts her contact with other men. If she communicates with another man, she is retaliated against and called names.

Many abusers got addicted to pornography in their teens (or earlier) and never developed beyond a fixation on reproductive organs. When you look at media with a discerning eye, it's not hard to see how pervasive this condition is—millions of teenagers walking around in adult bodies obsessed with reproductive organs. It's a form of mental slavery and spiritual disablement as well for the man and his partner(s). Some men carry unrealistic ideas of what his ideal woman should be like that were formed from his exposure to pornography. Since his ideals are unreal, he is never confronted with their unreality and so has unlimited ammunition to use against his partner about her various insufficiencies.

Over the years, pornography has become more intense, unnatural and violent as "soft" porn has broken out to move mainstream. An abuser can inflict pain on his partner without consequence because pornography has reframed what is normal sexual behavior in his head. This coupled with any psychopathic tendencies is a recipe for sexual savagery. As a result of pornography's influence, sexual mores have fallen or never formed in many toxic individuals. In addition to gratuitous sex in mass media, the masses are also being programmed to feel "compassion" for sexual predators, the damaged who can't help themselves and turn to strangers, children or animals for release.

The sad truth is that most men who use sex in ways that wound women are incapable of love. They can perform the sex act, but they cannot love. A high percentage of women who find themselves involved in a relationship that turns had sex with the man early on before she had gotten to know him. Many of them say later that had they known what he really was, they would have never consented to enter into any kind of a relationship with him. They report that they entered into sex when they thought he expected it to keep the relationship progressing. (This is not consent so much as a symptom of inadequate self-image.)

Sex has become such a commodity, and been so denigrated by media, that men expect sex and women give it almost by rote—as if there's not much else to experience than its physical component. Statistically, about half of females consent to sex as early as the third date and then wonder why the man excoriates them later for it. Many teenagers are sexually active these days; they say that the main reason they "do it" is boredom. If an anthropologist were to look at the behavior of these girls, they would quickly deduce that the females have been programmed to believe their cleavages are about all they have to offer. When these implanted feelings of inadequacy combine with the abuser's tendency to objectify his partner, the relationship doesn't have a chance and the stage is set for dehumanization. Relationship first, sex last.

Social engineering notwithstanding, at whatever point you became intimate with the man who later abuses you, you felt, at the time or afterwards, that there was a strange quality to the experience. It may have been so slight a feeling that you didn't pick up on it in the moment, or you may have been off-put by something at the time. Your expectations of prowess and finesse were met or not. You felt that something was missing although you couldn't put your finger on it. Chances are you were so compelled by him, that you attributed the minor misgivings you felt to the newness of that part of the relationship.

In the beginning of a sexual relationship with a predatory or psychopathic partner, the act itself may or may not be satisfying for you. Be assured, he will make sure it is satisfying for him. If little doubts creep into your mind, you dismiss them thinking that sex will lead to greater intimacy as you know it can. As the relationship progresses and other abuses come into play, the sex will inevitably become harmful. You will be taken too soon. You will be made raw. You will be torn. You will be forced when your body is not ready.

Sooner or later, you will come face to face with the harsh truth that real intimacy with him is not possible. You will not know why or what to do. You will work on the relationship so that the sexual part of it can heal. You will do more to satisfy your man. And so forth. The plain fact is that there is nothing you can do to improve sex when he does not have the capacity to love.

The sex act for the pathological is about control, gratification and destruction; it is not about love, union and intimacy. Though he probably knows enough to talk about your wants and needs, his actions say it all; they show that the sex is for him, and you matter less and less as time goes by.

One of the wages of the pathological's lifelong use and abuse of women is his organic inability to give and receive love. He can go through the motions, but this is all. He is incapable of showing tenderness, being intimate and creating transcendent moments. He cannot express affection, he can only be sexual.

You are groped, but never simply held.

You are tongued, but never kissed.

He criticizes your sexual expression.

His sex is devoid of love.

He demands and expects sex on his terms.

He constructs a sex routine that you are expected to follow.

He tells you how and when to respond to him because the sex act is all about him—you are just the body he is acting out with.

The man who seeks to control his partner's sexual response is capable of sadism. It begins with him telling you what kind of response he wants. It may lead him to resort to other behaviors as he searches for a way to get a response from you that fills the empty place inside him. After whatever you are forced to endure in bed, he may walk away snarling because you did not follow his instructions or satisfy him.

You go along to keep the peace for fear of what he'll do if you resist. Despite complying, you are condemned for not being enthusiastic, for not moaning or writhing or verbalizing the way he wants. If you submit in order to live another day, this part of the nightmare will become a grueling exercise of mind over matter to keep up the protective charade. This is not an uncommon choice that women in these relationships face. Sometimes it is necessary, but it is still a sort of rape.

But there will come a day when your body shuts down and you can no longer stifle your revulsion and submit. When this happens before you are able to escape, odds are you will be raped. Afterwards, you will be yelled at and blamed for deceiving him or ruining his sex life. He pronounces you "frigid" or accuses you of being homosexual. And all you want is to be out of his bed.

Sex may be important to him, but it's really nothing personal.

| 19 |

Red Flag #15
SLEEP

Sleep is when the body self repairs and the mind processes. It is meant to be done in one long block of time every 24 hours.

Sleep is a state of total vulnerability. Sleep is an absolute necessity.

Lack of sleep is a factor in many emotional and physical maladies. It is not to be interrupted or taken for granted or scrimped on. Any persistent experience can alter your consciousness, but perhaps none more than sleep deprivation.

Abuse is its own trance, but exacerbated by regular lack of sleep, it becomes dangerous.

In the beginning, when you're falling in love (and he is leading you down the garden path) you lose sleep because you're happy and excited. This is natural. But this will change in many ways for many reasons.

He insists on sleeping conditions that are uncomfortable for you. - yes kicking me in middle of p'm

He wakes you up to argue about something.

He delivers a threat just before bedtime. — yes! often

He wakes you up to have sex.

He demands that you stay up or get up to do something for him.

The most numerous reasons however come from the consequences of being in a dangerous relationship with a pathological partner. They sit upon you in the dark, squeezing your heart and tearing at your soul. On those nights, you lie awake with your heart and mind racing because you are so disturbed by the relationship—the things he says and does keep your mind going. You struggle to understand how and why he's behaving the way he is. Your emotions fight against your logic; they get stuck or stalemated, for years. The exhaustion is beyond language. Your heart and your mind go into dark places in a desperate search for reason, strength, hope. Instead of finding answers, you find more questions and you begin to go numb.

You expend your dwindling energy to keep from giving into his behavior or letting him see how scared you are. You know that standing up for yourself could trigger him and so you strive to rise above the abuse and keep him from goading you into a reaction. When you pass the point of no-return, you take a stand and try to fight back or you become the walking dead.

On top of your emotional, mental and spiritual exhaustion, the steady buildup of sleep deprivation ages and exhausts you. Your sleep deficit grows to such excess that your health suffers. You find yourself so exhausted that on the rare occasions when you're able to let go enough to get some real sleep, unusual things occur.

You begin to snore or gulp air.

You startle so much you fall out of bed.

You wet or nearly wet the bed.

You waken so ragged you can hardly rise.

These indignities are only more evidence of what your internal and external life has become. You don't feel, look or think like yourself. You are being reduced to a nervous wreck. When you see your face in the mirror or hear your voice in conversation, you are almost unrecognizable to yourself. As you get weaker and weaker, you realize your condition makes his manipulations and torments more painful for you and easier for him. In time, your exhaustion is such that you hardly care about what is happening to you, you care less and less about enduring, every thought you have is incomplete. Your strength is gone.

Sleep deprivation is debilitating to mind, body and spirit, which is why it is used by men who like to destroy women.

Sleep deprivation is used to break down the psyche. Now you know.

134

| 20 |

Red Flag #16
TIME

Time flies when you're having fun. Predators know how to put time on their side, whether they're exhausting their prey by long stalks or rushing them into distressed moves that end in their demise.

Time is not kind to abusers either because they don't have staying power because they don't have substance. This is why time is used against the prey so often by placing her in difficult situations and then applying pressure by prolongation or urgency to wear her out.

Charismatic con artists (like political tyrants) use time to wear down their victims. The pathological is in a huge rush to get the relationship nailed down. The uninformed, uninitiated woman mistakes this for love. He says he wants you. He wants to take a trip or move in together or get married. He can't wait, he wants it all now.

His urgencies make you feel urgent in return; they get you scrambling to make these things happen. The rising crescendo of rushing that his urgency imposes on the relationship heightens the normal excitement of falling in love. This can be perceived as the counterfeit it is when you know what to look for. If you can disconnect enough to observe, you will see cracks in his persona or holes in his plan. You will see other things, too.

He is always in a hurry, but he resists it when you push back. In the beginning, he'll relent, but as a predator, he wants things to happen fast before you see where this is going. He explains his rushing as "just who he is" and how he gets things done. In his mind, he's just a dynamic guy. He considers any pace less than *fast* to be dilly-dallying. This is just the beginning of it. Every day is soon filled with unexpected, intrusive time tricks. He uses rushing, time change and interruption as weapons of control to disrespect your needs and disassemble your boundaries.

He tells you to be ready at one time and then changes it to another without warning, putting you at considerable disadvantage and inconvenience, which only sets you up for more abuse because you are slow or incompetent or disorganized, etc.

He sets the schedule for your day, telling you when to get up, what to do throughout the day, when you can use the phone, work on the computer, fix the meals, take a walk, use the car and when to go to bed. Failure to adhere is grounds for punishment.

He assures you there will be plenty of time for you to do something you want to do later that day or that week, but he keeps you running, and you either never get to it or the opportunity passes.

He stages little emergencies to interfere with the few plans he allows you to make so that nothing ever comes to fruition. This is one of innumerable takeaways he gets to pull on you.

Whatever you do, he wants it done faster. He directs and interrupts every activity so much that simple tasks take many times longer than they should, and you are blamed for this. Rushing is used to ruin any activity, especially those that matter the most to you.

You struggle to keep up with your day-to-day responsibilities. He uses this against you. He interprets your struggles to mean that you lack time management skills, you procrastinate, you're lazy, disorganized and so forth. One of the costs of this red flag is that sooner or later, you will be living a life in which you have no time for yourself. Physical therapist, survivor and author Sarah Strudwick calls this his "putting your head in the washing machine."

He is not comfortable with spontaneity and not forgiving of delays. Using time tricks is easier and just as effective in derailing your activities and draining your energy. He uses time tricks without mercy against the things that feed your soul.

If you sit down to read, he interrupts you with conversation or puts you to task.

If he discovers you dislike being rushed or interrupted, he does it all the more.

If you question the need to rush, he either ignores the question or attacks you for being obstinate, lazy, selfish and so forth.

His time attacks demonstrate his emptiness and disconnectedness. He is a depleted person looking to you to fill him up. Like distraction, rushing makes him feel safe from the scrutiny and losses that could result if things were allowed to occur at a more normal, relaxed rate. The more difficulties he can impose on you, the more reasons he has to keep you hurrying along. He sucks the joy out of life. He feeds on the miseries he creates for you.

> *He is an energy vampire and the joy he sucks out of you is his blood feast.*

| 21 |

Red Flag #17
WITHHOLDING

There are many ways to lie and many kinds of deception to be accomplished with lying. Partial truth telling is an age-old deception tactic. The pathological liar skillfully declines to divulge certain information or talk about certain things without using avoidance tactics that raise suspicion. This can be done to steer a conversation to keep something concealed, to distract or to manipulate perception. Often times, the social predator will announce that he is honest and never lies before his credibility comes to the test. This is done to throw inquirers off balance.

When you step into a trap laid by a deceptive man, part of how he got you into the trap was to withhold information about himself. He knows what to say and what not to say so you are charmed, remain unaware you are being deceived and come to a conclusion that allows him to continue his con. It serves him for you to believe him. He gets away with it because he knows you'll give him the benefit of the doubt—this buys him control and time. Withholding requires the careful arrangement of information and emotion—it is a devious and vicious form of lying.

The ways that withholding occurs in an abusive relationship could include a man who declines to talk in any depth about his previous relationships in a way that suggests he's doing so to protect the dignity of his former partners and that he's over it—both of which reflect well on him. However, the real reason he hides the truth from you is because if you knew the truth, he would be exposed, you would exit the scene and the game would be over. Pathologicals live for the game. He could have trashed the lives of dozens and dozens of women already and yet the denial and delusions of grandeur of his mental illness allow him to say things like:

"No woman has ever been fool enough to leave me."

"You don't know how lucky you are."

There are women who would kill to be with me."

"My old girlfriends still write and call."

"The women I've been with—they know how good it is here."

Besides his past relationships, he declines to talk much about other topics like his family, his business, his background, his finances, his health and so forth. If you initiate conversation about the forbidden or ignored topics, he lies, gives you polite non-answers, he changes the subject or he walks away.

If you ask about his location, he may tell you that he's moved or relocated. He'll let you assume it was for business or retirement, that way he doesn't have to tell you he was run out of town.

If you ask about his marital status, he may tell you that he's divorced. He'll let you assume it was once, that way he won't have to tell you how many times and what he did to his other wives.

No matter how much you disclose about your life, no matter how attentive or polite he is in the beginning, he is not that interested except to have the information to use against you later. There is no such thing as sharing confidences with these types of men because they are not capable of being honest or responding in kind to the normal progression of sharing in an intimate relationship.

Besides information, he will also withhold things from you. If you have a particular line of personal products that you like, he promises to provide it for you and then without warning refuses to do so. If you want to watch a show on television, get your hair cut, return a library book, take a walk or see a show at the theatre, he could engineer a way to prevent it or stop you—not because he cares whether you do the thing but because it would give him a charge to withhold from you something that you want or need.

This is one of many behaviors that confirm what scientists report about the mental maturity level of the typical psychopath: 14 years of age.

The more important something is to you, the more you can be sure he will find a way to withhold it from you. For him, the means justify the end, which is to control you and the relationship so that he can get his needs met. The less you know, the easier it is for him to do this.

He is the most withholding about the sickest part of his life.

Part Three:
Personality Dynamics
of Subjugation

"While woman #1 is basking in the hyper-focus of his attention, he is trolling, in the middle of and ending other relationships with men and women... Of course, woman #1 is high on oxytocin and believes she has just met her soulmate."

Sandra M Brown, MA

Tom & Dina

Dina was a year shy of vesting her pension with FedEx when she met Tom on the last delivery of her day. She drove down the long drive to the large farmhouse and thought how lucky the owners were to live in such an idyllic place. He walked out, signed for the box, smiled and walked away. After several more deliveries over the next few months, Tom began to walk out to meet the truck and save her the time of running to the house. One day, he walked up with a pretty mare in hand, her young colt trotting alongside. "She's the same color as your hair."

He said it with a softness that took her back, like they'd known each other for years. He handled the mare with quiet authority. Dina could see that both horses were relaxed, which told her he knew what he was doing. Like her, he owned Belgians. She thought about Tom and his farm the rest of the day.

By early summer, the inevitable had happened: Tom had asked her out. They had a nice dinner made all the more enjoyable by his easy-going manners. He hardly took his eyes off her the entire evening, which felt alternately discomfiting and delicious. By the end of the fourth date, Dina realized how utterly safe and comfortable she felt with this man. He asked if she'd like to stop by his barn to see a late-season colt that had been born the previous week. She said yes immediately. They spent a half hour watching the foal with his dam and talking together easily. As they walked out of the barn, he hugged her shoulders and lightly kissed the side of her head. She felt his lips through her hair and nearly gasped. She wanted him to kiss her again, but he didn't. He opened the truck door for her and drove her home.

The summer went by in a blink. More dates, more time with horses, more kisses, more conversation, more knowing looks. For the first time in her life, Dina felt completely accepted and wanted. In their hurried encounters when she was making deliveries and their unrushed reveries on weekends, she slowly opened her heart to this kindred spirit, pouring out her deepest wounds and fondest wishes.

In the midst of all this, something happened to the first colt Dina had seen. The vet said he died of dehydration, but Tom said that didn't make sense because he was with his mother and she was fine. Dina stood in solemn witness as the backhoe dug the hole and Tom laid the beautiful young horse to rest. They stood over the grave, looking down. "I'm so sorry," she said. Tom shook his head.

He was a third-generation horseman. He was the sole heir of the family homestead with all of its equipment and some of his horses. Tom made a good living growing hay in the summer and logging trees in the winter. For fun, he'd started entering his horses in pulling competitions at the local level and quickly moved up through the ranks. Dina was also working with her horses and entering them in some shows, but without as much ease or success on account of her work schedule. She had a pair of powerful young geldings she dreamed of campaigning.

When Tom asked her to move in with him on Labor Day weekend, she laughed and said "Okay" without hesitation.

When he proposed two weeks later, she blinked back tears and said "Yes, yes."

When he suggested they elope, she shook her head, but he talked her into it and elope they did the next week. She really had to wrangle for time off on such short notice, but she did.

The first month of marriage was a continuation and enlargement of everything that had gone before it. Every day was a gift. Dina felt like she floated on air and reveled in the amazing turn her life had taken in the space of a few months. Tom made her feel welcome in his home, he made room for her horses. He helped her make dinner and they talked about everything.

A couple of her horses got banged up by his, but it was nothing serious and she knew horses would be horses. One evening she looked out and saw one of her horses limping badly. She ran out, lifted up his enormous hoof and was stunned to see a huge nail going straight up through it. She had to cut away part of the inner hoof to get purchase on the nail and pull it out. The horse was lame for three months, partially due to the size of the nail hole and partially due to infection. She was relieved he had been spared tetanus or sepsis.

Sounds familiar

The second month, she got a flat tire every week driving to work. When she called Tom for help, she got his voicemail, which meant he was outside without his cell phone—again. He was apologetic when she told him about the flat and her unanswered calls. He promised he would keep his cell phone on him. She didn't get any more flat tires after that.

The third month, her other horse must have run into something because she came home to find him with a three foot laceration running from his shoulder to his flank. It wasn't deep, but it was ugly. This required a vet call and as much follow-up care as the hoof injury. The vet said it looked like a blade cut because it was so clean. Dina couldn't imagine what was in the pasture that the horse had moved against. She scoured every square foot of the barns and pastures without finding anything. She was mystified. None of Tom's horses had ever picked up a nail or cut themselves the way hers had. The injury was going to leave a long flowing scar, like a tendril of smoke.

Tom kept an eye on the horses while Dina was at work and doctored their wounds, but they weren't healing easily or well. They were also becoming nervous and difficult to handle—something they had never been.

As the weather cooled, Dina felt weary with the growing burdens of her job, her marriage and her horses. Just as quickly as her luck had changed and she'd met and married Tom, now it seemed she was under a ban. Nothing was working out and everything seemed to be so time-consuming. She was so distracted, she started misplacing things. She'd spend frantic minutes every day searching for her keys, her wallet, her cell phone, her contact lenses, etc. She wondered why she was doing this all of a sudden. One Saturday afternoon, she was in the tack room looking for a headstall she knew she'd cleaned and hung up, but it was not there. She was fed up. Tom walked past just as she was about to swear in frustration. He looked at her and laughed in a way she hadn't heard in weeks. It melted her heart and she laughed, too. "I think you are working way too hard."

He wrapped his arms around her and she leaned into his bulk. His flannel shirt smelled like man and horse. She felt the visceral sense of his understanding for the first time in many weeks and it made her weak in the knees. How could she lose touch with how much he "got" her? It was one of the many gifts he'd given her and yet she'd let it slip in the drain of daily living.

The next morning it rained. It was Sunday, they sat in the sun room and looked out over the farm drinking their coffee. "Why don't you quit work, stay at home and do what you want to do?"

The thought had never crossed her mind. She just looked at him, speechless. That evening, he turned out the light and they lay there in the dark. "If you want to, you can, you know."

She closed her eyes, but didn't sleep. She chewed on the idea for weeks. She was six months away from vesting. She didn't dare quit before then--that would be too scary. Every few days, Tom encouraged her without pressure to think about the difference between continuing to run in the hamster wheel versus being home with him and the horses full time. He didn't need to tell her what it would mean to their hopes of campaigning their horses.

She felt inadequate in so many ways as she thought about the net effect of being pulled in so many directions. Once she'd married Tom, she had all but lost interest in her career. She was appalled at what it had meant to her before, when she'd needed it. *I am like a hamster running a wheel, and here's a chance to get off the wheel and out of the cage.* But if she stuck it out 25 more weeks, she'd have her pension. She told Tom that's what she was going to do.

She could stand it for six more months. He shrugged and nodded. "Whatever you want."

He didn't say he was disappointed, but she could tell. The next week, the steering went out in her truck on the way to work and she careened off the road. She hit a tree, went through a fence and hit the concrete casing of a field pump. The truck was totaled. She was bruised, but unhurt. Ten days later, one of her horses nearly gouged his eye out—another inexplicable injury and another big vet bill. The vet saved his eye, but barely. He was going to need months of care and separation from the other horses. Tom helped her tend him, which was a good thing, because her horse was wild with pain and she was in no shape to tend him herself. One evening, Tom turned loose of him too soon and Dina got knocked to the ground as the horse careened to get away from their ministrations. She lay against the wall looking up at her husband and her horse wondering why all of this was happening. Her formerly calm horse stood against the far wall regarding her with a cold eye. She stood up to go to him, but froze when she saw his flattened his ears. Tom grabbed her arm and pulled her out of the stall. He guided her into the house and walked her up the stairs to bed.

"What is going on here? I don't understand anything anymore." She lay down in her clothes and pulled a blanket over her.

The physicality of her delivery work that week was agony, she got more sore for three days running. Tom dutifully took care of the farm and her horses while she was at work, but she could see the strain in him. It seemed like a live wire was running through the herd, making every one of them agitated for no apparent reason.

One night when she couldn't sleep, she tiptoed down the stairs to the kitchen. She fixed some tea and sat alone at the table, feeling empty and sad. The house was quiet, the pasture was bathed in moonlight. It all looked peaceful, but it didn't feel peaceful. *What is wrong here?*

Later that week, a piece of equipment nearly fell on Tom when he was out by himself working on the tractor. That evening after dinner, she grabbed her coat and went out to survey the scene. She could see exactly what had happened and nearly happened. A chill ran up her spine and over her skull. The thought of him being pinned, or worse, with no one to come to his aid made her feel faint.

The following week, she went into her manager's office and started the paperwork for her resignation. He tried to talk her out of it, reminding her how close she was to vesting, but she said that what was at stake at home was more important than a supplemental income later on. She was walking away from about 2200 dollars a month that would kick in when she reached the age of 55. That sum of money would not matter now and probably would not matter at all in 20 years. Tom had a knack for making money and investing. He had told the truth when he'd said she didn't need to work.

When Dina told Tom she would be a full-time wife in three weeks, he leapt to his feet, grabbed her and tried to spin, but nearly dropped her because of his injury. She groaned too because she was still sore from wrecking her truck and getting knocked down in the stall. "What a pair!" he laughed.

She felt flooded with relief and prayed things would begin to calm down. Once she was free of her job, she dedicated herself to being a house wife. She got to walk out to wherever Tom was working and bring him hot coffee or something out of the oven. She got to see her horses several times a day. Life was good.

One morning, she was upstairs cleaning when she heard Tom come in the back door and bellow her name in a tone of voice she'd never heard from him. One of her horses had busted down a gate and was loose. She flew outside and got to her horse before he got out on the road. A close call. A freak occurrence, and not at all like her horses. She put him in another pasture and went to help Tom fix the gate. When she got to him, he glared at her and threw down his tools, "you can start cleaning up after these nags now."

She apologized and worked on the gate for two hours. Tom didn't say a word to her the rest of the day. Or the next day. She was in the house when she heard a loud report and a horse scream. She ran to the back door to see Tom and Lester explode out of the barn in opposite directions. Tom had a broken 2 by 4 in his hands. He strode into the tractor barn and slammed the door.

Dina stood frozen for several minutes, then ran to the barn to see what she could see. Blood on a post. She went out into the pasture and located Lester in a far corner.

She was halfway to him when she heard Tom yell her name. "He's okay. He ran past me and broke a board against the barn door."

She waved at him and continued. He yelled again and she thought she heard an obscenity, but pretended not to hear him. The tractor barn door slammed again.

Lester had a foot-long gash in his chest which was bleeding profusely. *He's okay? This is not okay. What the hell?!* She could see the whites of his eyes. In six months, each of her horses had been injured and her truck destroyed. Why were they all having such bad luck? Were Tom's horses really beating up on hers or was something else going on?

That evening Tom and Dina had their first real argument. She knew they disagreed about some things and held differing opinions about others, none of which concerned her or affected their relationship. Tom unloaded on her with a fury that scared her. He raged about everything—her cooking, her butt, her horses, her truck, her lovemaking, her baking and her lack of money. She sat dumbfounded, unable to respond. When he was finished, he stomped upstairs and slammed the bedroom door.

She cleaned up the kitchen, then sat in the study for hours before daring to go upstairs to bed. When at last she did, she found the door was locked.

In the ensuing months, Tom took one of her horses to a show 800 miles away and withheld water from him the entire time so that he would weigh less at weigh in—a supposed advantage. Bud collapsed in the arena and had to be dragged out with a tractor. They put him in a stall and he died there alone that night. Tom did not tell Dina until he got home without her horse.

As Tom's verbal rampages intensified and her horses continued to have unexplained sicknesses and injuries, Dina decided to leave. Tom had put her on an allowance so it took time for her to ferret away enough money to get away from him. She had lost touch with most of her friends and didn't feel she could call on them for help now.

When Tom went to the next out-of-town show, she loaded up her belongings and her horses and left. She drove 500 miles south and moved in to a house his family owned. It didn't take him 10 minutes to figure out where she'd gone once he got back to town and found her gone.

She began divorce proceedings and tried to get a restraining order, but couldn't because he hadn't threatened to kill her, which was the criteria. He turned off her cell phone and stalked her. She had to get a job and feared for her horses' safety when she was at work. She took a job as a retail clerk for eight dollars an hour and wondered how she would survive. She also wondered what she had been thinking when she'd given up her job at FedEx before being fully vested.

Tom stalked Dina for seven years. He called her at work so many times her employer reprimanded her, he defrauded her in the divorce, he got away with forging her signature on debt instruments that had been in his name, which ruined her credit, he set fire to her garage and he would have tried to kill more of her horses except they wouldn't come near him and he knew better than to try to go after them in the open pasture.

In the 10 years since she got away from Tom, Dina has endured many hardships as a direct result of her marriage. Despite working steadily, she has lived below the poverty level and become an alcoholic. She still has her beloved horses, but struggles to care for them. They are her responsibility and her only source of joy. They have all healed from their physical wounds, but their hearts and lives will never be the same. Dina has decided that when her last horse dies, she will die, too, since she has nothing left and life is so unkind.

| 22 |

The Stranger in Your Bed

Finding yourself in a relationship that "turns" is like waking up in a foreign land with a stranger in your bed. You feel confusion, embarrassment, vulnerability and *unmistakable menace.*

Living through it day to day is like being in a maze with a monster. You're frightened all the time, but you know you can't show it. You fumble along trying to keep your wits about you because you know panic could be fatal. You search for reason, safety and understanding, but find none.

The farther into the experience you go, the darker and more dire things get and the more lost you become. Your mind and your heart are at odds. You lie awake at night, your head throbs and your heart pounds. Your mind tells you something is wrong. Your heart tells you to keep on. You loved this man, you vowed to be with him; but what has happened to him, why is he acting this way and what is he going to do next?

You could lie awake at night for the rest of your life and never make sense of it because it makes no sense—until you get the big picture. It is a picture of many things from long ago—of heredity so horrendous or parenting so evil, that it creates a pathology so extreme it affects successive generations.

Family violence does irreparable harm. Abused baby boys grow up to be perpetrators who do more or less what was done to them. Abused baby girls grow up to be victims having become habituated to mistreatment, although a miniscule percent defy their DNA and grow up to be perpetrators. Horse trainers Monty Roberts and Buck Brannaman are examples of this rare outcome. Their fathers beat and brutalized their mothers, their siblings, them and the family horses (in two cases almost to the death), but both of them overcame the trauma of their childhoods to raise their own families without violence and to teach empathic, relationship-based methods of horsemanship.

Two Categories

Perpetrators of abuse fall into two broad categories: the *emotional disturbed* and the *mentally ill*.

Emotional Baggage

Emotionally disturbed men are capable of purging their emotional baggage to learn healthy ways of relating IF they want to. Their desire is the fulcrum upon which the future health and happiness of their relationships depend. When someone wants to get better and engages fully in the therapeutic process, chances are good, they will recover.

This principle applies to emotional and physical difficulties.

Brain Damage

Brain damaged men—*regardless* of what they say—do not have the *organic capacity* to recover. It's crucial to understand that a such man (mentally ill or personality disordered)—no matter how exciting, romantic or "right" he appears to be—is a ticking time bomb. He is not capable of love (or compassion or guilt or honor or shame) because one or more parts of his brain (frontal and/or temporal lobe) do not function normally. *He knows how to play the game of romance, but he does not know how to love. Any woman who gets caught in his trap will be harmed.*

What Is A Psychopath?

Beast. Brute. Demon. Devil. Evil. Fiend. Lunatic. Maniac. Monster. These are some of the words used by women to describe the nature of the men they fell for fast and hard who then abused them in multiple ways before they escaped. In every case, this man seemed "too-good-to-be-true" before he began to unleash hell in their lives. These women are describing *psychopathic* partners.

When psychopathy was first studied in the 19th century it was described as "moral insanity" because the behavior of the afflicted was so immoral and unscrupulous. The top-tier hallmark of this condition presents as "lack of empathy" and the group of characteristics (Cluster B) that manifest in psychopathic behavior is best described as a "lack of conscience."

In a narrow sense, conscience can be described as the internal mechanism that guides right-and-wrong decisions, perspectives and behaviors, which result in doing the right thing, even if no one is looking. A compassionate person of conscience stops to help an injured animal instead of driving by, returns a wallet they find on the street, works late to meet a deadline, does what they say they'll do. The implications of persons who do not possess this internal mechanism, who have no sense of right-and-wrong, who have no inner guidance to do the right thing are serious indeed. They hit a pedestrian and keep going, they take money out of a co-worker's desk, they make excuses for not doing their work, they lie to get what they want.

In some contexts, the psychopath can be distinguished as *primary* and *secondary*. They both participate in abuse for personal gratification and often for personal gain as well but at different levels.

- The primary psychopath has a principal role in causing pain and suffering to the victim—he applies the blows, metes out punishment, withholds food, etc.

- The secondary psychopath plays a supporting role— he performs necessary duties to support the primary psychopath, he observes or tolerates the abuse, he condones it by keeping quiet about it.

For example, in dog fighting or human trafficking, the primary psychopath would be the one who masterminds and abuses the victims for profit, the secondary psychopaths would be the ones who work for him and pay to watch the dog/woman perform and then exploit each one (bestiality/rape) when possible. Each psychopath participates at the level commensurate with his current level of pathology, which increases with age.

In relationships and organizations, the psychopath dishes up the Hegelian Dialectic as only the soulless can. He causes a problem, proffers a solution, which results in him gaining more control. He torments his victim(s) with unrelenting cruelty, pauses to catch his breath which gives them a moment of respite and then offers an excruciating condition or two if they wish relief from the current session. If they whimper or plead for mercy, his contempt erupts, he withdraws or worsens the condition(s) and resumes the torment.

The Predator/Prey Model

You always find the psychopath installed near their prey item of choice, such as women, children, animals, drugs, money and power. In any environment that draws a significant number of desirable prey, there will be psychopaths somewhere nearby:

- gyms and spas
- modeling and acting
- pediatrics and day-care centers
- elementary schools and child services
- animal shelters and research labs
- zoos and training facilities
- pharmacies and hospitals
- college campuses and casinos
- brokerage houses and financial counseling
- business schools and the professions

- capital venture and corporations
- all levels of government

Psychologists say that within the general population, one to four percent is psychopathic; within positions of influence, that percentage rises to six or more. These don't seem like significant numbers until you consider that each psychopath has many, many victims. The charismatic con artist that preys on women goes through many women each year. It has been reported that the average pedophile assaults more than 130 children in his lifetime. The corporate criminal can exploit millions, the political tyrant billions.

Psychopaths are uniquely disposed to conduct cons or frauds because they are masters of deceit and unimpeded by conscience. They deceive themselves with *denial* and *delusions of grandeur* (among other things), they deceive others with *charm* and *pathological lying* (among other things). Even though abundant red flags fly over their lives and their relationships, it's impossible to see through their game until you know their secret modus operandi. Their ability to camouflage their true nature and select their victim is chilling, which capabilities factor in their success at manipulating and using others. Besides being hard to detect, they succeed because their behavior is so egregious that it is *beyond belief.* The unreality of the extremity of their behavior is part of how they get away with it. These individuals *routinely* do things to their spouses, children, animals and associates so diabolical that these acts can only be described as "unbelievable" and "unconscionable."

The psychopath's condition is *permanent* and *progressive*, the rate of recidivism is 100 percent. Although the equivalent of a half trillion dollars has been spent worldwide on research for them, there have yet to be found any therapeutic options. Holland and Canada are just two countries where massive work has been done in recent decades to try to help the psychopath.

- According to Dutch Ministry of Justice Department Head Jacqueline Hockstenback, "We know there is no effective treatment for psychopathy."

- Before completing his four decades of research in the Canadian penal system, Robert Hare, PhD said, "Compared to other major clinical disorders... psychopathy ... is responsible for far more social distress and disruption than all other psychiatric disorders combined."

Another finding of all that research is that those who receive therapy do not become less dangerous, they become *more cunning*.

Generationally Transmitted Disease

Violence begets violence—it is the generationally transmitted disease that parents give to their children. With the exception of hereditary transmission, *the psychopath is made, not born* by:

- trauma in-utero (sensory, chemical, physical)
- trauma in early childhood (family violence, natural disaster, war)
- extreme substance abuse (alcohol, drugs, pharmaceuticals)
- traumatic head injury

Other factors discussed by psychopaths and their victims, that could contribute to the development of psychopathic traits may include:

- extreme spoiling
- pornography addiction
- violent media (games, movies)
- occult practices

The psychopath is predatory not passive. Whatever his particular hunger, he is always on the prowl to sate it. Even when newly married, the psychopath is always looking for new prey. Many wives have found out after the fact that their husband was not just a player, but a voracious predator.

The exception to this is the older predator whose pathology is so advanced that he has dropped his mask of sanity and is preying at every opportunity. This is a symptom of the progressive physiology behind psychopathy—the derangement intensifies with age and so does the predation. They need more blood, more money, more flesh, more drugs, more power, more thrill to be satisfied.

The Developing Psychopath

Note: one-time acts and mild or transitory manifestations do not indicate brain damage. Psychopathy is an affliction characterized by patterns of extreme behaviors pursued intensively to inflict ever greater harm.

After the brain has developed, the brain-damaged child will begin to reveal his affliction in the elementary and middle school years. As time goes by, whatever predilections begin to emerge will be pursued with more and more intensity. It is during these years that the developing psychopath samples many kinds of abuse and cruelty to find what gives him the most gratification. Once he has fastened upon his predation(s) of choice, he will spend the rest of his life refining his methods of procurement and dispatch.

Early hallmarks include *extreme*:

- Selfishness (drive for gratification)
- Self-centeredness (narcissism)
- Bullying (financial, physical, verbal)
- Sneaking (to abuse in private to maintain image)
- Perversity (personal habits, sexuality, thinking)
- Promiscuity (experimentation, bestiality)
- Criminality (juvenile delinquency to gang violence)
- Recklessness (financial, physical, sexual, verbal)
- Cruelty to animals (extreme callousness, savagery)
- Mimicry (for purposes of social acceptability)
- Shallowness (mental, emotional, social, sexual)

In the early school years, the developing psychopath displays a lack of natural awareness and genuine interest in anything outside himself. His primary motive is to get his needs met. He throws tantrums, sulks or withdraws when he doesn't get his way, he wets his bed well into childhood. He begins to practice manipulating others for his own ends.

In later childhood, he has developed into a bully and a sneak. He chooses Targets that are smaller and weaker than him, who have done nothing to provoke him. He frightens and torments them in secret. His Targets may be animal and human. If they can't defend themselves or don't fight back, the bullying will escalate until it stopped by the death of the victim or some external circumstance, such as being discovered or interrupted. He doesn't just want to dominate his victims, *he wants to torment them.*

In adolescence, the developing psychopath experiments with behaviors that give him a rush: alcohol, cars, crime, drugs, girls. He will experiment with animal torture, sexual sadism or pornography for gratification. He is beginning to understand two things: he is different and he needs to hide his true nature. His ambition and intelligence will either help or hinder the veneer of the persona he is crafting.

As the afflicted leaves childhood and the teen years, he knows what he likes and his predilections are becoming established as habits of mind and behavior. His methods are refined, too and will be more so with every passing year because they are what he lives for. Although not known to be of high intelligence, the psychopath possesses great predatory cunning. His ability to camouflage his true nature is the little hinge that swings the big door. This is what allows him to move through society undetected whereby he can get access to his prey of choice. His success as a predator depends upon his ability to conceal his deception. The psychopath whose prey of choice is a woman must be able to achieve intimate access in order to run his con.

By early adulthood, the abuser has developed one or more preferred channels for gratification. The 20s are spent refining the procurement of targets, self satisfaction and social acceptability. He knows people but has no close friends. He is involved in activities that provide rush and keep him from having to face himself like drinking, gambling, hunting, racing, burglarizing, carjacking, bronc busting, etc.

In mid-life, the abuser not only possesses advanced tools for trapping victims, but he has constructed an effective method and has the resources to be dangerous.

The Masked Man

Of course, no woman in her right mind would willingly admit such a predator into her life. This is why the psychopath wears a mask and develops a public persona. The mask he wears is one of the tools in his toolbox. He uses it to befriend, help, earn trust, fascinate and flatter, all of which he does with perfect pitch. This social predator has an uncanny ability to read his prey and fashion his pursuit to be effective.

Once the prey is under control (committed, compromised, exhausted, trapped, pressured), the games begin. The psychopath begins to reveal his true nature: joking turns into humiliation, criticism turns into character assassination, sex turns into sadism, demands turn into degradation and more.

Being on the receiving end of these private revelations is destabilizing. It is the betrayal of trust by the one you trusted most. All of this works to increase your vulnerability. You don't understand, you want things to go back to how they were, so you try harder. This is how the initial wounds buy him more time and set you up to for more pain. Too few women know what these behaviors mean and fewer still are able to react to avert further damage.

Emotional states of extreme anxiety, especially those laced with fear and horror, make you more impressionable and more vulnerable; this is why women who have been entrapped by psychopaths often exist in a sort of trance. When mental and emotional coping mechanisms get overwhelmed, they go into overdrive at first, then they go numb and finally they shut down from exhaustion—which sets them up for even worse predation. It's a vicious circle. Some women seek help, others do not.

The man and woman in an abusive relationship both function in different sorts of denial about what is taking place between them—both are in denial about what he is, what he is doing to her and how the abuse is affecting her. Since most psychopathy is created by genes or early childhood trauma, there is often partial or total lack of acknowledgment from the family, too. The parents, siblings and children of psychopaths wrote the book on "flanking" or surrounding the psychopath and denying his abuse. Let anyone question the behavior or inquire into the background of the psychopath and you will see them close ranks and flare off. When a psychopath is on trial, you will see his family in the courtroom decrying his accusation and proclaiming his innocence.

Most psychopaths get by with their intimate crimes; they know how to stay inside the law or outside detection for what they do. When suspicions are raised, they change locations, spouses, territories or methodologies. Of course, none of this lessens their pathology.

To the uninitiated, the psychopath is taken at face value. The prey responds to the promises made, which are crafted to be irresistible to her. The psychopath uses his best manners to be smooth and charming, even to the point of being unctuous. He is not necessarily polite, shy or inclined to observe social conventions *except* during the entrapment phase.

One of the ironies of the gregarious aspects of psychopathic predator is that while they know a lot of people and have many acquaintances, they have no real friends. They won't admit this, to the contrary, they will name-drop and talk up their social lives; but with the exception of psychopaths in high places, these claims are just part of the con.

A Little Lesson in Neuroscience

Neuroscience has made great strides in recent years, including how to apply it to people on both sides of the equation of an abusive relationship, which could be represented like this:

NEED TO CONTROL + INADEQUATE SELF IMAGE = ABUSE

What has been discovered about the human brain in recent years has great bearing on prospects (or lack of) for the abuser and the abused. From the latest research in neuroscience, we now know that the brain:

- Works as a full-time, unemotional, goal-seeking mechanism

- Subconsciously seeks to replicate or substantiate whatever it has been "fed" and accepted as reality, whether the input was true or false
- Is unable to distinguish between actual experience and virtual experience
- Is capable of making and breaking synapses (the physiological basis of mental habits) based on repetitious input (neuroplasticity)

In other words, the brain is highly *programmable*. This is how and why brainwashing works—and this is how and why women get *programmed* by abuse and succumb to its meta messages. Psychologists say that the universal would is "I'm not good enough." For millions of women, the meta message of abuse is like salt in the wound, "I'm nothing, I don't matter, I have no value."

Over time, these cruel and untrue messages go deep into the subconscious and become part of programming for life. If unchallenged and unchecked, they can do even more damage to self image and in some cases, the will to live. The good news is that neuroplasticity works both ways—when you want to, it helps you bounce back.

Once you notice a problem, your brain starts working toward the solution. The first step is noticing it.

Permanent and Progressive

As Drs Cleckley, Pritchard and others have documented in two centuries of study, the condition characterized as psychopathy is *permanent* and *progressive*. Every normal person would benefit from understanding the magnitude of this and would be wise to give it due thought because psychopathy affects them, whether they realize it or not.

Psychopathic behaviors differ in intimate and organizational relationships, but their goal is the same: to control and destroy. When you look around you and see how many things are getting worse, do you think it's an accident or do you see the fingerprints of psychopaths in high places? When you see a relationship in crisis, do you wonder what's behind the downward spiral?

Many of us have never experienced these things, but this is changing. Just like obesity used to be rare, now it is the new norm (and by design). It's the same thing with interpersonal abuse, which is the fastest growing social plague on the planet. Bullying, spousal battery, teen dating violence, sexual harassment, child abuse and family violence seem to be positioned to become the new norm.

History shows that the fate of many once great civilizations and organizations have been destroyed by traitors within whose behavior revealed psychopathic traits. Emotional abuse, financial control and sexual immorality are touchstones of destruction in intimate relationships. Economic injustice, political hypocrisy and moral decay are touchstones of destruction in societies. These are all expressions of the moral insanity of the psychopath, whose compulsion is to *annihilate*.

The progressive nature of psychopathy can be seen in the escalation of his behaviors:

- acts of betrayal and deceit
- sophisticated cunning
- impersonal sexual behavior

- pathological lying
- insatiable greed and avarice
- reckless theft and thrill seeking
- ruthless cons and schemes
- relentless harassment and pursuit
- remorseless damage and violence

It is essential to acquire a working knowledge of key patterns of behavior so that you can spot trouble at a safe distance.

Personality Dynamics of Abuse

The underlying personality dynamics of the pathological abuser include characteristics that express automatically as well as other attributes that he uses at will:

ANGER
COMPULSION
EGOTISM
HYPOCRISY
IMMATURITY
INDIFFERENCE

If you ever attempt to show an abuser that he is being compulsive, hypocritical, etc., he will deny it (and so will his family)—unless it serves him to apologize, go to counseling and so forth. Denial is the mental foundation upon which toxic relationships are constructed. Until a problem is admitted, no remedial action can begin.

| 23 |

Red Flag #18
ANGER

Like alcohol, anger is a convenient and convincing excuse for loss of self control. The pathological uses the display and threat of outburst to control his victim. He uses explosions of anger to instill fear, doubt, minimization and insult. The payoff for him is the emotional and practical damage his outbursts inflict and the chilling effect they exert in the aftermath.

The pathological use of anger is corrosive. It is out of all proportion to reason and reality. He blows up at the slightest thing or at nothing at all, making his anger a frightening and unpredictable weapon.

Pathological anger outbursts have none of the remedial characteristics of healthy anger expressions, which can help resolve problems and deepen the relationship. The victim is kept off balance, kept scared, made to feel inadequate and helpless, which hinders her need to think clearly and take steps to protect herself.

You miss an exit on the highway. Instead of letting you make the needed correction without comment, he becomes enraged, grabs the wheel, etc.

His anger displays range from annoyance to fury. They can be a shock to witness and terrifying to receive. His first reaction to the slightest infraction is anger.

You water the plants too much or not enough, you leave water drops on the counter and he erupts with fury.

You put an object on a shelf instead of into a drawer, or vice versa. When he discovers this mistake he bludgeons you with it.

His primary problem with anger was seeded in him when he was a child. It is now a learned behavior that he knows how to use at will to manipulate and terrorize. The controlling behaviors he expresses through anger can cause physical and emotional harm right then that haunts you for years. His outbursts will be followed with apology or contrition, albeit without sincere accountability. He apologizes for his less threatening displays while making no remark at all about his full-blown eruptions. He says you make him "lose control" when in fact in his wrath he is trying to "take control" of you. He denies or minimizes his behaviors. There are two sides to this red flag: his suppressed (undirected) anger at "something" and his expressed (directed) anger at you.

Among other things, his anger can be an expression of his belief about his role in the relationship and his reaction when it is breached. The pathological believes he is above reproach and above rules: he alone is justified. When you get angry yourself or become the object to his anger, he responds with wrath. So, you learn to maintain a poker face, squash your feelings, edit your words and stifle self expression to avoid his ire. This muting of the self is an act of self preservation, but it is not healthy. In the long term, it is debilitating.

The stress of living with a human volcano takes a heavy toll on your health that should not be underestimated. It can cause a range of visible health problems as well as many that don't show, for a while. (Rash, headaches and stomach aches are common, so are adrenal and lymphatic exhaustion. Victims of abuse are known to suffer heart attack and stroke later on.) Anger displays (and threats) occur along a continuum, from mild to extreme; likewise, the reactions it elicits from you can range from a slight startle to utter terror. There is raw power in the honest expression of healthy anger. He knows this subconsciously, but he has a vested interest in keeping you from accessing that power.

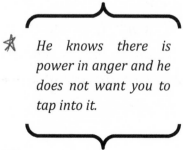

🌟 *He knows there is power in anger and he does not want you to tap into it.*

| 24 |

Red Flag #19
COMPULSION

The more pathological the abuser, the more compulsive his behavior. He is driven by private urges, worn routines and inflexible opinions.

One of the characteristics that feeds the compulsion of the toxic person is insatiability. Whatever he has or does, he wants more. For example, if he's a charismatic con artist that preys on women, his predations must feed his insatiable ego and sexual appetite. If he's a financial con man, he has the money disease and is driven to defraud to quench his hunger for money. If he has succeeded in his work life and is in a position of power or influence, he is compelled to have his woman subordinate to him and at his beck and call.

The ruthlessness of the psychopath allows him to succeed in certain occupations, which provides him the means to indulge in his depredations to an uncommon degree. Whatever his age, he is set in his ways and used to getting his way. He knows how to wear his compulsions so that they appear as extraordinary disciplines or high passions—at first. He uses them to awe and attract—at first. Later, he will reveal them to be weapons of coercion which he uses at will against his partner.

His compulsion is your coercion. He is rigid about how certain things are to be done and the burden of performance is on you. Chances are none of it matters at the end of the day, but the routines are required nevertheless. Being "employed" in the fulfillment of someone else's compulsions can become mind-numbing and soul-deadening by virtue of the pointless repetition alone. Day in. Day out. Over and over. Ad nauseum. No creativity. No spontaneity. No satisfaction. No choice.

His compulsion about cleanliness could mean you spend many of your waking hours dusting, washing, wiping, scrubbing and so forth.

His compulsion about order could mean you have to memorize the exact placement of every object in every room of the house.

His compulsion about sex could mean you have to submit to certain activities at night before you can go to sleep or in the morning before you can get out of bed.

His compulsion about money could mean he controls it and you have little or none or you live like you have none.

Compulsion introduces a measure of unreality into daily life. Trivial things are made oppressively important. Everyday tasks are made intrusive and burdensome. You are not to ask why. You are not allowed to have any preferences or priorities of your own. You are to capitulate. There is no let-up. He adds to his compulsions at will. Any new object or event presents an opportunity for a new compulsion.

In his mind, his compulsions are your sacred duties to him—but in reality, they are endless, pointless, petty and tedious.

| 25 |

Red Flag #20
EGOTISM

Egotism derives from an inflated sense of self and an immature perspective—it comes from delusions of grandeur and shallowness. The young abuser tends to be arrogant and egotistical, the older abuser cloaks his egotism with false humility. Some psychologists say that psychopaths are unable to learn from their experience except in ways that serve them in the moment. This has to do as much with their insatiability as it does with their lack of self control. The predator refines his methods with each new opportunity, but despite this, his predation ultimately exposes him and he is run out of (another) town (job) because of the number of women he's victimized there. Every toxic person has his own style: he may strut about like a young buck, be the strong, silent type, the reserved retiree or

177

play some other role. Whatever face he shows in public does not betray the enormous ego inside. He has cultivated his mask(s) over time to ensure that his outward appearance serves his predation by confirming his persona. The way that the abuser cloaks his ego is telling—the way he presents himself in public provides clues about two things: the way he thinks of himself and the way he wants his ego fed. For example, the young buck wants to be admired, the strong, silent type wants to be sought after, the reserved retiree wants to be worshipped.

The bottom line about the veiled egotism of the toxic partner is that it is another lie. The way he presented himself to you does not reflect who he is. If you responded to his mask, chances are he did a good job of hiding his predatory nature and his egotism. If he is an experienced abuser, all of this has gotten by you because he has become so proficient in hiding his true nature in order to reel in a steady stream of victims. When you fall for the mask, your emotions fail you by keeping you from seeing the monster behind it.

Delusions of grandeur infuse the abuser's egotism. Although he thinks well of himself, he knows to lead with his strong suit according to the prey he is trying to bring down; that is, he puts forward the qualities he knows you will respond to, based on his assessment of you. For example, if you are financially burdened, he leads with his financial strength and offers to help relieve some of your burdens. If you are struggling with a difficult child, he leads with his paternal prowess and offers to share his parenting wisdom. If you were dealing with a difficult person, he leads with his diplomatic mind and offers to counsel you or mediate a meeting.

As a shallow, superficial person, he carries a high opinion of himself, but he doesn't admit this. Instead, he says his success is due to the fact that things come easily to him or he had great parents or he worked hard or he was blessed by dumb luck. If he has had material success, there is little chance he will mention anything going wrong on his watch—ever—unless it's caused by someone else. This lack of accountability is another function of egotism and in the extreme, a hallmark of psychopathy. His initial easy-going ways and self-deprecating humor are crafted and delivered to be charming, disarming and engaging. And they are—for a while.

He is self centered, but not self aware.

He is his own little "g" god.

He is consumed with getting his own needs met.

He pursues his wants to the exclusion of all else.

Among other things, his life is arranged to serve his pleasure seeking and enhance his well being. And that's where you come in. You are the embodiment of his security, ego-building faculty. Your job is to feed and enlarge his ego by being his "Yes" woman, by attending to his every whim and by being his audience 24/7.

The pathological spends an inordinate amount of his personal resources on himself. If he is getting on in years, his pursuit of the fountain of youth may be nothing short of spectacular as he spends hours a day:

- Grooming himself
- Working on his health or fitness
- Planning his entertainments
- Shopping for new possessions
- Playing with his toys
- Surrounding himself with trophies
- Making himself more comfortable
- Fussing over himself and his things

If illness or injury befalls him, it dominates your waking hours until he has recovered. If something happens to you, there will not only be little or no care, he will apply pressure to get you back to your job of taking care of him.

> There is no mishap too insignificant when it happens to him. If he stubs his toe or pops a button, you will hear about it for weeks or months.

| 26 |

Red Flag # 21
HYPOCRISY

His being and doing give mixed messages. He describes and thinks of himself as one sort of person but behaves in the opposite manner. Hypocrisy is another form of emotional dishonesty that reveals lack of conscience, immaturity and shallowness. This man does not walk his talk. His talk drips with largesse and passion, while his walk is mean and indifferent. It's not that he's acting, it's that he's empty.

Hypocrisy runs on emotional dishonesty in its many forms. In the toxic individual, these qualities exist with an attenuated conscience as well.

He tells you he's a one-woman man, but later reveals himself to be an online predator.

He tells you he's an honest man, yet you learn he has lied to you and others extensively and substantively.

He tells you he's sensitive, but he treats you cruelly.

He gives you books to read so that you will be a better partner to him, but declines to do likewise himself.

He tells you he's a people person, yet you do not witness him say or do a kind thing for anyone else.

He tells you he's a family man, but he has unhealthy or superficial relationships with family members.

He tells you he wants to take care of you, yet he harms you.

He uses other behaviors and tactics in his hypocrisies. Blaming, denying, lying, minimizing and withholding information are all enabling and useful tools to the hypocrite.

When a neighbor calls to ask a small favor, he doesn't go to the door or answer the phone. When he runs into the neighbor later, without flinching, he says how sorry he is he wasn't home or never got the message. He even blames you for failing to relay the message!

If he does do something for you, no matter how minor, he will talk it up for months as if it is one of the greatest, most heroic, most self-sacrificial gift ever given.

Whatever he promised you, he is quick to forget or take away. In this way, his hypocrisy can be cruelly employed. He is the speaker of weasel words.

"I was not put on this earth to take care of you."

"You can go back where you came from."

"I don't owe you a damn thing."

He requires profuse thanks and regular apologies from you all the while he denies your experiences and refuses to give you the thanks and apologies you are truly due. The message to you is clear: your feelings do not matter and you do not matter outside of enabling him to gratify himself. If he asked you to quit your job, leave your business or otherwise deplete your own financial resources to be with him, he does not hesitate to threaten you with abandonment or expulsion if your efforts don't live up to his expectations.

> *He derives pleasure from roaring at you to get out of his house knowing that you have no way to leave.*

| 27 |

Red Flag #22
IMMATURITY

His immaturity can be breathtaking. Regardless of his age and life experience, his behavior shows that his emotional maturity was arrested a long time ago. The way he spends his time can provide clues to the nature and extent of his immaturity. He is more or less a child in an adult's body. His devices and maladjustments are the adult manipulations of a child's anxieties.

However he acts out, his immaturity will express itself in:

- Shallowness
- Vindictiveness
- Inconsistency
- Instability
- Meanness
- Selfishness

- Hyper-vigilance
- Inattentiveness
- Immorality
- Insatiability
- Infidelity
- Violence

No matter what situation you find yourself in with him, you cannot count on him to be mature, fair, predictable, stable, thorough or reliable. This is not due to his lacking these life skills or being *unable* to use them, this is due to his being *unwilling* to use them.

One of the ironies of the toxic individual is that they demand from others what they are unwilling to provide in their turn. They expect others to be honest, prompt, etc., yet they themselves are disinclined to act that way unless it serves them. You can be sure he uses diplomacy at work and out in public, but when he gets home to you, he tosses all forms of civility and reverts to type.

Part of the role of the woman in a toxic relationship can be likened to a sort of mothering—but mothering as it was never meant to be. When your partner is toxic, the relationship is unbalanced and unhealthy. All emotional enrichment and nourishment comes from you. All apology, patience, willingness to forbear, compassion, forgiveness, supplication comes from you. Whether it's sex, forgiveness, another chance or self sacrifice, you give, he takes. He demands, you supply.

He expresses his immaturity in ways to make you feel sorry for him. This is base manipulation. Feeling sorry for him is a trap.

- He mopes or sulks extravagantly.
- He refuses to talk.
- He slams doors.
- He eats alone.
- He closes himself off in a room.
- He drives off in a rage.
- He bellows when he doesn't get his way.
- He threatens you to compel performance.

His emotional maturity is stuck at the level of a child or adolescent. There is no emotional depth or resonance, only the appearance of it. His shows of love were all fake. He is a counterfeit.

After the literal or figurative honeymoon, the relationship "turns." You realize you have married a 14-year old boy in a man's body.

| 28 |

Red Flag #23
INDIFFERENCE

In the beginning, he displays the ability to be laid-back and take in stride the stresses of life. Later, his partner sees that he does not take things in stride, at least not with her, when she finds herself on the receiving end of a vicious tirade and realizes with no small amount of shock that he's not laid-back—he's indifferent, even unfeeling.

He is unaffected by and uninterested in other people's experience and personhood. If he reacts at all, it is with indifference or impatience.

He shows no compassion or empathy for others because he feels none.

He expresses hot impatience when another person's situation, no matter how grave, if it poses even the most minor inconvenience to him.

If another driver is slow to respond, he honks and gives him the finger instead of driving around him or waiting.

You cannot depend upon him to look after your animals or children because he is indifferent to their existence. He does not care if they are safe and comfortable.

Indifference is said to be the opposite of love and a second cousin to aversion. The more outright indifference an abuser displays, the more he demonstrates the extent of his emotional limitations and the risks of relying upon him.

In public, he knows he must feign compassion and concern, and he plays this part to perfection. He knows he has to make a show of catering to you in front of other people. His loving husband act is convincing to others. But in private, he reverts to type.

He inquires of your comfort on a cold night, but then forbids you to put another blanket on the bed when you say you are cold.

He asks what entrée you'd like to have at a restaurant, but
 then tells you to order something else. *— Jes or very strongly suggest*

He does not react to human or animal suffering or his reactions are not normal—he mocks, gloats, get enraged or even contemptuous.

He laughs when he sees a man pounding the steering wheel in a car while screaming at his wife who has her head in her hands.

If you sustain a visible wound, he tells you to stay home so no one else sees it and to cover it up so he doesn't see it.

Serious Consequences — passive agressive!

If you suffer a loss, even one which he causes, he <u>offers</u> no acknowledgment, apology, comfort, condolence or help.

Consider what he would do if you were ever badly hurt while alone with him and prepare.

Yes! When my dad was dying!

— He went to the neighbors and asked them to play baseball.

Car accident
Treated me cruelly
Driving me to the urgent care while in terrible pain on purpose Turning sharply so that I could not tell what was happening The nurse ran a stern for Bob had a stern message for Bob

Only to the emergency room "can etc.," "can extend with is." "The one I'm really concerned with is." Bills mad at me — wasn't my fault 4 can pile up and side swiped, yet The worst was Bob's anger in a car accident

189

Part Four:
Masks and Personas
of the Charismatic Con

"Good people are rarely suspicious; they cannot imagine others doing the things they themselves are incapable of doing...."

William March, THE BAD SEED

Leonard & Angela

What most people noticed about Leonard at first were his big smile and his humility. He was as plain and unremarkable as could be—dammit. He did not want to be plain, he wanted to be complex and intelligent, he wanted to have admiration and authority. When people met Angela, they quickly saw a pretty girl utterly without guile. Both children were raised

190

to be humble, but they expressed it in different ways as they grew.

Leonard learned how to cover his personal deficiencies by wearing his humility like a badge. He found this to be effective in socializing with girls who would not otherwise be willing to talk to him. By the time he was out of college, he had refined his use of humility as a social tool into a layered persona that included intellectualism, pomposity and self righteousness. He got so proficient at wearing his mask that he came to believe he was intellectual and righteous.

To no one's surprise, Leonard picked Angela out of a church choir as the girl he would marry. He was two years into a menial job after college, she was fresh faced and soon to graduate.

Leonard's parents were ... Angela's parents were ambitious professionals who devoted their lives to medical missionary work with children in foreign countries. As a result of their priorities, their own children got shipped off to relatives during the summer and boarding schools during the school year. The impact this had on the three children was profound. For the two girls, it set them up with such low self images, that they were both snapped up young by men consumed with the need to control them. Angela's sister was abused by her husband for many years before she escaped.

Angela's under-nourished self image expressed itself as intense desire for children—it gnawed at her from a young age. She believed, in her heart of hearts, that she was somehow unworthy of love, but she was determined to be as good a person as possible. As she grew, she did not act out with promiscuity or self harm because of her pure heart and clean mind. Kind and whip-smart, Angela matured into an obedient, broken-hearted woman. She was possessed of many admirable and useful attributes, yet something in her never flowered. She camouflaged her pain by putting her best foot forward and making the most of things. She became so adept it was often unnerving to others. No matter what happened, she sailed on. She learned to endure great emotional pain without letting on to anyone except God. In this way, the mental maturity she gained early on morphed into spiritual detachment and self sacrifice, all of which she learned to hide behind a mask of happiness. Although she was friendly and warm, she didn't let anyone in until Leonard came along.

They dated for an appropriate amount of time and then married. Leonard wore his mask of humility adorned with gratitude about how lucky he was. Angela wore her mask of happiness adorned with purpose: to be a good wife and mother.

During the first decade of their marriage, he pursued non-descript jobs, while she encouraged him and empowered him behind the scenes. She served him from sunrise to sunset as his cook, housekeeper, secretary, editor, travel agent and business assistant.

All this time, Angela prayed for children but never conceived. It was decades later, when she went through menopause that she gave in to the years of unanswered longing. An afternoon when she was alone in the house, she uttered her grief with a long, drenching cry to God. Leonard had intellectual ideas about why they had not been able to have children and comforted his wife, thusly. Angela carried the pain of her empty womb for the rest of her life.

At some point, Leonard became interested in the ministry. It occurred to him that it would be intellectually stimulating as well as deliver to him some of the social leverage in life he was missing. This was the beginning a new and complex layer of control that he would apply to his wife. They joined one little church after another in search of a congregation that could support them so they could put down roots. Things always started out well. They were both model believers, engaged and knowledgeable. Angela was welcomed by the women, but Leonard struggled to be well received by the men. As time went by, this became a thorn in his side because although he could control his wife, he could not control other people who always liked Angela, but not him. As he grew into his role of pastor, he could not understand why success in starting or taking over a church continued to elude him. In some places, they never progressed beyond being members; in others, Leonard worked his way into pastoral duties only to be asked to leave when he made his move to claim or usurp the position of senior pastor.

Because they moved often neither of them made deep emotional investments outside the marriage. They stayed in touch with their families, but their life did not include close personal friends. Leonard communicated with a number of people about business and attended conferences that interested him. For the most part, he traveled alone, leaving his wife to "keep the home fires burning."

Early in his transition to the ministry, Leonard decided to keep Angela at home. He did not consider what this would do to her, only that it's what he wanted (and would serve his ego by keeping her from being around too many other people). He made some exceptions—he let her visit her aging parents and he took her on the occasional weekend getaway. Angela, being dutiful and obedient to the core, went along with all of it. She helped him with his work and stayed in the house. She did not even have to leave the house to go to the grocery store—he did that.

About 30 years into their marriage, Leonard let her go to a working lunch with two church friends. She was out of the house for over two hours and nervous as a cat the whole time. Her friends noticed her anxiety, but they didn't wonder out loud about it to each other or understand it until a few years later.

A little while after that, Leonard let her go to a three-day business conference with the same friends. He thought it was magnanimous of him to allow it, which he did for a couple of reasons: it would make him look good and it could lead to additional income. He told her to call him every evening and she did. The first day of the conference was jam-packed with excitement and enthusiasm. By the end of the day, they were too animated to go to sleep, so they decided to order room service and have a little pajama party. Back at their hotel room, Angela went out on the small deck to check in with Leonard. When she came back in, her face was ashen and her animation was gone. In the blink of an eye, the fun ended. She caught herself quickly, but not before the mood was lost and both of her friends got a good look at the phone call's effect on her. The scene repeated itself the next two nights, dampening the otherwise exceptional experience they were all having.

Her friends noticed two things on that trip: that Angela had great fun in her (far more than expected) but that her light was always tamped out by her phone calls with Leonard. What they observed allowed them to connect those dots, but go no further. They did not realize the meaning of the behavior they were witnessing. Besides, she was a pastor's wife.

Leonard and Angela fit together like a hand and a glove, their respective backgrounds paving the way for the marriage they have today. It is biblically correct according to the letter of the law, but not the spirit of the law. She is owned but not cherished. She is not allowed to wear makeup, except for lip gloss, even though she would like to. She is not allowed to wear attractive clothing. The years of overwork, exacerbated by her heart of service have harmed her health and aged her prematurely. If she has personal interests, no one has ever seen the evidence.

Angela's parents changed their minds about Leonard over the years to the point that he was no longer welcome in their home. They knew he never raised a hand to their daughter, never yelled at her or anything like that, but they despised him for what he had wrought in her just the same. Angela always defended him to her family and deflected their concerns so that she didn't have to face them. It was perhaps the one way her sharp intellect failed her.

It took Angela over a half century to realize that she had been orphaned by her living parents. Despite this betrayal, she remained dutiful to them to the end. She will never see what others see when they look at her marriage. No one dares call it abuse.

|29|

Red Flags

The numbers of people who suffer and die for lack of knowledge about dangerous relationships are similar to those who die in natural disasters every year. But unlike, extreme weather and earth changes, relationship storms cannot be identified by equipment, they can only be detected by discernment that comes from specialized knowledge. By and large, these storms do not happen in public, but behind closed doors. And often, the damage these storms do is hidden from view or denied for a long time.

These signs work like weather warnings; they broadcast the presence of conditions that could threaten life. They pick up circumstantial anomalies like weather-sensing equipment picks up changes in barometric pressure, tectonic movement, wind speed and so forth.

Relationship red flags are warning signs of conditions that are not evident to the untrained eye. They give those who understand them a chance to change course and spare themselves. Heeding these signals can be every bit as expensive and inconvenient as heeding forecasts of flood, fire, earthquake, tsunami and blizzard. It can also make the difference between life and death.

Back before we knew how to forecast weather and earth changes, immense destruction regularly befell entire populations for lack of knowledge of the warning signs. In the 1930s, the dust bowl devastated America's breadbasket for a decade. It could have been avoided altogether if people had understood the consequences of certain agricultural and industrial practices. Instead, the lives of millions of people and animals were annihilated as the long-term fertility of more than 100 million acres was destroyed.

Appearances

In the context of pathological individuals, the lesson is this: normal people do not seek to destroy others, but abnormal people do. Those with an anti-social predilection tend to be successful because their characteristics deliver a predatory advantage to them.

Dealing with the psychopath means you are constantly having pieces on your chess board moved without your knowledge and consent. In the end, they win and you lose. If you're lucky, you lose time and money; if you're unlucky, you lose relationships and sometimes your life. All they have to do is engage you, enroll you, entrap you and then play you—which they will do whenever you give them the chance to get close to you. How do they do it? By fooling you with appearances. They know how to use first impression to win your trust and get you to "open the door" so they can "get into you." Once inside, what they do will show that they are fearless, shameless, relentless and ruthless.

It's crucial to understand that even when the red flags are hiding in plain sight, chances are you're not going to see them because:

- You're falling in love (it feels so right...I have waited for him for so long).
- Destruction is the last thing on your mind (he'd never hurt me...he is the ideal man for me).
- It don't look ominous in the beginning (it couldn't be more perfect...everything just works).

The individual whose behavior and life is covered in red flags can be *anyone*—a clean-cut guy with a good job who goes to church; a successful retiree who keeps an immaculate yard; a volunteer fireman who likes kids; a nice neighbor who always waves; an indefatigable boy scout leader; a doting husband and hard-working dad; a dedicated school teacher; a well regarded pastor; an established banker, a beloved doctor and so forth.

The persona that an abuser creates for himself can be telling because it contains clues about some of his egotistical investments and interpersonal expectations:

- who he thinks he is (egotism)
- who he wants you to think he is (narcissism)
- how he wants to be perceived by society (delusion)

Since deceit and image play major roles in a charismatic con, abusers have to construct convincing façades. The more sophisticated he is, the more elaborate and convincing the façade he builds. This façade does two things: it hides his true nature and assists his predation.

Something else needs to be mentioned about appearances. Because psychopathy is a progressive disorder, those in the advanced stages are losing their ability to camouflage their true nature. They are beginning to have outbursts in public and even starting to look odd. Many serial murderers exhibit this progression. They get stopped (caught or killed) because they get sloppy because their depravity is overtaking them.

Ted Bundy is an example of a psychopathic serial killer who began his murderous career by engaging with women so that they went with him of their own accord before being raped and killed. At the end of his cross-country rampage, he had deteriorated to the point of having to sneak up on sleeping women to kill them. The ferocity and frenzy of his later attacks were also more extreme.

Relationships That "Turn"

Relationships are unique, but the warning signs of abusive ones or those that "turn" are universal. In these relationships, the perpetrators:

- first appear as benign, charming, compelling
- slowly change to influence your thinking
- begin to exert pressure on your behavior
- begin to isolate you from who and what you love
- crowd your emotions and emotional expressions
- program your thinking and beliefs about yourself
- strangle your spirituality and connection with Source
- constrict your social life
- limit your financial resources and future ability to earn
- degrade and destroy your best attributes

- adversely affect every aspect of your life in the long term

Individuals and relationships vary, but toxic behaviors do not. The red flags you experience will be similar to those described here with slight variations according to the personality of the abuser and the forms of abuse he dispenses. The purpose of breaking down these behaviors is to get you thinking and seeing to help you avoid or foreshorten these life shattering experiences.

Dishonesty permeates almost everything an abuser does. Abuse, be it mild or severe, is a sick sort of performance art. Some of the most common masks that abusers wear to disguise their true nature include:

- The Gentleman
- The Fun Seeker
- The Animal Lover
- The Family Man
- The Wounded Man
- The Wired Guy
- The Great Guy

Some abusers mask their agenda successfully in the beginning but do not maintain the guise for more than a few months. Many toxic individuals are adept at wearing more than one mask, and within each persona there can be variation.

One of the things that abusers have in common is that the man behind the mask, the man whose deceit requires the use of personas, does not think there is anything questionable about his behavior. The other thing is his insane tally of his partner's transgressions. Part of his mindset is retaliatory, and this is what he gets to indulge when the mask comes off.

The woman in an unhealthy relationship is stressed and oppressed, but often misunderstood because people outside the relationship believe the mask. Without knowledgeable support and without being able to learn how to see through the mask, she can't begin to understand the counter-intuitive world she's living in. She has no protection against the wiles of her abuser and she will sustain great harm until she gains some understanding. She may have been so controlled and so unequipped to counter abusive attacks that she comes to believe what her abuser tells her. This happens to even the strongest and most independent women.

The toxic partner acts one way in public when he's wearing his mask and quite another when he's not. Here are seven common personas used by pathological men to deceive the public and destroy his partner.

| 30 |

Red Flag #24
THE PERFECT GENTLEMAN

There are two sides to this man, a public side and a private side. His public side is acceptable and respectable (i.e., he is well spoken, calm, reassuring, gentle); he is comfortable in his own skin, a man at peace with the world and with no need to prove anything to anyone. He has done it all.

In conversation he is able to show interest and understanding. He is a master of drawing people out and making them feel special. He can call upon books, movies or news to suggest that he is informed and to punctuate his appropriate convictions about the issues of the day. He plays the role of the gentleman to the hilt, he even sheds a tear to underscore his refinement and sensitivity.

Not only do women fall for this, but so does everyone else. He fools her, her family, her friends, everyone. Although he doesn't appear to be calculated, his moves are well rehearsed and he never lets his mask slip in public. Later, when he begins to wall her in, she will doubt her perceptions because of the gentleman mask he can don in the blink of an eye and because no one will believe what this gentleman is doing to her.

The reality is that his public side bears little or no relation to his private side, which is unpredictable, cruel and repugnant. His behavior is dishonest and manipulative in both arenas. He is an ego-driven actor and an expert deceiver. This is part of why it's so hard to see his true nature. When a woman doesn't know to look for a schism between his public and private side, she won't see it until it's too late.

When people ask how you ever got involved with a man who later mistreated you, this is how: he played the role of the perfect gentleman for as long as it took to get you into his trap. Of course he didn't mistreat you at first.

Abusers succeed because they have adopted winning ways, which they are able to maintain for limited periods of time. Setting up a relationship takes time and he knows that. Subconsciously he knows he has to entrap his victims with an act. He also knows he can get anyone he wants as long as he uses the right trap. The Perfect

Gentleman knows if he dropped his act and revealed his private side too early, you would flee and he does not want you to get away.

His act is designed to draw you in.

His public self is one of easy-going self assurance.

His first impression is fabulous; his conduct unimpeachable.

He knows how to be charming and mannerly.

The Perfect Gentleman has no awareness of any trespass he commits against you, he just wants your absolute adoration and undivided attention. He manipulates your perceptions of him to win your admiration. He acts humble, even self-effacing.

"I don't like to talk about myself."

"I don't take myself too seriously."

The Perfect Gentleman leads you and everyone else to believe he is something other than what he is—often the opposite.

- He acts magnanimous when he is petty.
- He makes a show of generosity, when he is miserly.
- He plays a man of honor, when he is dishonorable.
- He paints pretty pictures with his words and promises you more than you ever asked for, when he has no interest in your happiness and no intention of carrying through on his promises—any of them.

"I just want to make you happy."

"You deserve this and so much more."

"I want to be everything to you."

Take note of his persona. His public self reveals a lot about who and what he thinks himself to be. This is how he functions in society. It is an expertly crafted persona that is attractive and appealing. This is who his co-workers, neighbors and others in the community know him to be. This type of man knows what buttons to push. He knows what to say and how to say it. His delivery has perfect pitch. This is because he has been refining his method for most of his life.

When he begins to be abusive and you object or recoil, he will tell you that you are hurting him! Then he will enroll you in making it up to him, this will become an unwritten rule in the relationship which will be your burden for the duration, and which will undermine the balance of power since you will be put in the position of making it up to him. This rule will not apply to any hurt feelings you experience—double standards redux.

His hurt feelings are all your fault. When he's not abusing you over his, he puts on his Perfect Gentleman mask to show you how to "rise above it" or "do the right thing" or "think of someone besides yourself" for a change!

The Perfect Gentleman Mindset

The principles at work underneath this mask express:

- "I'm above the coarseness of life and petty squabbles, I would never do anything base."
- "I am a desirable man. I know it and women know it, so take good care of me because men like me don't come along often."

- "I expect to be catered to, noblesse oblige and all that, you know. The least you can do is please me."

- "I understand you better than you understand yourself and I expect you to respond to the things I tell you in this regard."

- "I have a lot of experience with women so I know more than you and you would be wise to take my advice."

The eventual revelation of his real character will be in sharp contrast to his Perfect Gentleman act. Be aware that he will deliver his coup de grace on you.

| 31 |

Red Flag #25
THE FUN SEEKER

The Fun Seeker leads with light-heartedness and zest for life, which is often wrapped in an appealing mix of energy, libido and ego. This is an effortless mask for the psychopath to wear because it gives him free rein to indulge himself—his favorite thing. It lets him be insatiable, immature, youthful and self-centered.

The beginning of an intrigue with the Fun Seeker can be mesmerizing because it plays to the woman's sense of fun with lots of partying, adventuring, lovemaking, etc. The fun she has will make her fall for this man harder and faster than she would without the excitement factor. The Fun Seeker is the type of man who can make every activity compelling and spectacular. He can make a woman feel special by including her in his "exciting" and "extraordinary" daily existence.

The Fun Seeker traffics in fun, but when it comes to anything else, like the commitment of exclusivity, he starts back-peddling. If you can see through the haze, you'll see that his devotion to fun is devotion to himself because it feeds his selfishness, lack of control, denial, minimizing and sneaking or lying. It also feeds his addictions.

When the Fun Seeker overindulges in his substance of choice and then abuses you, you think there's a connection between the two, but there's not. Abusive people don't abuse because they're drunk or stoned, they abuse because they're abusive. Their altered state is just a convenient excuse and something they can use to appeal to your compassion or patience. Altering substances function as dis-inhibitors, but they are not the cause of abuse, the cause is something far deeper than their blood alcohol level.

Substance abuse alters perception and introduces a torpor that comes from chemical imbalance. It allows the Fun Seeker to keep from facing himself and his behavior. Chemical alteration only deepens the individual and collective quicksand you're already in. There are numerous risks you face in dealing with the Fun Seeker. His substance use heightens all forms of his risky behavior, such as driving, spending and physical or sexual assault.

When you see his fun seeking intensify, you'll also see his level of interest wane; his attention will begin to wander because he is getting restless for the thrill of the hunt for his next victim. The chances of being in an exclusive relationship with a Fun Seeker are nil, he just doesn't work that way, no matter what he says. Remember, he lives by distraction and thrill seeking. The Fun Seeker is playing you like he's played others, taking things as far as he can to squeeze every last drop of "fun" out of each involvement.

If you are a woman who can't see the writing on the wall and tries to "stand by her man" you will soon find that your formerly fascinating romantic partner—except when he wants his needs met—is able to treat you with great callousness and neglect you for long periods of time. If you stick around after this revelation, your self image is going to take a beating. If you try to take a stand on his playing field in spite of everything you are doing to keep him "satisfied" and at home, you are in for disappointment and violence because you are, in fact, dealing with an abusive and immature man who doesn't care about anyone but himself. You face the most risk when you catch him in the act or confront him with evidence of his cheating. It's important for you to understand that:

- Getting him off _____ will not eradicate the problems in the relationship because _____ is not the root cause of his abuse of you.

- Getting him off _____ will only reduce the substance-related excuses he can draw on to justify his behavior. If he gets off _____, be assured he will find other ways to excuse his abuse of you.

The Fun Seeker has considerable charm and expertise in keeping you focused on his enjoyment rather than what you need to do to protect yourself from the consequences of being involved with him. He even claims he wants to reform in order to string you along for a little while longer.

The Fun Seeker Mindset

The principles at work underneath this mask express:

- Life is short and he deserves every good thing he can grab
- Exclusivity is too limiting
- His fun seeking should be supported
- He can't help it if he overdoes it (alcohol, drugs, sex, etc.)

Yet another pitfall you face in dealing with the Fun Seeker is falling into destructive fun-seeking behaviors yourself. This occurs as a means of distraction, peace-seeking or self-medicating to help you cope with being abused and having none of your own needs met.

> *He doesn't abuse you because he uses. He abuses you because he is abusive.*

| 32 |

Red Flag #26
THE ANIMAL LOVER

This man uses animals because they deliver gratification to him. They allow him to engage with compassionate women as well as being ever-present objects for mistreatment; both of which deliver strokes to his insatiable ego. An animal's utility for social leverage pays off with messages about his character—that he is kind, patient, protective, responsible. It also creates opportunities for shared activities that will increase access and accelerate relationship—like walks, rides, shows, lessons, shopping. In whatever context he presents himself, he uses animals to serve as a conduit through which he can connect with desirable women.

When the predator posing as an Animal Lover targets a woman who is highly involved with animals (such as an equestrian, breeder, groomer, trainer, rancher) he will posture extravagantly to convey his standing as like-minded. For example, he might share pictures of himself with animals that suggest he hikes with his dog, takes care of his horses, relaxes with his cat, when the pictures are actually of animals that belong to someone else. He presents himself as animal-friendly, but he is not, he is animal indifferent. The most pathological of this type run this con without worry of being found out should the relationship take form.

This man's animals, if he has any, tell the real story. His animal(s) will exhibit the classic signs of the defensiveness that come about when any sentient creature lives in an unsafe environment. They will show themselves to be disengaged, neurotic, timid or vicious—and all of this reflects the treatment they have endured at the hands of the pathological, it does not reflect their true nature.

The Animal Lover trades on the assumptions his mask affords him. It allows him to play the part of a sensitive person, milk that persona for all it's worth while working towards the ultimate goal of delivering pain and suffering to his woman, his animals and hers. The older Animal Lover may have had the time to learn some of the tricks of the trade, he may mimic the calm demeanor and quiet authority of real animal trainers with you—he may even use hand signals!

The Animal Lover acts out his sense of entitlement with animals because he can. There is no give and take—he demands compliance and punishes them when they fail to obey. When you see it, this foreshadows what he will do to you. Most animals retreat in the face of pain and punishment, so life with an animal abuser masquerading as an Animal Lover is not a long or happy one.

He may indulge in cruelty to animals through rituals such as hunting or rodeo, or cruelty may be part of his everyday life because it is how he gets thing done. Callousness to animals is epidemic in "cowboy country" where animals live lives of unrelenting stress from overwork, poor nutrition and exposure. The animal holocaust in "research" demonstrates the most extreme moral insanity; hiding behind the façade of the trillion dollar medical/pharmaceutical/academic complex. In urban areas, millions of animals are abused and killed in fighting and sacrificial rituals.

Animal exploitation, neglect and torture are hallmarks of primary psychopathy. All animal abuse demonstrates the diminished capacities of secondary psychopathy.

When you get involved with the Animal Lover, you may see the truth behind his mask in the lives of his animals before you see it in your own. The baseline of his treatment of animals occurs between neglect and abuse. You may witness extreme punishment and violence committed against them. If you try to intervene, he will turn on you. The mistreatment of animals is a witness his lack of compassion, his inability to accord respect and his lack of conscience.

He treats animals more like equipment than creatures with feelings.

He is covertly cruel or overtly savage with animals.

He "tries" to be patient with you, but not with your animals.

He becomes enraged over any consideration you give your animals as if it's an affront to him.

Predators go where there is prey. Animals, like children, are easy to take down. Over 71 percent of family violence and domestic abuse cases involve long-standing animal abuse, too. Often, the toxic adult as well as one or more of the children have become habituated to dealing with their anxiety by torturing animals. If you live with or marry an abusive man, you will observe that your once-friendly, well-adjusted animals avoid him or start misbehaving. Your animals will disappear, turn up with curious injuries or die. As animal casualties occur, the Animal Lover will say he's sorry or he will not react. The truth is he is pleased or relieved that something you care about has been hurt or removed. What he wants is for it to be just him and you, with nothing else to matter to you and nothing else to take your attention away from him.

Ensure that your animals are protected. Do not delay in getting them to a safe place at the first sign of the potential for cruelty to occur. Once he discerns what your animals mean to you, he will begin a campaign to separate you from them:

He comes up with logistical reasons, like wanting to travel.

He begins an emotional attack, like insinuating that you have an abnormal affection for or sexual attraction to your animals.

He proposes a deal, wherein if you give up your animals he will provide something he knows you want.

He does not hesitate to use your animals to control and manipulate you to include killing them or taking them away without your knowledge.

"You can be emotionally lazy with animals and that's why you have them."

"Your animals just stick around because you feed them."

"You have animals because you don't know how to relate to people—and you never will."

"Your animals are just a substitute for children."

The Animal Lover twists your affection for your animals every way he can to break you down. In his mind, he believes that your interest in your animals indicates lack of character and capacity for human relationships. He expresses this directly in words or deeds. You and your animals will suffer in ways that violate the dignity of life.

The Animal Lover Mindset

The principles at work underneath this mask express:

- Animals are his for the using—period. He and he alone has intrinsic value.
- They don't have feelings (they are "dumb" animals).
- If his woman cares about animals, she is defective and needs to be punished and so do her animals.

- Animals are useful tools for manipulating people—to attract, control and punish them.

- Seeing his partner or family upset over his torture of animals excites him.

- He derives power from holding an animal's life in his hand and all the implications that holds for the people he is trying to control.

Damaged boys often torment animals on their way to tormenting women. Many of the most heinous serial criminals began their "careers" torturing and killing animals.

It is one thing to see your inanimate property lost, mishandled or destroyed; it is another to see your animals who have known love, who have blossomed under compassion and respect experience the hatred of your partner. If you are not able to exit without delay, you could see them suffer and die without mercy at his hands.

His animals will tell you what he is if you know how to observe them. And animals do not lie.

| 33 |

Red Flag #27
THE FAMILY MAN

Like the Animal Lover, the Family Man professes a love of something in order to attract a certain kind of prey item, a compassionate and nurturing woman.

The truth is that children are merely commodities for him to use in his war against goodness. He knows posturing as a man with a heart for children works to his benefit by suggesting he is normal, stable and safe. One irrefutable fact in the creation of nearly all pathological individuals is love hunger.

His grotesque acting out as a Family Man would be ludicrous if it weren't for the agony it visits upon those who fall into his hands. He is not capable of bestowing anything positive on any children who come into his care; he is only capable of abusing them, soiling their purity, blunting their life force, polluting their innocence, eviscerating their developing self image and twisting any healthy characteristics they have. Why? Because he hates them because they are of you. If you have children, you can be sure he will use your love of your children to great advantage—his.

The Family Man knows children are the most powerful tools of all with which he can manipulate and control you and them.

He impregnates you to get himself into your life.

If you have small children, he uses their need of a daddy to compel you to marry or live with him.

If he has small children, he uses their need of a mommy to draw you in.

If he has grown children, without a doubt they have serious issues of their own, which could threaten your wellbeing in the years to come. If you marry this man, pay close attention to what provisions he makes for you and what provisions he makes for his children. Chances are you will be left out in the cold should you trust him to do the right thing. Even from the grave, he could abuse you! The Family Man may attempt to impersonate a Patriarch, but you can be sure it will be in the meanest way possible.

Later, he abuses or neglects your children. He may mistreat your children in front of you, such as by disciplining them, but more likely he will do it when you're not around using techniques that do not leave a mark on the child, like shaking or suffocation. Do not allow this man unsupervised access to your children. It could cost them their souls, their lives and their futures.

Five million children witness the abuse of their mothers and thousands are killed by their fathers or stepfathers during violent episodes. If you cannot stick up for your children, get help from someone who will or get the children to a safe place and do this without delay.

He imposes rules on how you treat your own children.

He threatens to kidnap or kill them.

He concocts charges against you to have the state seize your children.

He institutes one set of rules for your children and one set for his.

He tries to coerce your children or his to testify against you in child custody hearings.

The Family Man Mindset

The principles at work underneath this mask express:

- He believes his family exists to serve him, he is entitled to their primary allegiance.
- His family is expected to cover his responsibilities and accept his excuses.
- He is the head of the household and therefore always right.
- If compliance is not forthcoming, it is incumbent upon him to dish out the appropriate punishment.

- No one in the family can have anything in their life that matters more than him.

One of the latest legal hurdles used against women by their abusers is the invocation of "parental alienation" actions. This is a claim that the effects of the mother's abuse have alienated the children from the abuser. This has now become a legal liability for the abused woman! A contest for child custody against an abuser may be the fight of your life. If you need legal counsel, get referrals only from a women's shelter or other organization that specializes in domestic violence or child abuse.

> *Because the Family Man has no conscience and is in denial about his abuse, none of this is hard for him to do and he has no remorse for his ill treatment of them or you.*

| 34 |

Red Flag #28
THE WOUNDED MAN

The Wounded Man uses tales of woe to engage and play upon the emotions of his victim. He engages his prey by making a first impression that shows and tells how he has been overlooked, disrespected, impoverished, abused (!), wronged and violated by others. His story may be large or small. It might center on the treatment he received by his ex-girlfriend or ex-wife or it encompass his entire life.

His purpose in crafting this tale is to find women who are not only compassionate, but gullible, naive and maternal. He wants to be relieved of it all. One of the implicit expectations of the Wounded Man is that of getting special treatment—this is the set-up for a behavioral blank check. He knows what he is going to do, but his

222

woman does not, so manipulating her into a maternal and all-suffering position is crucial to the longevity and success of his ruse. The Wounded Man blames any of his own limitations (like being addicted, broke, sick, injured, unemployed, on the run) on persecution. What he doesn't say, but what his victim will find out is that he considers his status as persecuted to be his badge or mantle of his supreme entitlement.

The stories that the Wounded Man comes up with to snow women comprise the laughable, the impressive and everything in-between. His wounds can be real or imagined. They derive from a difficult childhood, poor health (addiction, injury, disease), financial loss, emotional distress, spiritual torment and more. His stories might be based on something factual and then enlarged to suit his needs or they may be fabricated. The most effective stories are those that contain at least one fact that can be demonstrated—this small bit of truth is often enough to enroll the victim, who needs no further evidence of his woundedness because she is falling for his other ploys— charms and promises.

He is most successful with women who don't know his history and are not likely to find out about it. If he is an adept abuser, he has covered his tracks by moving, changing jobs, expunging his record, changing his appearance, preying on women in another locale, etc.

The Wounded Man often goes after rich women who will take care of him. There is no caretaking and relief of responsibility that would be too much for him to accept. When his victim begins to weary of the burden of his unending needs—which can go on for years if he has chosen well for himself—he wraps his abuse in *inversion* and *projection*:

- When she objects or resists, he accuses her of being "just like all the others" who have treated him so unfairly
- When she expresses the wish that he could get on his feet or rise above his past, he accuses her of doing to him what he is doing to her—using and abusing

These techniques give the abuser a way to tighten controls and gain more ground while also setting up the victim to feel more defective, obligated and guilty.

The Wounded Man Mindset

The principles at work underneath this mask express:

- He has suffered great wrongs and is therefore entitled to unending loyalty and support.
- The abuses he has endured make him unassailable because he is the perennial victim, which state he milks ad nauseum.
- He should be allowed to do whatever he wants to do without question or limitation because of all that he has suffered.
- He is unconstrained in his predations because he is blameless and anyone who thinks otherwise is out to get him.

Like all abusers, the Wounded Man is empty and blameless. His mistreatment by others when he is such a blameless, innocent, righteous man can compound the emotional ammunition and penetrate even the most sophisticated heart with the seamless lying that only a psychopath can deliver.

> *He has an insatiable need for attention which is inserted, like a long needle, into the assets, character, and reserves of his victim.*

Bob crying when
suing his change
of command
speaker - inappropriate!

| 35 |

Red Flag #29
THE WIRED GUY

The Wired Guy is connected to electronics— they are part of who and what he is. This shows up as addiction to and obsession with video games, web surfing, texting, work, programming, the news, pornography, stocks, etc. The Wired Guy will interrupt any interpersonal activity, from casual conversation to sex, to take a phone call, read a text, look at an alert, etc.

If he grew up addicted to electronics (pornography, video games, horror films) by the time he was 18, he was exposed to about a quarter million images of violence, of which about 50 thousand included scenes of murder, some with a considerable gore factor. Interactive electronic entertainments are calibrated to engage and arouse in order to sell more. The result of this "formula" for the consumer is in the virtual world, it is seen and interacted with, but not felt. This is dangerous territory because the perpetrator acts with impunity no matter what he does to his victim(s). Without real consequence there is no psychological impact, no emotional reckoning, no opportunity to think about what is being done. Social media is built on the same principle, and as such, will lead to its own demise—like cancer that kills it victim.

The Wired Guy tends to grow up not taking anything too seriously, including life and death. His behavior is based on lack of feeling and comprehension. His socializing consists of exchanges with strangers and is devoid of emotional connection. He probably had a "NO FEAR" bumper sticker on his first car. When you don't feel, respect or understand emotions, fear is just one of them.

Some of the best paying jobs happen to be the most technological and the best-selling entertainments happen to be the most pathological. Being immersed in the virtual world blurs the distinction between the real and the unreal, between accountability and unaccountability. It also retards personal growth and social development. It is no secret that high tech has its own culture, and one of its characteristics is the absence of social skills. When this is magnified by intimate abuse, the effects on you can be terrifying. When you are further compromised by an inadequate self image, you will endure much mistreatment.

He spends his waking hours in front of his electronic device(s).

He interrupts any activity with you, including sex, to take a call, check email, etc.

He spends inordinate amounts of money on hardware, software, memberships and subscriptions that allow him greater access to his wiredness.

He becomes enraged when anyone says to "put that thing down."

When he does disconnect, he is distracted, sullen, wrathful until he gets back in front of his device.

During the last two decades of the 20th century, 15 billion dollars was spent by consumers on electronic entertainments, a high number of which contained graphical violence. These depictions were (and are) amplified; that is, violent acts are rendered as more gruesome rather than more realistic. Over time, this does things to the human mind because interactive engagement exerts greater influence than passive observation. As the Wired Guy becomes more addicted, he becomes more dangerous.

The Wired Guy Mindset

The principles at work underneath this mask express:

- He is accustomed to acting with the impunity he has in the virtual world no matter what he does to his victim.

- He does not need to develop personally to excel in the virtual world, he does not want to do this for his partner either.

- He is capable of over-the-top abuse because his wiredness removes the reality of consequences.

- He does not think twice about using his technological expertise to sabotage or destroy his partner.

- When his victim tries to leave him, he cyber stalks her.

An addiction to any electronic media, but especially to violent electronic media is a red flag. It often precedes live acts of bullying, teen dating abuse, online predation, domestic violence, animal torture, elder abuse. It does not just depend on the neurological subsets of psychopathy but conveys its own dulling of right and wrong.

In the wired realm, there are unlimited games to play without having to get dirty, deal with blowback or clean up any carnage—it is a psychopath's wet dream.

| 36 |

Red Flag #30
THE GREAT GUY

His social interactions are all choreographed so that he can gain the upper hand in any exchange. When it serves him, he initiates his activities with flattery, friendliness or posturing to charm and disarm the other person. It is like a game to him and he plays it without inhibition because he knows it well.

The Great Guy is cunning in how he presents himself to people. Despite his studied assertions to the contrary, this man is preoccupied with achieving advantage, promoting image and elevating position—his!

Nothing that he does is out of regard for anyone but himself. He is self-serving to an extreme degree.

He name drops.

He attends church.

He makes appearances.

He pursues his goals.

He flaunts his resources.

He indulges his desires.

The type of person he presents himself to be can give you clues to his capabilities as an intimate partner. It can tell you things about the nature of his childhood and his familial relations. It can explain things to you about other aspects of his life, now or later. For example, he may tell you that he's from a great family, has great relationships with his parents and children. However, you witness nothing to confirm these claims and you learn later that this is all false. You may also observe that the entire family participates in this charade of greatness.

The Great Guy is often formulaic with people. He may greet different people the same way, such as with a hearty handshake, a clap on the back, or some show of over-friendliness. Depending on how well he's known, if you look carefully, you will see cracks in the act:

You see he takes the initiative.

You see people put off by him.

You see he is more animated than those he talks to.

You also see they avoid him or move away first.

When you go out with him, you never know if it is going to be a normal, peaceful outing or not. When he's in a mood, you find yourself more or less abandoned while he drinks, talks loudly, hits on other women and so forth.

You'll be ignored except for dirty looks from across the room. When the event is over, he may seethe in silence or unload on you in the car on the way home. In either case, you're in trouble because of something you did or did not do. And this transgression of yours is his excuse for whatever he decides to do to you afterwards.

The Great Guy Mindset

The principles at work underneath this mask express:

- He is not responsible for his actions because he is so great.
- His woman should be grateful to be with him, anything less is unacceptable.
- His great guy reputation sets him apart, entitles him and belongs to him forever.
- Anyone who can't see what a great guy he is, is an idiot and not to be tolerated.

No matter how social you once were, you find yourself anticipating public outings with equal parts longing and dread.

When it's too late to matter, you may realize that the friends he has talked up were from long ago or far away.

| 37 |

The "Other"

Thousands of years ago, they were called *demons*, *demonaics* and *demon-possessed*. Hundreds of years ago, they were called beasts, fiends, evil and monsters—some were the stuff of legends. In the last two centuries, they have been called *insane without delirium*, *morally insane* and in modern times, *psychopathic*. Though the names have changed, their reality has not; they are *Other*.

The psychopathic and the possessed want you to think they look like lunatics or monsters, but in fact, they make sure they look normal and many of them make the effort to be appealing. There is little about their appearance that gives them away—until they reach that point in adulthood when their pathology has grown beyond their ability to manage their behavior. It becomes too intense for them to camouflage and they are too ill to care. Organic brain damage is progressive, so there comes a time when the mask begins to crack and public conduct begins to reveal his true nature. This is a small relief. By the time the mask cracks however, the abuse he has been dishing out behind closed doors has been prolonged and pronounced.

Although the social predator lives to achieve control over others, he has little control over himself. He denies, justifies and minimizes his abuse by saying that sometimes he "just loses control of himself" when what he is doing is creating or manipulating circumstances to seize more control of her. This critical distinction comes from a professional who has worked for over three decades with abusive men:

> "An abusive man often considers it his right to control where his partner goes, with whom she associates, what she wears, and when she needs to be back home. He therefore feels that she should be grateful for any freedoms he does grant her…"

> Lundy Bancroft
> WHY DOES HE DO THAT?

We have a reliable basis for identifying and assessing of the attributes of the psychopath. A good place to begin is to know what causes this condition:

- genetics
- early childhood trauma
- head injury
- substance abuse
- demonic possession

Babies who are born with a genetic predisposition to psychopathy grow into it. By childhood, there can be the first signs of cruelty. Toddlers damaged by violence in the home begin to exhibit self-centeredness. Individuals who sustain severe head injuries or abuse mind-altering substances (to include many pharmaceutical drugs) begin to show signs of altered behavior and cognition. A priest who worked with doctors and psychiatrists, noted that half of the psychiatric patients he saw were not psychopathic, but demon possessed. He reported that *all* of his cases were resolved through exorcism.

Dr Hare has studied psychopaths in prison and taught at the university level for four decades. He developed the diagnostic standard used today to establish psychopathic traits present and whether or not they add up to a diagnosis of full psychopathy.

Note: According to some clinicians and researchers, an individual can possess several traits without that leading to a diagnosis of full psychopathy. It takes a preponderance of these traits expressed to an extreme degree to warrant a clinical diagnosis. A person who uses charm for example is not necessarily psychopathic unless there is a history (pattern of behavior) of their using that charm to deceive and damage others in the extreme.

There is a growing movement to use this assessment tool as well as *f*MRI brain scans on individuals in corporate and governmental positions to help halt high level corruption. On PsychCentral, functional magnetic resonance imaging, or *f*MRI, is described as:

> "a technique for measuring brain activity. It works by detecting the changes in blood oxygenation and flow that occur in response to neural activity – when a brain area is more active it consumes more oxygen and to meet this increased demand blood flow increases to the active area. fMRI can be used to produce activation maps showing which parts of the brain are involved in a particular mental process."

One of the distinctions between the sane and the insane is access to higher emotions; this distinction is not hard to see when you know to look for it, but it takes practice to discern the feigned emotions expressed through the pleasing personality of the psychopath (persona) from his real feelings expressed through his true nature (predatory). In personal relationships, this dichotomy expresses the counterfeit nature of a psychopathic bond. It also explains more of what women experience when they are being abused by a partner who is incapable of higher emotions. In the public arena, this dichotomy expresses the age-old struggle between good and *evil*.

> "Many psychopaths are master manipulators and game players; they will use every trick in the book to achieve their goals... The chance to con and manipulate others is a primary motivator for someone with a psychopathic personality disorder; psychopaths like to play games with people.
>
> Paul Babiak, PhD
> SNAKES IN SUITS

| 38 |

Spiritual Battles

When they are being abused, one of the first questions many women ask is, "What's wrong with me?" This question evidences a willingness to be accountable and take the blame for the dreamy relationship that has turned into a nightmare. This is a willingness that wants to face the problem, (which her abuser has said is all her fault) so the relationship can heal, become "normal" and move forward. Such a journey often stays within the confines of psychology. This is where I turned when logic, intuition and experience failed to help. When a chance conversation introduced the subject of psychopathy, I knew I needed explore it. Later, when a chance radio show delved into demonic possession, another jurisdiction came into view.

> "Mental illness is an aspect of a post-fall world. There was no mental illness in Eden. There is mental illness now. What has changed? Sin, that virus of self-centered blindness to the truth and glory of God, has twisted and broken every aspect of human nature, from the clarity of our mental processes to the bio-chemical make-up of our brains. Sin has multi-generational effects.

It is embedded in every aspect of the social make-up of human communities and relationships. It has altered everything about the world."

The Internet Monk

The following are primary themes in the Bible about the relationship between illness and demonic activity:

- When it is in the body, it develops as a result of inherent sin nature. It can cause additional problems that affect physical health.

- When it is in the will (mind and heart), it develops as a result of giving in to baser nature. Corrupted behavior can lead to corrupted thoughts and vice versa.

- When it is in the spirit, it comes as result of direct attack by a demon or influence by a demonic spirit.

- A person without faith in God is open to demonic possession.

- A person who is firm in their faith, even if it is new, is not subject to possession, but can be oppressed by demonic spirits or by a demon itself.

Some say demonic activity can lead to additional problems. Each cause of mental illness responds to or requires a particular treatment for healing to occur:

- Neurological disturbances, such as brain dysfunction, respond to physical treatment.

- Psychological disorders require confession, counseling and the implementation of higher principles of conduct.

- Supernatural disturbances, such as demon possession, require spiritual intervention and the use of Christ's name.

Spiritual Oppression and Demonic Possession

Oppression and possession are two distinct categories of demonic activity, which differ in *nature* and *degree*. Both can afflict the victim in multiple ways and both can be caused by more than one spirit. In the 2000 Bulletin of the World Health Organization, Director General, Dr G H Brundtland listed major depression, schizophrenia, bipolar disorders, alcohol abuse and obsessive-compulsive disorders as the most serious mental health illnesses. The Bible says these disorders can be caused and relieved through spiritual means.

Demonic oppression refers to having demons and spirits acting in opposition to the victim. To be vexed means to be harassed, tormented or troubled. Demonic oppression most often manifests as "work of the flesh" which is another expression for sin.

Symptoms of Spiritual Oppression

The afflicted is more cognizant of demonic oppression than those around him. He tries to hide the symptoms. When he can't hide them, he makes up reasons for them to deflect blame or responsibility from him, and to deny or minimize consequences for others.

Note: This behavior is congruent with how psychopaths handle their "slip ups."

- Anxiety and fear that is irrational, unusual and intense
- Lapses in rational thinking and acceptable behavior
- Extreme emptiness, loneliness and feelings of loss

- Uncharacteristic conflicts and emotional outbursts
- Unprecedented lack of self control (verbal expression, substance use)
- Loss of direction and interest, aimlessness
- Inability to discern things spiritually
- Overwhelming desire for control, power, material possessions
- Loss of connection to God, lack of fear of God

Causes of Spiritual Oppression

Demonic oppression is predatory and opportunistic. In the latter case, all it takes is a single, casual contact with something or someone demonic to unleash hell:

- Emotional dishonesty to self and others
- Hedonism to the point of immorality
- Sexual congress with the oppressed or possessed
- Looking at pornography
- Over use of mind-altering substances
- Trying out or joining false religions
- Exploring the occult
- Playing with psychic phenomena
- Having or acquiring possessed objects
- Venting rage or wrath on strangers *grocery store*
- Developing extreme jealousy in relationship
- Accepting violence that is unjust (video games)
- Going without sleep or sleeping little
- Being angry at God

Symptoms of Demonic Possession

The goal of a demon or spiritual evil is to destroy (kill) the afflicted by his own hand or through the rigor of the possession. If others can be destroyed, they will be. It is reported that some possessions last for years without dramatic events; however, when help is sought to expel the demon, the battle becomes pitched.

Note: The last four symptoms (italicized) are held to be the most conclusive evidence of true demonic possession by spiritual authorities.

- hyper-sensitivity to light, sound, touch
- lack of interest in food
- intense loneliness with desire to be alone
- personal and social recklessness (appearance and conduct)
- uncontrollable verbal rages with extreme profanity
- speaking in foreign languages unknown to the afflicted (including ancient ones no longer in use)
- refusal to submit to any human or spiritual authority other than the occupying demon(s)
- mental insensibility that renders the person unable to grasp simple spiritual concepts (keeping God at bay)
- display of occult knowledge (necromancy, astral projection)
- utter inattention to physical appearance and wellbeing
- complete lack of restraint (urination, masturbation, sexual advances)
- attempting or wanting to commit suicide
- display of superhuman abilities (levitation, psychokinesis, strength)
- expression of multiple and distinct personalities
- threatening and terrifying behavior involving heights, fire, weapons, temperature, animals
- intense and violent reaction to Christ's name or mention of His crucifixion

Causes of Demonic Possession

Demonic possession happens by exposure to someone or something that is associated with the demonic. Most cases of possession result in the death of the possessed after prolonged suffering.

Note: This corresponds to Levels 20, 21 and 22 of Dr Stone's Scale of Evil and the highest scores on Dr Hare's Psychopathy Checklist.

- experimenting with or leading an immoral lifestyle
- having or using occult objects
- seeking or using occult abilities
- giving occult practitioners spiritual access (fortune telling, astrology, psychic reading)
- overtly or covertly rebelling against biblical authority
- blaspheming the Holy Spirit
- spiritual immaturity that includes disrespect of God and His anointed

Some of the foregoing material was sourced from: healingdeliverance.net, eternaldestiny.com, prophecyoffellowship.com

| 39 |

Measuring Evil

The public was introduced to forensic psychiatrist Dr Michael Stone in 2006, when the television show, "Most Evil" which was based on his work debuted on the Discovery Channel. In each show he profiled murderers (mass and serial) and explored the nature of human evil, which he equated to the psychopath.

Michael Stone, MD is a professor of Clinical Psychiatry at the College of Physicians and Surgeons at Columbia University and an attending physician in Forensic Psychiatry at Creedmoor Psychiatric Center in New York. At the Mid-Hudson Psychiatric Center in New York he undertook an in-depth study of the biographies of 500 murderers from case files. His purpose was two-fold:

- to determine why these killers did what they did
- to identify the underlying traits that facilitated their violence

From this, he formulated a list of behavior interpretations he called the "22 Levels of Evil" (similar to the circles of Hell in Dante's epic poem, "The_Divine Comedy").

Levels of Evil

In explaining his list, Dr Stone said that the first classification is not evil but self defense; he used it as a starting point from which to follow the descending trajectory to evil. (Dr Stone's words are in quotation marks.)

Level 1: "Those who kill in *self defense* and do not show psychopathic tendencies."

Dr Stone describes the second through eighth classifications as impulse crimes arising out of overwhelming emotions, situations as well as poor impulse control. These behaviors are reactive, but not premeditated. They could be described as crimes of passion, which are committed when someone finds himself in an intense and unrestrained situation. Perpetrators of these crimes often feel remorse, such as the jealous lover (Level 2) and the traumatized person who kills in desperation, such as an abused child or battered wife (Level 6).

Level 2: "*Jealous* lovers who, though *egocentric* or *immature*, are not psychopathic; crime of passion."

Level 3: "*Willing* companions of killers: *aberrant* personality; probably *impulse-ridden*, with some anti-social traits."

Level 4: "Those who kill in self-defense, after extremely *provocative* behavior toward the victim."

Level 5: "Highly *narcissistic*, but not distinctly psychopathic persons, with a *psychotic* core, who kill loved ones or family members out of *jealousy*."

Level 6: "*Traumatized, desperate* people who kill abusive relatives and others (to escape abuse) but lack significant psychopathic traits. Genuinely remorseful."

Level 7: "*Impetuous, hot-headed* murderers without psychopathic features."

Level 8: "*Highly narcissistic*, but not distinctly psychopathic people."

Levels nine through 16 classify acts of rage and ruthlessness, only some of which require low-level psychopathic traits. These killers got into situations using their charm, then acted out through murder. On the periphery of this group are murderers whose crimes escalate from stalking activities. Dr Stone describes these as "... people who are hungry for attachment but who know no bounds. There's no brake system preventing them from bothering, pestering and sometimes even harming the object of their interest."

This corresponds to lower levels of self control ("braking") observable in youth. Perpetrators of this level of violence do not hesitate to murder someone they feel is "in the way" (Level 11) or kill because they want to (Level 15).

Level 9: "Non-psychopathic people with *smoldering rage* who kill when that rage is ignited."

Level 10: "*Jealous lovers* with marked *psychopathic* features."

Level 11: "Killers of people who were in the way (such as witnesses), *egocentric*, but not distinctly psychopathic."

Level 12: "*Power-hungry* psychopaths who kill when cornered."

Level 13: "Murderers with inadequate, *rage-filled* personalities and psychopathic features with a *psychotic* core, who kill those close to them. Jealously is an underlying motive."

Level 14: "*Ruthlessly self-centered* psychopathic schemers"

Level 15: "Psychopathic or *cold-blooded spree-killers* who have committed *multiple* murders."

Level 16: "*Psychopaths* committing *multiple vicious* acts."

The final six levels of evil express full-blown psychopathy in extreme acts of premeditated cruelty and inhumane behavior. The psychopath is driven by an insatiable quest for gratification. When he possesses a majority of entrenched anti-social traits, the result is someone who thrives on delivering pain and watching others suffer. These are the incomprehensible and unimaginable crimes that often end up in the news.

Dr Stone identifies children who develop "with no sense of empathy or compassion for others" as "callous-unemotional youths." These are children who develop into psychopaths in adulthood and commit this level of crime. Perpetrators of this type take their time with their victims. They possess an unnerving calm as they commit their acts of perversion, murder and torture (Level 17). It is not uncommon for them to make their crimes into rituals that go on for hours or days because torture is the source of their greatest gratification (Level 22).

Psychopaths in this state of pathology are incapable of relationship. Their sex life consists of rape and one-night stands. Their crimes are likewise done on the fly. They inflict extreme suffering on their victims and then they murder them. They derive more pleasure from the torture than from the murder. When their victims plead for their lives, the psychopath only feels more contempt. The extent to which they are enlivened by extreme psychological and physical anguish is the measure of their sickness.

Level 17: *"Sexually perverse serial murderers and/or torture-murderers.* Murder is the primary motive, following prolonged torture (among males rape is the primary motive, with murder to hide the evidence), systematic torture is not a primary factor."

Level 18: "Torture murderers with *murder the primary motive."*

Level 19: "Psychopaths driven to terrorism, subjugation, intimidation and rape, but short of murder."

Level 20: "Torture murderers with *torture as the primary motive* but in psychopathic personalities."

Level 21: "Psychopaths *preoccupied with torture in the extreme*, but not known to have committed murder."

Level 22: "Psychopathic, serial torture-murderers, with torture the primary motive."

Dr Stone relates that about 90 percent of serial murderers can be classified as psychopaths. He believes that more than half of these were damaged as young children by the failure of their parents to love and protect them. The stress this caused those children altered their brain chemistry to the point that the organ did not develop as it should. As a result, they wander the earth alone, incapable of love (or any of the higher emotions) and act out their primal wounds by abusing themselves and others. Early exposure and subsequent addictions to alcohol, drugs, pornography and video violence can also figure in the formation of human evil.

Dr Stone summarized what he saw in the minds of serial killers this way:

> "... more than 90 percent meet criteria, hard criteria for psychopathy. Almost all of them are sadists... where there's enjoyment of the suffering of others as a key quality, and a love of control and domination of others, etc. Half of them are loners, men that can't make long relationships with others. So in effect, some of them use serial killing as a way of having a one-night stand where they rape the woman and then kill her to destroy evidence...

> "Some of them seek revenge... so they're constantly getting back at the parents who abused them or neglected them...

> "And another motive... killing a specific parent over and over, but not actually killing the parent... terrible, terrible childhoods... So the bulk of them; however, have come from horrible homes where the early damage and misery becomes a motivating force later for seeking revenge... they don't have the social

skills to compensate for that and to make a good relationship anyway and kind of get past it. So they're stuck, they're mired in the misery of their childhood forever."

Dr Stone's work does not explore other realms of evil such as the white-collar criminal. This type of psychopath operates in a position of influence that allows him access to his preferred prey and form of gratification. Most of these organizational psychopaths do not commit murder, but their actions can lead to large-scale suffering of all kinds, including death.

SNAKES IN SUITS, WHEN PSYCHOPATHS GO TO WORK by Paul Babiak, PhD and Robert Hare, PhD delves into evil in high places. The 2012 film, "Fishead" also depicts the world of the organizational psychopath through interviews with leading thinkers from diverse vantage points. Both provide valuable introductions into what happens in an organization when a psychopath gets into a position of power. Almost all abuse is perpetrated out of sight; none is so diabolical as that of the human being who has been taken over by spiritual evil.

| 40 |

Battling Demons

Before man came up with the psychological disciplines, violent people were considered possessed and treated as such—they were removed from society. I found a series of interviews with a Jesuit priest who participated in thousands exorcisms during his lifetime and later wrote about them. Father Malachi Martin criticized the Catholic Church, the Vatican and some governments in his writings and in his later interviews. Toward the end of his life he admitted to being in fear because of the organizations he had criticized and exposed as evil. He died in 1999 at the age of 78 under circumstances that those closest to him considered questionable. In his books, Father Martin shared his observations and experiences:

> "Like a mongoose playing a cobra, the priest will attempt to work the demon into a position first of disadvantage, then of vulnerability. He begins by demanding, with the authority of prayer, to know its name. The demons are not always willing to play this game. They lie silent, sullen and hidden. When this happens, the exorcist must provoke them into breaking cover. You have to tease them out."

According to Father Martin, there are different types of possession, with "perfect possession" being the worst, the state in which a person has lost complete control and is at the mercy of spiritual evil:

- There is a difference between spiritual oppression and demonic possession
- In his lifetime, he saw a staggering increase in evil in general and recorded an 800 percent increase in possession
- Half of psychiatric patients diagnosed as insane were not, but were possessed
- Exorcisms were only performed at the request of the possessed and/or the family
- Exorcisms did not go forward until the possessed passed a medical and psychiatric evaluation
- At least one medical doctor was present at every exorcism
- The possessed were all found to have done something that created an opening for evil to enter them
- Playing with a Ouija board was one of the most common conduits for demonic entry
- Channeling was another activity that opened the practitioner and participant(s) to demonic influences
- Other forms of dabbling in occult practices are also dangerous
- The purpose of evil and the goal of a demon is to destroy the possessed
- Nominal Christians appear to be their preferred prey
- The dominant energy of the demonic is hatred so extreme it defies language
- More than one psychiatrist left his profession after witnessing an exorcism

- Many atheists converted to Christianity after witnessing an exorcism
- Many participants in exorcism die in the months following the ritual
- Exorcisms can last a few hours to a few months
- The exorcised spirits are not destroyed, they are evicted from the possessed
- Demonic spirits are around us at all times
- Cases of perfect possession are beyond the scope of exorcism, there is no deliverance for them

Father Martin describes the battle with demons this way:

"The demon does not physically inhabit the body; it possesses the person's will. We have to compel the thing to reveal itself and its purpose. It can be slow and difficult, with the demon taunting, scorning, abusing you–speaking through the mouth of the possessed, but not in his or her voice... In the end, though, it does come out – and when that happens you experience the sensation we call 'presence'. At that moment you know you are in the company of the purest evil. I have felt the claws of invisible animals tearing at my face. I have been knocked off my feet, blinded and winded. But it is then, when you've sensed the 'presence' that the real attack on the demon can begin... The whole nature of the thing changes. The demon knows it's losing. Instead of screaming abuse, it begins to plead for mercy. It says it's sorry, it begs to be spared. It promises to go home... Where they go, I do not know. We do not destroy them, we drive them out. Sometime I encounter the same ones again. As the demon disappears, the person it has possessed is 'cleared' and a wondrous wave of peace comes over them."

The overlay between the psychopathic and the possessed is staggering. The sole distinction seems to be the supernatural repertoire of the possessed. The psychopath, like the possessed is driven to destroy. The psychopath is driven by the absence of conscience, the possessed is driven by the presence of hatred; the actions of both embody evil and lead to *inevitable harm*. As many people on the planet are guided into the baser pursuits of ever more primitive and secular interests, evil has, unsurprisingly continued to become more prominent in society. The careless and the uninformed continue to be at greatest risk.

Part Six:
Mind Games for
Soul Destruction

"To die is nothing; but it is terrible not to live."

Victor Hugo

Howard & Melody

Howard and Melody grew up in the same small town. They grew from childhood playmates into teenage boyfriend and girlfriend as tenaciously as a vine wraps itself around a pole. She had dreams of being his wife, he just wanted her to be his.

Howard's family had farmed and ranched the rich bottomlands there for five generations. They were steeped in raising crops and livestock and the callousness that so often shows up in that way of life. Melody's family had moved to the country the year before she was born after deciding to leave the overload of urban living behind.

Unlike the women in Howard's family, Melody's mother and grandmother and great grandmother had not grown up in homes where they were brutalized by their husbands. The notion of being mistreated was foreign to them. Several times during her teen years Melody observed Howard's father, brothers and uncles being as brutal with their women and children as they were with their animals and equipment. Melody would later wonder where this cruelty came from and why it got worse with time.

When Howard and Melody got married, no one was surprised. It had long been understood that she belonged to him and that anyone who came near her or bothered her would have a can of whoop-ass opened on them. To say Howard was protective of Melody did not tell the whole story, he was *proprietary* about her. Nobody ever challenged him and nothing he did ever crossed the line, but somehow everyone knew that he considered Melody his treasure and he would protect her with his life. Melody basked in his protectiveness; it was unlike anything she'd ever known before. Growing up in a large family where both parents were spread too thin, it was like a salve on a wound she didn't even know she had. She sometimes felt she didn't deserve it, but she cherished the feeling of being cherished by Howard. It was part of what she loved about him. She imagined that it would be the fabric of their life together, an impregnable bond woven over time that would comfort and protect them.

The odd thing was, this was not what happened after they got married. The honeymoon was wonderful, but once they got back and began to settle into the rhythm of living together, the spark of love was slowly extinguished by something else. Howard's maleness and size exerted a different energy without the protective affection Melody had once enjoyed. In its place, something else began to rise up; something she couldn't identify at first. It seemed that Howard was turning into an angry man and that he was unleashing his anger on her. He had not been an angry or hostile boy, although he knew how to convey menace without making a move. This was something else. Had he hidden this from her for all these years?

The day after Thanksgiving, Melody got a taste of Howard's wrath. When Howard came in early from the fields to find Melody talking on the phone to her mother, he waited for her in the kitchen. As soon as she walked in, he felled the refrigerator like a sawn tree to protest her talking on the phone instead of getting his supper ready. "It's the least you could do," he had roared as he stormed out of the house and left in his truck. When he returned hours later, obviously well fed, he exhibited no guilt over the mess his tantrum had caused. After he righted the refrigerator, he went upstairs and went to bed. The message was clear: his mess was Melody's to clean up.

When she gave birth to their first child that fall, Howard began to compete with the baby for her attention. One day she sat in a large rocking chair nursing her infant son. She sat facing the window, gazing at her baby and watching the breeze stir the curtains. Her heart swelled with the joy of having her baby in her arms. Birdsong fluttered up the stairwell. She did not hear Howard walk up behind her. In the blink of an eye the rocking chair was lifted and up-ended, hurling her to the floor. Her son lost his grip, but Melody curled into a protective ball and held him fast. She landed on her forehead, one hand and both knees. Dazed and shaken, she looked up uncomprehendingly. Her husband walked around and glared down at her with unfeeling eyes and clenched fists, "Where's my lunch?" he spat.

Melody drew strength from having the baby and poured herself into his rearing. They were extremely close. Howard on the other hand seemed largely indifferent, even contemptuous of his son. He only exhibited interest in the child when other people were around, tossing him in the air, bouncing him on his knee or slapping him on his diapered bottom. Consequently, little Howie cried or ran whenever his father came near. Melody saw this and was tormented by it.

One evening when little Howie was two, he was playing with his toys on the kitchen floor while his mother stood nearby cleaning up after the evening meal. This was their ritual, this was when it was usually safe for Howie to be let out of his playpen. Heavy footfalls came down the hall. Doors and windows rattled in their frames, the house shook. Melody took a deep breath and kept washing dishes. *What now?* Without any prompting from his mother, Howie knew to try to get out of sight. He scooted far under the kitchen table and grasped a chair leg. His father stormed in, his face red with anger. Melody had no idea what was he mad about, and really, it didn't matter.

This is how they lived—he blew up, she placated him. His voice boomed and shook the room like thunder again and again. His mother's voice responded softly, like summer rain. He towered over her and smacked the counter with one hand. She startled and took a step backward.

Howie began to whimper—he had seen this many times before and had the primal understanding of a child that he was not safe. His body knew when it was in the presence of danger. At the sound of his son's crying, Howard bent down and grabbed his small arm, pinching the fragile skin between his calloused fingers. He pulled him out from under the table and threw him at his mother who groaned as his weight hit her. She caught him with her wet hands and instinctively hugged him tight even though she knew that would further enrage Howard. *Get away.* "And shut that kid up, or I will…"

When little Howie was three, Melody was told to get a job and start bringing in some money. They didn't need the money, but Howard needed to know his wife would be separated from their son some hours every day. This was actually his mother's idea and when she offered to babysit, it became an easy fix to what Howard considered his son's excessive attachment to his mother. It was time the apron strings got cut. He knew the slice would make his wife, who was a shadow of her former self, reel.

So, Howie went to his paternal grandparents' farm five days a week while his mother toiled in the hot kitchen of a bread bakery. She spent her days alone, aching for her son and wondering what had happened to her life. Lonely for his mommy, Howie shadowed his grandmother around their big house, and later, around the grounds. His grandparents ran a small dairy and near the house was a barn where ailing cows and calves came to either recover or expire. One day, his grandmother took him into the barn so she could check on an ailing calf. Howie had never seen a baby cow (or baby anything). He sat spellbound as she ministered to the glossy little newborn. To her, it was just another calf, which she handled perfunctorily, but to Howie it was a wonder.

After that, he began to toddle out to the barn every chance he got. He loved its hugeness and its smells, and most of all, he loved the animals in it. It didn't take long until his personal explorations netted him a big discovery, a shy barn cat, who he called Kitty. Every afternoon, he took her a strip of lunchmeat from his sandwich and waited patiently for her to emerge from her hidey-hole to grab it.

At the end of one summer afternoon, Howie wandered into the barn by himself with a piece of chicken he'd grabbed in the kitchen. He started towards the back of the barn as usual, but stopped short when he saw a man bending down in front of the hidey hole that Kitty used. As Howie approached, the situation came into view. The man, a dairy worker was killing Kitty's kittens. They squealed weakly as he pulled them away from their distraught mother, dispatched them and then dropped their limp bodies into a burlap sack. Mouth agape and transfixed in horror, Howie stood frozen. When he snapped out of it, he turned and fled.

Running fast, blinded by hot tears, he bolted out of the barn as fast as his short legs would carry him, but then fell hard on the gravel outside. His grandmother heard his wails from the house and was rushing down the steps toward him as he clambered to his feet. By the time he found her arms, he was hysterical. Expecting a physical injury, she was bemused to learn the source of his upset was just the killing of cats.

When she discussed this incident with Howard, he listened without reaction, as was his custom with his mother. On the drive home, he became livid that his wife was turning his son into such a "pussy." He drove like a madman and when his son whimpered, he reached back and boxed him in his car seat. By this time, Howie had learned not to cry in front of his father. When Howard threw the truck into the driveway, he had decided to deal with Melody that night. *I'll put a stop to this. No woman is going to turn my son into a girl.*

He was silent as a stone through dinner to let her know she was in trouble. He knew she was racking her brain for what he could be mad about. It almost made him snort with self satisfaction.

He waited until she came up to the bedroom to let her have it. After the usual one-sided argument—she never had a good excuse—he let himself hit her—just once. He'd wanted to hit her before, but hadn't. Now, in the moment, it was a sensation worth waiting for. Tonight he felt justified because she was turning his boy into a sissy. When his open hand landed on her cheek and her head snapped sideways and she flew through the air, he felt vindication flowing through his veins. He also felt aroused. When he realized he'd become hard, he opened her clothing and took her.

He wasn't thinking about her, he didn't notice the expression on her face, that her hair was wet with tears or that there was a trickle of blood coming out of her nose. No, he was thinking about how he was going to deal with her from then on. The harder he pumped, the limper she became but he didn't notice because a new day was dawning for him and it was going to change his life. He knew it. The last bit of power in the marriage had just been delivered to him. There was nothing he could not have his way about now.

The week of Howie's fifth birthday, his parents took him to the store to pick out a present. He sat in the cart gazing at all the toys as his mother pushed the cart down the aisle listlessly, the handle bar across the middle of her pregnant belly. His father walked behind them, glowering. Howie pointed to a toy soldier. His mother stopped the cart and put the box in his hands so he could look at it. "Let's hurry it up," came from his father.

Melody stood pale and expressionless while he examined the soldier and looked around at other toys. Another little boy, smaller than Howie, took a few steps across the aisle and away from his mother, who was distracted by some fine print on another toy box. Grinning, the little boy reached up toward the toy soldier Howie was holding. Without a word, Howie clutched the box to his chest and kicked out at the pint-sized interloper, striking him in the temple with the side of his shoe. The blow knocked the child off his feet and onto his bottom, from which position he then fell backward, hitting his head on the floor. Across the aisle, his mother spun around in disbelief, dropping her box on the floor with a loud report.

No longer occupied with the toy soldier, Howie watched the results of his action with equal parts satisfaction and fascination. The long moment of silence ended as the toddler's first howl emerged from his throat. He clutched his tiny hand to his head and screamed as his mother lifted him into her arms. She glared at Howie, then at Howard and Melody as she kneeled down to comfort her shrieking son.

Feeling the wrath to come, Melody snatched the box away from Howie and shoved it back on the shelf. In a fluid motion, she whisked him out of the cart as Howard grabbed her arm, spun her around and led her roughly out of the store—away from the screaming toddler, the shocked mother and the consequences.

When they were all three back in the truck, Howard let loose. He swung his head around at Melody like a mad bull. He pounded the steering wheel and the seat with his fists. His face red and contorted, spittle flying, he roared on and on. She stared blankly ahead and didn't flinch even when his fists came near her face. The car rocked with his violent gestures. Then Howard turned around, and took hold of his son. Melody squeezed her eyes shut and clenched her fists. Howie looked at his father with terror-swollen eyes and peed in his pants. Undeterred by his son's fear, Howard grabbed the rail-thin shoulders and shook the living daylights out of his little boy.

| 41 |

The Alchemy of a Con

A con is the purposeful deceit by one person (or group of persons) of another person (or group of persons). The modus operandi of a national con to achieve political tyranny illustrates how psychopaths in high places manipulate information and living conditions to control and destroy their prey items, their citizens. These principles also apply to the primary relationship:

> "The greatest threat to mankind and civilization is the spread of the totalitarian philosophy. Its best ally is not the devotion of its followers but the confusion of its enemies. To fight it, we must understand it. Totalitarianism is collectivism. Collectivism means the subjugation of the individual to a group—whether to a race, class or state does not matter. Collectivism holds that man must be chained to collective action and collective thought for the sake of what is called 'the common good... No tyrant has ever lasted long by force of arms alone. Men have been enslaved primarily by spiritual

277

weapons. And the greatest of these is the collectivist doctrine that the supremacy of the state over the individual constitutes the common good."

Ayn Rand
"The Only Path to Tomorrow"

Rand understood that mental control could only be achieved by presenting a pleasing image which plays on emotion and gives the *illusion* of "the common good."

The method of a charismatic con to achieve personal tyranny expresses the same psychological anatomy. The same principles that corporate tyrants use are employed to different extents by pathological men to manipulate information and circumstance to control and destroy their prey items.

The Structure of Abuse

Whether a woman is involved with a low-level abuser, a psychopathic or possessed person, the relationship will be structured in a predictable way. It is called the Cycle of Abuse, the Escalation Cycle, the Wheel of Violence, etc. because it has distinct, repeating phases. The end result of each complete cycle delivers more damage to the victim and more power to the abuser. Its dynamics are not easy to for the victim to identify, even though they are continuously in motion because of the way she is affected by it. The escalation cycle has these main components:

- Increasing Tension
- Explosive Outburst

- Quiet Manipulation

The Increasing Tension Stage

During the first stage, the victim "walks on eggshells" as she seeks to delay or mitigate an outburst. The abuser knows he is in control and taunts her. He knows the chances of any challenge or resistance to his provocations are small. The victim tries to protect herself and her dependents (children and animals) by staying out of his way. Denial and withdrawal are other strategies she uses i to cope with the stress of inevitable, but unpredictable abuse. The Increasing Tension stage can last for days or weeks.

The Explosive Outburst Stage

Then comes the Explosive Outburst stage when the abuser gets violent, vents his rage and unleashes his torments. This is when mental, emotional and spiritual abuse intensify and sometimes transmogrify into acts of physical injury, sexual assault, murder, animal abuse, property damage. Sometimes the violence is verbal and mental with explicit condemnations and threats. Except in cases where the abuser has caused visible damage, he is unlikely to acknowledge what he has done. In his mind, he has asserted his ownership and put his victim in her place. This is how he lives. The victim has little or no control of outcomes at this time. Women who are wounded during physical attacks sometimes say they don't feel their injuries until much later. They "check out" or "trance out" as a means of coping with the horror. The Explosive Outburst stage is the most violent part of the escalation cycle, but also the briefest, lasting a minute, an hour, perhaps a day.

The Quiet Manipulation Stage

After energies are spent, the Manipulation Stage is set. Even though the psychopathic partner is incapable of emotions like guilt, shame or embarrassment, he has mental awareness of them and knows how and when to "employ" them for his own benefit. His victim may not be able to distinguish his feigned contrition for the real thing the first time or two, but she will learn that it is an act. He may apologize to her, romance her and promise never to "lose it" again or he may not say a thing. Either way, it is an uneasy quiet for the victim, a temporary respite. After his outburst, he has soothed the beast, vented his wrath, discharged his tension. The household is allowed to return to "normal" and things are quiet for while. This is a time of increased vulnerability for the victim; this is when she may find herself succumbing to emotions described as Stockholm Syndrome in an effort to survive. The abuser will later reveal that he uses the time in-between his explosive outbursts to justify a previous event or set up a future event. The Quiet Manipulation stage can be the longest part of the cycle.

Most of the descriptions of the repetitive phases of an toxic relationship express its intrusiveness, imbalance of power, inequality of rights, diversity of forms and social tolerance of mistreatment. It is valuable to grasp the operative principles so they can be recognized, avoided and where possible, remedied.

Two Kinds of Fear

The abused live with instinctive emotion on a daily basis; fear is one that figures prominently in their stories. As Gavin de Becker reveals, there are two kinds of fear: one that can save you and one that can kill you. The first kind of fear is *primal*—your body knows it before your head gets it.

- It's the hair on the back of your neck standing up.

- It's a surge of clear-eyed determination to survive without hesitation or panic.

- It's action without second guessing.

This is the kind of fear that can save you.

The other kind of fear is *cerebral*, it is not so insistent because mind and heart are at cross purposes.

- It's wrapped in confusion, doubt, terror, immobility that enervates.

- Your mind is blank or a roar of conflicting messages.

- Your heart pounds, but your legs turn to lead.

- You say the wrong thing, your face gives you away, you freeze or you panic.

This is the kind of fear that can kill you.

Unproductive fear comes from various places; it comes most especially from early childhood. The nature of brain development between birth and age five consists of downloading experience and observation as truth. The basis of much fear and illusion of fear comes from those early programs, which were based on inaccurate information about the self and incomplete information about the world.

Other fears come from experience later in life— failures, losses, misunderstandings, injuries, injustices. Emotionally charged issues become amalgams in the spirit; some can serve you, but many do not.

In addition to developing insight about the telltale signs of the psychopath as he or she moves through society, it is also valuable to know some of the most common responses to their actions.

Normalcy Bias

A common reaction to an encounter with the unreality that only the deranged can arrange (emphasis on the concept of unreality) is *normalcy bias*. It is a natural, but uninformed reaction to a misperceived risk that leads to disaster. It's like trying to run from a grizzly bear, it's an all-but impossible situation that leads to a violent end.

Over time, normalcy bias depletes and incapacitates because it is a reaction to the worst kind of stress there is: unrelenting (which also happens to be a characteristic of psychopathic abuse). Normalcy bias can be described as inaccurate, inadequate thinking that makes things worse. It occurs in the most dire circumstances as a freeze or panic response.

The freeze response is withering; it shows up as the too-little-too-late of timidity or the never-even-trying of immobility. Caution and circumspection serve, immobility and timidity prohibit. Immobility is not just never leaping, it's never looking. The immobilized watch the world go by; they lead a "sort of" life. Some become armchair critics, some become bitter, some become dull.

The psychological run-up to normalcy bias is this: the person thinks that since something has never happened before, it never will. It is one of the ravages of abuse you can observe–if you know what to look for–in the behavior of someone who is being abused. Normalcy bias can show up like this in language:

- "Oh, he would never hurt me."
- "I leave my kids with her all the time."
- "His first wife just didn't understand him."
- "She's not after my money."

Abusive relationships are counterfeit and counter-intuitive experiences. They're counterfeit in that they start out like romance but turn into assault. They're counter-intuitive in that what works in a healthy relationship does not work in an unhealthy one. Normalcy bias comes from not knowing what you're dealing with. It can manifest as both a *cause* and a *result*.

As a cause factor, normalcy bias means you do not see the red flags and do not grasp the gravity of the situation—which works in you like *denial*. This is one reason bad things happen to good people: they're uninformed (gullibility, naiveté) and therefore unprepared for the unthinkable. When you're faced with a situation you've never anticipated or experienced, the typical reaction is to overlook its seriousness and go with the flow. In a pathological relationship this kind of thinking can lead to ruin.

Denial and naiveté, real or postured, may delay the onslaught, but they will not save you from the ravages of an dangerous individual. In fact, this frame of mind actually makes you more vulnerable. Denial does not change reality. Naiveté does not change reality. Just because you cannot imagine or refuse to accept something doesn't mean it doesn't exist. This kind of mindset sets you up to be less able to deal with the extreme circumstances that are heading your way.

> After just two months of marriage, the wife realizes that all three of her animals have been harmed in the same time frame. The cat appeared with a broken leg, the dog became ill after ingesting something poisonous and the parrot started dropping feathers. She tells herself it's coincidental. She knows her husband knows she loves her animals. In the extra-full days of being a newlywed, she doesn't notice that her cat has become nervous, her dog defensive and both have had multiple accidents indoors despite being housetrained for years. Six months later, the cat has disappeared, the dog has been euthanized after being hit by a car when the wife wasn't home and the parrot has died in her cage of unexplained causes.

When you face a situation you've ever imagined, it's not uncommon to downplay the risks and go along in hopes of nothing out of the ordinary happening. However, when a worst-case scenario unfolds, you become prone to over- or under-react in order to escape pain and return to normalcy. In an abusive relationship, an over-reaction can lead to violent reprisal, an under-reaction can lead to abject submission; either of which can be life-changing or life-ending.

As a result factor, normalcy bias sets in when you are beginning to break down under the strain of unrelenting stress. This is the kind of stress that kills. It depletes body, mind and spirit. It impairs thinking, dulls feelings and shuts down life force. This is the experience that leads to the post-traumatic stress disorder (PTSD) suffered by veterans of war and veterans of domestic violence. Normalcy bias accelerates when you're weak and getting weaker; it exacerbates the crumbling of your faculties. As a result, you make poorer and poorer decisions. And as you do, the consequences become more and more grave, which effects lead to added, unnecessary suffering and death.

> During a day-long hike in the back country, the wife becomes aware that her husband is getting farther and farther ahead of her. He is in great shape and he is familiar with the territory; she is neither. She doesn't want to hold him back, so she doesn't ask him to slow down. She climbs and hikes as fast as she can. Within half an hour, he is out of range and she is, for all practical purposes, alone. As anxiety wraps its cold fingers around her, she scolds herself for letting it happen. She imagines a mountain lion behind every boulder and a grizzly bear in each stand of trees. Her husband has the flashlight, ponchos, bear spray and water bottle. She comes to a fork in the trail and cannot see his foot prints. She does not know which way to go. She screams and waits for a response that doesn't come. Unable to contain her panic, she

begins to run and trips over a tree root. She falls hard, splitting her lip and spraining her ankle. Shivering in the coming cold of a mountain night, she crawls to a fir tree and gets up under its skirt. It is late in the tourist season and it could be weeks, even months, before anyone comes this way. And it is.

Normalcy bias is an important but little known factor of being trapped in a pathological situation. Millions of people waste their lives in toxic relationships because they do not realize and cannot accept that their difficult partner is dangerous because he is without conscience and incapable of love.

The final nine red flags can be thought of as "water-torture" behaviors because they are applied in a steady, relentless drip.

Note: Like the other red flags, there can be overlaps in the application of these behaviors. For example, immorality is a universal characteristic, but it is not limited to infidelity. Rules are another common tactic, but they are not imposed consistently. Most toxic relationships do not include direct physical violence, yet many women sustain serious injuries even if their partner doesn't hit them.

ENTITLEMENT

IMMORALITY

INJURY

INSATIABILITY

"NO"

OTHER WOMEN

RIGHTS

ROAD RAGE

RULES

Most toxic partners know it's better for them to avoid acts of overt physical aggression and violence. Women innately know this, too, which is why they almost always take steps to mitigate escalation. Abusive relationships in which there is extreme control but little or no physical violence evidence the abuser's self interest and the victim's resourcefulness. This is the rule, not the exception, in documented cases. It is not an indication of low pathology or low danger, as it exists in cases where the victim is murdered.

| 42 |

Red Flag #31
ENTITLEMENT

Entitlement is not by definition a negative thing, but when taken to extremes, it can become harmful. Some feel one of the root causes of toxic relationships is a warped sense of male entitlement. This can be attributed to DNA, misapplied patriarchal values or cultural conditioning.

Some of the most advanced civilizations on earth have succeeded because the male went out into the world to hunt, legislate, fight and earn a living while the female stayed home to raise children, keep the home and nurture her mate. It's not hard to see how emotionally immature or socially undeveloped males could exploit this situation to the point of abusing their wives. In some cultures for example, a female is not permitted to leave the house without being accompanied by a male relative. This requirement assumes that the female and males at large are untrustworthy and might engage in immoral behavior without the presence of a protective male.

A review of the roles that males have fulfilled through history as well as current statistics show that males are more inclined than females to engage in acts of aggression (including sexual aggression), whether it be sparring with a co-worker, challenging a competitor or dominating his wife.

Cultural observations have identified certain pressure points that can trigger this aggression in behaviors that express an entitlement mindset. When ill-expressed, such as through deceit and domination, entitlement is an abnegation of responsibility rather than the assumption of responsibility. It is an assumptive mindset not based on a reality in which fairness, logic and justice apply. This is the playing field of the psychopathic and the possessed.

In the beginning, entitlement can be expressed in ways that are unique and appealing, such as by conveying a man's masculinity and prowess. He carries himself with confidence; he lives with zeal and high expectation. This self assurance makes his choice of you thrilling—at first. His ways are winning. His energies impress. If he has had success in his work, you may suppose that his confidence and sense of entitlement are two reasons for it. Taken as a whole, early signs of entitlement can reflect well on him and on you. As the relationship proceeds, he begins to turn that zeal, expectation and sense of entitlement on you. It may seem that the quality of his attention changes into something else. You begin to see things that cause you to question his emotional maturity. Something is coming forth that does not value you—it is not considerate, appropriate or fair. As it creeps into more and more of your space and the relationship, you begin to feel crowded and pushed around by this thing.

Because he believes he deserves whatever he wants, his demands begin to increase in number and complexity; they occupy more and more of your time, energy and emotions. Some of your duties and many shared activities exist only to feed his ego.

Like double standards and hypocrisy, he seems to be unaware of the unfairness and recklessness of his behavior and the ways in which it affects you. This could be due to denial and narcissism. Pushing his sense of entitlement on you doesn't have anything to do with loving you, it's all about his need to fill his insatiability. He says he's entitled to having his way about something because he knows more about it than you do or because he's wanted it longer or more than you or because he deserves it because he supports you.

The plain truth is that he believes he is entitled to whatever he wants, including you. His entitlement is all-encompassing and he is quick to deny or justify its encroachment if challenged. Unchecked entitlement can turn into usurpation, where he takes over your life.

> He sets himself up as the sole authority in the relationship so he can function as its god.
>
> He believes he has the right to dominate you to achieve his purposes.
>
> He overrules you.
>
> He uses weasel words to play on your emotions.
>
> He expects you to agree with him and bullies you if you do not.
>
> If he persuades you to enter into an agreement with him claiming it's mutually beneficial, which it is not.
>
> There is a lot of smallness and sameness in daily life, except for the misery, which grows and twists.
>
> His entitlements expand and grow exponentially until your energy is sapped and you collapse.

An entitlement mindset expresses elements of lower behaviors that are repressed until the romance has got you in the trap. Once you've been seduced into the "deal" the encroachments and taking and usurpation begin. Entitlement can be implemented sexually, financially, emotionally, socially, physically and so forth. It can go on until you are drained of resources, life force and vital energy. The entitlement flag is not unlike cooking a frog. You put it in cold water so it doesn't protest and then you turn the heat on. You cook it slowly. By the time the frog realizes it's in trouble, it's too far gone to escape.

> *You are there to be consumed by him.*

| 43 |

Red Flag #32
IMMORALITY

Immorality is a deficiency of decency, which is defined as "a system of reliable conduct based on principles of uprightness." In a relationship, morality is expressed by baseline behaviors that are fair and honest, that bequeath a reasonable expectation of a person who is guided by their conscience to do the right thing. It is not unsafe to turn your back on them.

Brain-damaged psychopaths are not disposed to do the right thing (unless it serves them) and display a host of behaviors that exhibit immorality. It is not safe to turn your back on them. The absence of morality means that they remain unconcerned about the deficits they cannot detect. They are comfortable with and well served by their immorality. Their mindset is focused on their gratification. Period. The mindset of the non-psychopathic abuser fluctuates between getting away with abuse when he can and trying to do better the rest of the time.

Society is awash in messages that feed baser instincts from demanding authorities to violent media, which often lead people to a choice between the lesser of two evils. These add up to implied norms that condone laxity, selfishness and disrespect. These can lead to social chaos as those most vulnerable turn into parasitical and predatory creatures. Interpersonal abuse is at plague level now and it will continue to increase unless personal and social solutions are brought to bear.

Except for blatant opportunistic predation, an abusive individual may not display his immorality, except to perhaps drop hints about whatever he most wants from you. He is charming and appealing, which hides his dishonesty and perversity. He is adept at something, which hides his insanity. If he is in a position that requires persuasive selling, he is successful. He could sell an igloo to a desert rat, he could talk a hunter out of his gun and he could talk you out of whatever he wants.

He is convincing because he has been lying for so long he believes his own fictions. He has no awareness of the immorality of manipulating you and he is so good at it that you don't question him for a while. As he wins your trust and gains access to your inner life and your home, he plays you and sizes you up at the same time. It's a relationship to you, but it's just a game to him. He is there to take, you are there to give.

He rushes you to be sexually intimate by playing the sort of man you most want him to be.

He carefully inquires into your assets.

He finds out who your closest friends are.

He identifies your vulnerabilities, physical, mental, emotional, financial, spiritual, etc.

He takes careful note of your deepest emotional wound.

It is fun and exciting. There is "something" about him. He pushes you in some ways and you go along because you like it. When you give in to him, you tell yourself you're growing and pushing your limits. Sometimes when you are alone you feel an undercurrent of resentment, but the next time he walks in the room, it vanishes. His "something" keeps you engaged. You always want more of him than you get. He keeps you hungry and you wonder if it's on purpose to draw you out.

He is adventurous and daring; he can play conventional or unconventional convincingly. He lives by his own rules. He avoids the things that pain him and gives in every time to the things that tempt him. He courts the forbidden and lets it hold sway over him. When his mind says he must have it, he does. He is his sole authority.

If his primary temptation is sex, you may find yourself carrying one or more infectious diseases.

If his primary temptation is drugs, you may find your house vulnerable to a drug bust.

If his primary temptation is money, you may be cleaned out or expected to participate in a heist.

Then, there begin to be incidences. They will test your patience and your boundaries. They may seem spontaneous, but they have been time-tested on dozens of other willing women.

He forgets to put gas in your car after using it.

He doesn't give your kids their snack when they get home from school.

He leaves the gate open, your dog(s) get out of the yard and hit.

He doesn't return your _____ that he had to borrow.

He forgets to give you your mail and your phone messages.

He deposits your check into his account.

He books himself on a trip without telling or including you.

He apologizes or makes excuses. You either accept them and things go on or you don't and things change. Things change when you draw your line in the sand. Even if there's not a confrontation, he will feel it when his ways are beginning to grate.

> *Immorality is an easy way out because it requires no character.*

| 44 |

Red Flag #33
INJURY

In a contest between a male and female of same or similar age, there is little chance that she will be able to hold her own for even a few minutes, much less win the contest. The man who likes to hurt his woman knows this. There are men who batter their women, there are men who arrange accidents and there are men who inflict non-physical injuries. To paraphrase the 70s bestseller, THE WOMEN'S ROOM by Marilyn French, "You don't have to murder a woman, you can just let her work in your office for 300 dollars a week."

The injuries that abusive men cause to their women run the gamut and a third of the men that batter are white-collar. Injury can mean disablement, maiming and death. A third of women who are abused by their husband or boyfriend never recover and a number of them choose suicide to escape the pain. Extreme injuries can be sustained in any relationship. He may proclaim, "But, I never hit her..."

This is not the issue. The issue is his need to control her. This is what drives escalation over the cliff.

When you fall for a man, the last thing that crosses your mind is whether or not he would ever harm you or cause you to be harmed. Injury can take many forms— some seen, some unseen. An abusive man knows there are lots of ways to hurt a woman that are not physical, although they do a lot of damage. He knows he doesn't have to hit you or run over you or push you off a ledge to get you to do what he wants.

He can get you to quit your job or leave your business to impoverish you.

He can talk you out of buying or keeping a car to immobilize you.

He can get you to relocate with him to isolate you.

He can take away your animals to weaken you.

He can confuse and demean you to the point that you are second-guessing yourself and not thinking clearly.

He can tire you so much that you're having accidents around the house and getting hurt.

Then, he will deride you for being dumb and clumsy to drive home his general contention that you are unloved, unwelcome and unworthy. If he can lure you into bed, he will try to shame you. If he is a craven distempered type of psychopath, he injures you in bed.

He likes the rush of sex in strange places.

He likes the thrill of taking you against your will.

He flies into rages and vents himself sexually.

His physical demands leave you sore, torn, bleeding.

Many women who have been injured in various ways by their abusers report that physical injuries are easier to get over than non-physical injuries. A broken bone heals faster than a broken spirit. Nevertheless, at some point he may hurt you physically.

He rapes you.

He pushes you or rushes you so that you misstep and sprain your ankle.

He swings you into the sharp edge of a large piece of furniture.

He leaves something on the stair at night, like a tennis ball or a sharp rock.

He hits your fingers while you're holding a nail for him or slams a door on your fingers "accidentally on purpose."

He arranges something to break under or fall on top of you.

He makes a loud noise to startle you and the animal you are working with.

He banishes you to the basement in the middle of winter for days at a time and turns off the heat because you _____.

He locks you out of the house without anything but the clothes on your back because you _____.

Whether he does it in your face or behind your back, you feel damage just the same. You hide it if you can—for a while because whatever his method, your internal and external injuries are minor—at first. But, they become more serious because it takes more to satisfy him each time. Because he is devoid of conscience, then there is no limit to the lengths he might go to gratify himself by hurting you. You may not be able to predict his methods and his weapons for hurting you, but you can bet whatever they are, they will be employed with more cunning and force to do more damage next time.

Note: The time during which you are most vulnerable to attack (of any and all kinds) is when you are leaving a toxic relationship and can last for six to nine months following your exit. This is when the most vicious assaults occur. Even if he has never laid a hand on you before, he could then.

He feeds on your pain and suffering.

| 45 |

Red Flag #34
INSATIABILITY

The pathological is a woman-hating, woman-hurting junkie. He is as consumed with getting his fix as any drug addict; he may be an addict in addition to being an abuser and use this as an excuse for his behavior if he is challenged. (But remember, he does not abuse because he is drunk or high, he abuses because he is mentally ill.)

His fix comes from controlling and destroying his prey. He is self centered, but not self aware. There is no such thing as enough for him. His careful withholding of needful things from his partner is in total contrast to his fiendish pursuit of whatever he wants and needs. When he discovers what he likes and how he can get it, there is no stopping him. Whether it is money, sex, drugs, power, property or sensation, once is not enough. A thousand is not enough. A million is not enough.

When, in the course of his development as a toxic personality and the refinement of his "craft" he discovers what it is that makes his engine hum, his soullessness gets its first fix and his predation begins in earnest. His insatiability is fed by other personality dynamics, such as denial, delusions of grandeur, resistance to authority, irresponsibility and so forth.

His insatiability can be of such magnitude that he seeks prey outside of his relationship with you. If his fix is sexual sadism, for example, he may have become a sex addict or a serial rapist. He will hide this from you as long as he needs to. His exertions will intensify over time in his quest for more and more gratification until his predations become lethal to one of his partners. He may have been raping her for hours, but he was so obsessed with himself that he did not notice she was losing consciousness because she was hemorrhaging.

As you're getting involved, you suspect none of this because you do not know better than to take him at face value. Besides, you're falling in love or you're married to him when the first big cracks in the mask appear. You are turned on by his vigor. You think his lust for life carries implicit promises for you of good things to come. You think the adventure, money or whatever he seeks will be shared with you. You think you can learn from him. The way he carries himself does not betray the insatiability that you have not seen yet.

He gets advancement at a work and gets off on the sensation of power. He goes to work behind the scenes undermining the next person in his way on his climb up the ladder.

He goes online for women. He develops a sequence of luring messages, which he uses on every willing prospect in this unlimited pool of victims. As fast as he can, he sets up profiles at dozens of sites and has hundreds of women on the line at any given time.

In the beginning, you have no idea that this other side of him exists because you can't see the insatiability for what it is. His lies and manipulations are wrapped in romance or reason; this makes them more effective for him, but more compromising for you. Although you may do what he asks, it stings you.

Insatiability is a function of lack of conscience and soullessness. He directs a good portion of its energy into dispossessing you of what you have—this applies to tangibles and intangibles.

If you have close friends, he will not rest until he has relocated you or ruined those bonds.

If you have animals, he will go about taking them away from you.

If you have financial assets, he will use whatever influence he has with you to become involved and thereby begin to take control.

At the same time, his insatiability is at work getting, not just into your business, but into your mind. This is a big part of abuse: seizing control, separating you from your emotional and mental reserves and deriving pleasure from watching your suffering.

An abuser takes you apart bit by bit, day by day. The more proficient he is as a predator, the less you will realize that you are being continually assessed and weakened. He may want to see what you know, what you think, how you have accomplished things in your own life or he may simply go about deleting the parts of your personality that do not feed him and replacing them with something else. This sort of usurpation is one of the ultimate aims of non-physical abuse—it takes you away from you.

Remember, many predatory men go after high-functioning women precisely because they have the qualities required for him to run the con. The net effect of this is that your kindness, loyalty, etc., enables his insatiability, at least for a while.

He encourages you to get (more) fit by buying you clothes that are too small, withholding food, shaming you, hitting on athletic women, forcing you to exercise, etc.

He wants you to be a better wife and he is willing to assist you in this by giving you books to read, tapes to listen to. He points out women in movies or women on the street as examples of how he wants you to be. If you don't challenge this, it becomes the norm and as such, is an indicator of his inability to feel compassion, guilt or shame.

He wants you to be sexier. He asks for more initiative in the bedroom. He wants you to walk around the bedroom unclothed, then around the house, then outside.

He wants you to bathe with the bathroom door open. (He does not do any of these things, himself.)

No matter what you concede to—and there are many reasons to concede, mental exhaustion being one of them—there is always more that is required.

> *He has an endless store of things he wants from you, things he wants you to do for him, attributes he wants to implant in your mind—most of all, he wants to see the suffering and waste he has wrought so he can gloat in the shambles of your life.*

| 46 |

Red Flag #35
"NO"

Words are the most powerful thing in the universe. In the mouth of a toxic partner their power is awful. Some abusers use words with astonishing skill. Their actions, when the cognitive dissonance is great, show that words do not mean the same things to them as they do to normals.

In his landmark work, THE MASK OF SANITY, Hervey Cleckley, MD described a condition he called "semantic aphasia" as the inability to grasp the meaning of one's own words. He attributed this condition to primary psychopaths, who do not respond to disapproval and do not feel stress. Even though they are anti-social, they are cunning enough to control these impulses when it serves them. Lying, hypocrisy, double standards and manipulation are all in play when an abuser opens his mouth.

When you're getting to know him, you see him deftly decline to take "no" for an answer. The way he pulls it off seems to be his turning a negative into a positive and you are impressed. You see him ask for special consideration and somehow get it.

He gets a restaurant to let him in just before closing or after hours.

He gets a free upgrade for a car or plane seat.

He gets discount tickets not available to the public.

What you don't realize at first is that he charms and lies his way through life. What you also don't realize is that he does not like to take "no" for an answer. It costs him nothing to lean on service people to get more than he pays for, but if/when they say "no" to him, the stakes rise. He plays it like a game at first, but it gets ugly fast if it matters.

Over time, he begins to do this to you. The first time it happens, it may be over the pace of the relationship. He wants something that you don't want or are not ready for. He will charm, promise, lie, cajole, play, taunt to get you to compel. In the early part of the relationship, it will be fun and light. He will flatter and reassure. If you resist and stand your ground, the unspoken rules of the game will change. Once you have stepped into the trap so that he has you, he won't take "no" for an answer, and he might not be nice about it. This should tell you two things:

- He cares only about getting what he wants
- You do not matter

If the relationship progresses, you discover that in his mind, only he is entitled to say "no." This is a red flag and this is one you would be wise to test early on. As far as he's concerned, your job is to reply in the affirmative no matter what he asks of you. In his mind, you are not you; you are his possession, his prey object. This is part of why problems arise when you express your true self by something as simple as saying "no."

You are there to gratify and indulge him.

You are there to reflect what he wants to see.

You are there to support what he wants to experience: <u>himself in female form.</u>

You do not have the right to deny him anything.

You do not have permission to express yourself.

You do not have the right to complain about or criticize anything.

Whenever it serves him, he will give lip service to your wants and needs but in truth, they do not matter and are not considered. Words do not matter or have meaning beyond getting him what he wants. He does not admit it, but this is what you come to realize after you have spent hours explaining, pleading or reminding him of his words. It is all for naught. There is no level playing field and your eloquence is wasted on his emptied being.

The first few times you say "no", he acts accepting, perhaps with a little incredulity thrown in for good measure.

Later on, he'll respond to a "no" from you as an act of war.

He rejects it outright or he launches a counter-attack to demand you do whatever you've declined.

To assure the outcome he wants, he'll maneuver circumstances to force you if need be.

He does not hesitate to threaten you if you don't comply and will sabotage your work or kill your cat to make sure you get the message.

He does not deal well with any form of external authority, adversity or inconvenience.

He cannot tolerate challenge, complaint, critical comment or question from anyone although he dispenses them liberally.

At some point, he dispenses with asking you things at all, you are told what to do, and you do it or else. He does not care what you think or how you feel. He does not care that you've kept all your promises and he's broken all of his. In his mind, he is the sole conferrer of rights and the sole possessor of authority in the relationship. As such, he has the power to allow or disallow your right to say "no." He is unaware of the unfairness of the imbalance of power in the relationship because it serves him to have the upper hand—this is how he lives.

By this time, whatever you have with this man no longer resembles a marriage or a relationship. It is more like a train wreck in a prison yard.

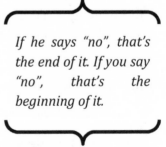

If he says "no", that's the end of it. If you say "no", that's the beginning of it.

| 47 |

Red Flag #36
OTHER WOMEN

The toxic individual at core is predatory; for many such men, other women are just prey items—outlets for gratification. There is no love or affection involved, just ego stroking and animalistic, impersonal sex. Other women supply him with content for threats (expressed or insinuated) to his wife or girlfriend. In all likelihood, he has at least one other woman on the hook at all times.

Continuous predation allows him to perfect his game. He feels entitled to and justified in his pursuit of other women, even if he is married. If he is young, he brags about it to his peers, if he is older, he has learned to hide it and lie about it.

Other women are his favorite compulsion. He could no more give it up than he could quit breathing. If he lives in a small town, he may be forced to look elsewhere for women. The easiest place to hunt for prey is the unlimited pool of willing women on the internet. He may be registered with one dating or sex service or with many. He may be a novice user or an accomplished online predator. Preying on women on the internet is easy because it gives him free rein while assuring his anonymity and providing abundant free feedback on his methodology. He may use the same profile, messages and methods with hundreds of women. People often behave while driving in ways they would not dare behave face-to-face. This same principle applies to conduct on the internet.

This type of man tends to be uncreative and methodical, so the internet dating world is pleasing because it allows him to systematize, which gives him a lot of leverage and practice. He perfects his offer continually; he has learned what to lead with and what kind of bait to use for the kind of woman he wants. He has developed the knack for finding and engaging nice, trusting women who fall under his spell. He is adept at dispelling the doubts that this kind of woman is sure to have if he does encounter her on the internet:

"Don't worry, I am not a player."

"I'm a one-woman man."

"Obviously, I am seriously looking for a long-term or permanent relationship."

Whether he hunts for women on the internet, in the paper, in bars or just in town, he uses the same general operating procedure, tailored for every woman he makes contact with. He plays varied roles with aplomb. If he hooks up with or marries one of these women, his predation is seldom interrupted for long. He is back online as soon as the honeymoon is over.

As he secures you, he continues to keep other prospects in the background so he can develop them and play with them on an as-needed basis. He may even taunt you with this information later to force your hand in some way. Like sex, his other women pursuits are important to him, but none of it is lasting, personal or sacred because he is empty inside. He has nothing to offer except the sex act, which is likely unremarkable. Other women are just a routine by which he gratifies his need to control and destroy. That's what he gets off on.

> *You can be sure everything he said to you, he has said and will say to countless other women.*

| 48 |

Red Flag #37
RIGHTS

In the beginning, he looks after your every need. He acts chivalrous, considerate, sensitive and correct. This doesn't last long. In an abusive relationship, one person has rights and the other person has none. These are some of the first to go once the gloves come off:

- Freedom to defend yourself
- Freedom from damage to and loss of your property
- Freedom to express yourself
- Freedom from arbitrary actions
- Freedom to exercise your own judgment

A healthy relationship allows and enriches each person's freedoms, often without the need for extensive discussion or negotiation. Each person retains their self determination, which they adjust *willingly* because they love their partner, not because they are coerced. This is what you expect and this may be how it starts. It all just works, but because toxic relationships are counterfeit, you discover that what it is now, is not what it appeared to be before. As he manipulates circumstances to acquire more control the balance of power shifts. You have some awareness of this, but you don't realize it's the prelude to abuse. You chalk it up to your inexperience, or lack of confidence, you tell yourself it's just the give-and-take of relationships. The things you notice seem too insignificant to bring up. You decide to rise above them, and you do, for a while.

The amount of space your things occupy in the house shrinks.

The amount of freedom you have to come and go is restricted.

The amount of respect shown for your feelings and needs is minimal, even grudging.

Your access to your children, animals or property may be made conditional upon your behavior so that it is diminished, threatened or eliminated.

If you are dependent on him or married to him, you will watch as your rights disappear. When he doesn't have to be bothered with considering you at all, everything is so much easier for him. If you still love him, you may be able to face the fact that your love has been lied to, your trust has been deceived, your vulnerability exploited and your force spent. It is the 21st century and your rights have been removed. As your life becomes less and less, it's harder and harder to believe you are worthy.

You are never given a car key, a house key or a check book.

You are told not to lock the bathroom door and he checks for compliance.

Your absences from him are timed and monitored.

You are quizzed about everything you do while not under his direct surveillance and supervision.

You are to start dinner after coming in work.

You are not to question why he sits around all day like his arms are broken and whines about being alone and having nothing to do.

While you were doing dishes, he was sitting back letting time work to his advantage. He is breaking you in and wearing you out. He's been down this road before. Once your resources were gone, he took you over like a warlord. He has usurped everything. You can't believe what he is doing to you as he is doing it to you.

You begin to believe you don't deserve any rights. Most days, you are too exhausted and numb to care about the losses you live with. You may accept the position he's put you in. Your head is filled with self-blame and self-doubt—that he put there and that you allowed. The removal of rights is just one way to rub salt in the universal wound of "I'm not good enough."

Rights are soon things you only remember.

| 49 |

Red Flag #38
ROAD RAGE

Rage is part of abuse and road rage, the equivalent of an adult temper tantrum, is one of its expressions. People sometimes do things behind the wheel they would never do face-to-face because the jurisdiction of the roadway offers its own kind of anonymity and leverage (like the internet).

In a relationship, road rage is inflicted to punish or terrorize the passenger. But, because it occurs behind the wheel, it can kill or injure other innocent people as well as do lots of property damage. (Drunk drivers can create like results with their brand of loss of control. Road rage is similar to abusers who intimidate his partner by killing or injuring one of her animals or destroying a valuable possession of hers.)

As discussed earlier, the most pathological abusers lack impulse control and are quick to "fly off the handle." When this happens, he declines to heed any requests from his partner to "back off" or "slow down" or in any way de-escalate the situation and things can get serious, fast. Driving may be the behavior that first reveals a hidden nature.

In a 2008 study, some doctors described road rage as *intermittent explosive disorder* (IED) and found that it affects 16 million Americans (more than the number who suffer from bipolar disorder or schizophrenia). When they considered the question: is road rage a mental illness, the consensus was in the affirmative. Dr Emil Coccaro, Chairman of Psychiatry at the University of Chicago Medical School explained, "People think it's bad behavior and that you just need an attitude adjustment, but what they don't know ... is there's a biology and cognitive science to this."

Road rage is a dangerous, immature, selfish and hostile set of learned behaviors. Abusers are often "mad men" behind the wheel.

He honks at, cuts in front of and tails cars that get in his way.

He makes obscene gestures and yells at other drivers.

He passes other vehicles when it is dangerous and illegal to do so.

He assumes he has the right of way in all circumstances and gets provoked when challenged.

He becomes enraged if he encounters other drivers who drive the way he does.

These behaviors can erupt for the slightest reason or for no reason at all. A man who exhibits road rage is showing you:

- His lack of concern for safety.
- His willingness to do harm.
- His need to get his way.
- His intolerance of others.
- The lengths to which he'll go to terrorize you.

If you have a history of car crashes or you are just a nervous passenger, you can be sure he'll make use of that fact for his own purposes every time you get in the car with him. Being trapped in a speeding car with an out-of-control driver is a form of torture. He knows this.

Note: According to the National Safety Council there were over 36 thousand traffic fatalities, over six million injuries and costs in excess of 200 billion dollars on American roads because of car crashes in 2012. How many of these are caused by deliberate acts of road rage where a psychopath is behind the wheel?

Road rage is just one barometer of the extent of his sickness.

| 50 |

Red Flag #39
RULES

An abuser's self-glorification is part of toxic relationships. He prides himself on his control of his partner, his antipathy, his manipulation of all things.

As time takes its toll on the victim, she becomes more subdued; this makes it easier for him to express his pathology in ways that would have been intolerable to her at the beginning of the relationship.

Rules have more impact on the victim in the early stages because the long-term effects of abuse have not yet blunted her spirit or poisoned her heart. When one partner dominates a relationship through rules, the other partner resists, withdraws and then goes numb.

When the dominated partner has succumbed, the abuser is able to revel in what he perceives to be his own glory. He has no one to think about but himself. He is not restrained by guilt, shame or morality. His self centeredness gives him the feeling of omnipotent control, which is confirmed daily by his partner's fearful obedience and exhausted compliance.

Like every other form of abuse, rules are not in evidence at first or are so slight as to be small details in daily life. They can be communicated or demonstrated, like kicking off your shoes before going in the house or being careful not to slam the car door. They are so minor, you don't notice them or give them a second thought. Your thoughts are about him and your relationship with him. Not walking on his floors in your shoes and not closing his car doors too forcefully do not register with you as rules or burdens.

Things proceed. You fall for all of it, you get married or move in together. You don't know it yet, but few if any of the promises he's made and the agreements you've entered into will bear fruit. He begins to find ways of separating you from what you care about and he shows you that rules are a handy method for doing this.

If you have a dog, he concocts an objection and makes a rule that the dog must stay outside whether it's 20 degrees below zero or 120 in the shade.

If you have a job, he decides that you must work less and makes a rule that if dinner isn't on the table by such-and-such a time, there will be trouble.

If you like to take walks, he will tell you when you can walk, where and for how long.

If you belong to a group, he announces he will attend a meeting and decide if you may continue in it.

As time goes by, the constriction is intentional and unmistakable.

A dangerous element of a ruled relationship is its implied misogyny and alienation from decency. The rules express his pettiness, vulgarity, egotism, greed and so on. Compared to the reasons you fell for this man, the reality you now face with him is void of the poetry of love. And even his rules about sex can't hide that.

Misogyny and violence are two strong indications that a relationship, and indeed a society, has "turned."

- What seemed personal is impersonal
- What seemed intimate is anti-social
- What seemed wonderful is horrible

The counterfeit has been revealed.

The normal behaviors of sharing food, making love, laughing and crying, talking for hours, running errands, cleaning the garage together, etc., become grotesque aberrations of the simple joys of sharing your life with someone you love, respect and trust.

It crosses your mind that this is worse than being a slave because you can't get away from him, you can't go home for the night. The unwritten rule that underscores all the others is that he suffers you to be there. The feeling that comes through—if you can face it—is that he hates you.

Daily life has been ground you into powder. Every rule was introduced, one subtle change after another over time—like a political takeover—requested with reason and a smile, urged with propaganda and delivered with a threat of annihilation.

Rules for every room in the house.

Rules for every meal.

Rules for morning and rules for evening.

Rules for crumbs and rules for water spots.

Rules for phone calls and computer use.

Rules for folding towels and rolling socks.

Rules for going out and coming in.

Rules for smiling and for crying.

Rules for dressing and undressing.

Rules for sleeping and for waking.

The rules are all his and they are to be followed. In his mind, they are for his care and maintenance. They are for the smooth operation of the relationship and the running of the household according to him. The fact that it is all one-sided escapes him.

Like rights, all benefits of the rules go to him.

Chances are, it may not be until someone else reacts to one of the rules you are observing that you see it. When you see it, you are thunder struck at the depth and breadth of the repression you've been living under. He has made the rules and he has reasons for each one of them.

They express some of the worst fundamentals emerging from a postmodern society—normal people held hostage by the callous dramas of the morally insane.

Rules are the necessaries of a small mind and a mean spirit.

Part Seven:
Choices at the Threshold

"Nothing splendid has ever been achieved except by those who dared believe that something inside them was superior to circumstance."

Bruce Barton

Roger & Sunny

It was another weekend. Slumped against the wall where he'd thrown her, her thoughts drifted. She lay on her side, her back to him, one arm over her head and said nothing while Roger vented himself. He walked over to her and she wondered if he was going to haul her up to continue or kick her; he did neither. She had learned to be still and act dazed or unconscious when he got violent. Eventually, he would lose interest, stomp out of the room and, storm around the house for a while. As she waited him out, she noticed faint smudges of blood and makeup on the wall, and a lone, long hair caught in a nick in the baseboard from earlier incidents. *How many times have I been flung across this room?*

She waited for Roger's next move so she could make hers—she knew he was still full of wrath, which he couldn't vent on her because she was out of it. He would clomp around for a while and then leave the house. He would be gone for anywhere from an hour to the rest of the day. This day would be different, however. This day, when he came home as if nothing had happened, she would be gone. *Gone.*

She had thought about leaving for a long time, but not done anything towards it because the whole thing was so surreal. During the first few years, she did not know why the marriage no longer felt good and why her husband was so difficult. Once married, Roger had changed from a friendly man to a hostile one. Something in her kept her from pressing him, instead she took it on herself to be a better wife and love him through it. She read self-help books and applied their best advice. She learned a language, she gardened, she lost weight, she changed her hair, she took up sports, she worked on herself and waited for the dark cloud to pass—all in vain—nothing she did mitigated any of his problems. After years of verbal and emotional abuse, Roger finally got physical. He'd meant it just as a push, but his rage came through and when his hand hit Sunny's back, she flew forward. She stumbled and feel all the way to the floor, hitting her face on the kitchen counter. She hit so hard it split her lip and chipped a tooth.

Her face was bruised for two weeks. He never forgot the expression on her face when she sat up and looked at him. It surged through him like liquid steel.

In hindsight, this should have been her defining moment. She wanted it to be, but it wasn't. His blow ups continued, but after the time in the kitchen, she knew they could get physical. And he knew she knew. Again and again, she wavered on the precipice of his lies and her hopes until she lost her nerve. It took months for the memory of who he used to be, the only man she had ever loved, to begin to dissolve. He was someone else now, but she didn't know who, or what. After considering Roger, she realized she, too had changed. She began to see how she had become the things he called her.

After his physical rages, Roger would apologize, act mollified and then slowly reel her back in over the following days and weeks with promises of "never again." For reasons she could not fathom, she stayed. Between the words and the shoves, the abuse had ground her to powder and she came to accept her fate: she was a defective person and a poor wife, and she should feel fortunate that Roger allowed her under his roof. She decided their unhappiness was due to intractable personality problems—hers. She decided to stay with him because that would be easier than starting over on her own and besides, who would ever want her?

The library was one of the few places Roger let her go by herself—and it was there that Sunny's mind caught fire. By chance she overheard a long conversation between two women she did not know who were talking about their marriages. From this, she deduced that Roger wasn't moody, he was abusive.

Curious and motivated, she began her own investigations. She learned the difference between difficult and dangerous relationships. She learned what she had tolerated would continue to increase—which told her what she could expect in the coming years. Every revelation came with case stories and statistics that made the hair on the back of her neck stand up. A silent shift began to deep inside her. What had gone silent in her mind began to whisper and come back to life. It happened ever so slowly, it gave new context to her daily life, it altered her perception of Roger, it gave her strength from who she was before and she marveled at it. Sunny decided she wanted to live. For years, she had accepted whatever she got. *It could be worse. I can deal with it. It'll get better.*

She changed her mind and had her epiphany, but without letting on. She decided she was not going to take it anymore. The new knowledge shocked her and shook her out of her complacency as it showed her what Roger's behavior meant. Her eyes were opened. Her clandestine and voracious reading delivered dozens of "ah-ha" moments to her like they were shaking her awake. Sometimes she had to clap her hand over her mouth to keep from squealing. *It will get worse. I am not going to stick around and deal with it. The only way I'm going to live is if I leave.*

So, she lay there on the floor until she heard Roger drive off. *This is my momentous day.*

Following instructions she'd gotten earlier from secret visits to the women's shelter, Sunny had worked methodically for weeks to put everything into readiness for this moment. Personal possessions had been transported, documents copied and taken out of the house for safekeeping. Sure that Roger was gone, she rose, packed her overnight bag and dialed her best friend's cell. Her hands shook with determination, fear and excitement. She put her bag on the slate floor and paced up and down the front hall while waiting for Jeanie's car. She wondered if it could really be this easy. *I'm walking out of here and never coming back. Ever.*

She heard a car approach and looked out the little window in the front door. It was not Jeanie, but Roger heading back toward the house in his blue Saab. *No!*

He swung into the driveway and coasted toward the garage. She hadn't planned on this. *What now?* Shaking all over and knees knocking in fear, she slung her bag over her shoulder and bolted down to the basement. Her legs felt like lead, but she kept going. She slipped out of the back door and sprinted across the backyard into the trees. She heard the garage door bang shut about the time she got to their property line. She kept going until she had made a big loop through adjacent properties and emerged from the woods between two houses a half block away. Out of breath, shaking and sweating, she stood next to a big tree and prayed for Jeanie's white Lexus to appear. Minutes later it did. She flagged it down and sank into the passenger seat as Jeanie made a tight U-turn and sped away.

As planned well in advance, they drove to a small motel on the outskirts of town and parked in the back. They sat on a small balcony overlooking a creek and let things sink in. Sunny felt elated and exhausted. Jeanie felt hopeful for her friend, but also scared. She knew the plan and the chances. They were following a good plan and drew comfort from knowing that it had worked for countless other women across the country. The police had been advised of Sunny's escape so that no resources would be spent on Roger's missing person report. Jeanie's husband was also on board. He was stationed at their house and prepared for a call or visit from Roger. Since Jeanie was Sunny's closest friend and the only one with whom she'd been able to maintain contact, it would be a matter of time until Roger tried to corner Jeanie. The two women holed up at the motel for 36 hours until it was confirmed that Roger had gone to work Monday morning and it was deemed safe for Sunny to be transported to another location for the next leg of her journey.

Even though she'd been told what to expect, Sunny was still amazed by the predictability of Roger's response. Following her escape, she'd gotten a new cell phone, a loaner car (with tinted windows) and a spare bedroom in a succession of safe houses so that Roger couldn't locate her or cyber stalk her. She thought of it as the underground railway for women fleeing abuse. The plan was for her to lay low until the divorce was final and then move out of the area. If she moved before the divorce was final, Roger could find out her new location through the discovery part of the proceedings. All communications would go through her attorney. *I will never have to hear his voice again.*

Roger's calls started the next morning. Jeanie reported to Sunny that it sounded like he had been up half the night rehearsing his speech and planning his calls. He called everyone he could think of to ask if they'd seen "his dear wife." As coached by the shelter staff, several of them had suggested he call the police. Sunny would have her attorney contact Roger in a few days to initiate the divorce, which she counted on his not contesting since she was walking away with nothing except the cash she had when they got married. If Roger had been neglectful instead of abusive, she'd have left him the way Meryl Streep left Dustin Hoffman in "Kramer vs Kramer" which she'd long regarded as a poignant and elegant exit. Watching it as a child, she had no idea it would ever figure in any way in her own life.

What she didn't count on was Roger contacting her clients. Her heart melted like wax as she imagined the damage he could do if he decided to try to destroy her part-time income. She had alerted her clients to her new phone number but not the reason for it. After agonizing over a possible security breach, Sunny called each of her clients to tell them why she had a new number. To her great relief, she did not lose any business over it and in fact, received much encouragement and support.

Over the ensuing weeks, Roger went on the warpath. His calls to her clients and friends became so frequent and frenzied that he found himself being threatened with charges of harassment. Sunny's attorney was fielding calls from him on an hourly basis. She later learned this was a common tactic to drive up the wife's legal costs.

Despite much howling by Roger, the judge found Roger in contempt and granted Sunny her divorce in less than a year. He also awarded her half of their savings and stock portfolio, which she desperately needed. If she had not had the shelter's expert guidance and an abuse-savvy attorney, it could have had a different ending. She packed her few belongings in an older SUV bought in her new business name and headed west. She moved 900 miles away and rented a small house on a large lot in a university town where she could live quietly and do some teaching. Money was tight, but the joy of personal freedom was delicious. The enormity of her years of false imprisonment revealed itself as each day came and went without having to walk on eggshells or keep an eye on the clock or account for her activities. Gone were the insults, interruption and intimidation. The first time she took a bath without Roger coming to the door several times to hurry her or waiting for her in the hall was revelatory.

She took the shelter's cautions to heart, and retrofitted her car, house and office for personal safety *just in case*. She checked the car for an external GPS device, stayed off social media, changed all of her online settings and used her new business name as a proxy for all transactions. This gave her complete privacy by removing any trail with her name attached to it. She did not change her name or social security number and sometimes wondered if she'd live to regret it. She was betting that Roger would get bored and go off in search of easier prey.

Month after month, all was quiet while Sunny waited for the other shoe to drop. She went through the release of the hyper-vigilance that had built up in her during the marriage. From time to time, she startled herself out of a sound sleep, flinched if someone touched her and laughed too quickly. Some days she had no appetite, others she was ravenous.

Once she caught herself becoming belligerent behind the wheel, exited the highway, pulled into a parking lot and sat and stared off into space. For a good long while, she second-guessed herself and struggled to appear certain and confident when she felt neither. She didn't know what normal was. She didn't know who she was anymore. All she knew was that stumbling through the aftermath by herself was better than living day-in, day-out in Roger's prison.

The only time he came to mind was when she caught herself acting on thoughts she realized he had planted in her head long ago. "If you knew how to be a wife, I wouldn't have to be like this" and "I guess no one has ever cared enough to tell you these things about yourself" and "You can't do anything right" and "You will stay right here, I didn't get married to be alone" and "You have absolutely no personality" and "You are a complete waste of protoplasm."

She was careful to look at each ugly thing that came to the surface, grab it and rip it out by the roots.

Sometimes she talked to herself to shore up her spirit when she felt ragged, "You can do it" and "It's okay" and "You have survived this for a reason" and "Someday, you will look back on this and laugh."

She taught part time and mostly enjoyed it. The students were self absorbed and disaffected, but the teaching staff was considerate. She went out to dinner with a few of the other single women, and began to feel willing to make new friends. She felt comfortable and relaxed until one of the male teachers asked her out. Inside, she recoiled, but recovered quickly enough to decline gracefully. She tried not to let it show, but she felt uncomfortable around him for the rest of the year. *Too soon, too soon.*

After that, Sunny did something she'd longed to do since marrying Roger—she decided to get a dog. She went to the animal shelter, checked Craigslist and put the word out. She met several dogs, but didn't feel moved to adopt any of them. Then a student stopped by her desk after class to say his neighbor was going overseas and had to find a good home for his retired K9. If he couldn't find something suitable soon, he would have to euthanize him.

Sunny met them that weekend at the dog park. Michael and Gustav were both tall and reserved. Gustav was a seven year old Malinois that stood 27 inches at the shoulder. He had worked with Michael until a year before when he'd torn a tendon that didn't heal well enough. Rather than risk a repeat injury Michael let his partner transition to civilian life as a companion dog, which suited both of them. Michael had been in law enforcement for a decade and was going overseas for two years. He was relaxed but matter-of-fact about Gustav's destiny. The whole time they talked, Gustav sat quietly at his side.

Michael put Gustav through his paces to show Sunny what she might be getting into. His abilities were astonishing. They walked for a half hour talking the whole time about Gustav. Midway through their walk out, Michael put Gustav between them and at the same point on their walk in, he put Gustav on Sunny's far side. And in this way, the matter was decided consensually. When they returned to the parking lot, Michael knelt, said a few words to Gustav, shook Sunny's hand and walked to his car without looking back. She stood speechless, looking back and forth between man and dog. He sent Gustav's papers, but no instructions on where to send the agreed-upon price. His loss was her gain in every way.

Gustav was remote, but obedient. She knew working dogs changed hands in early life to keep them from forming attachments that would hinder their careers. She saw in Gustav the result, which she took to be both impressive and sad. He was a trooper and so was she. In the second month, his depression lifted and his countenance brightened.

She marveled at the difference the dog made in her daily life. They took their time getting used to each other as nothing but time would create the room for the bond she wanted. Day by day, room by room, his sane, solid presence filled the house; it helped her relax and gave her hope for the future. They became regulars at the city parks and on the county trails. They walked and walked and walked. As promised, she "worked" him every day—a few minutes of hand signals and voice commands and a few runs through the obstacle courses at the dog parks. He took his work seriously Sunny felt blessed and inadequate as she watched him. His precision, strength and tenacity often got other people's attention, too. Working was in his blood, doing his work at the dog parks was one of his purposes, protecting Sunny was his other.

With every outing she felt clearer about herself and closer to her four-legged guardian. When she watched him, the word that always came to her mind was "noble." He was nobility in the form of a dog. He didn't know he was noble, but she did. It was not lost on her that she had not been around anyone who possessed a noble character in many years. As she began to feel safe, she also began to feel more of her feelings. It wasn't anything she tried to do, it just happened that way. She found she could feel frustrated, happy, rushed or irritated but still feel peace. It was like moving down a long, long path toward a big, glowing door.

It was almost two years before she finally arrived at the door, and then she wondered what to do. She felt no need to rush, she was content to wait for a signal, so she did. She continued to marvel at her new-found peace, which she likened to being sprinkled with fairy dust in her phone calls with Jeanie. Not too long after their last conversation, without fanfare or warning, the big door opened.

One evening while tossing a salad and listening to a book on tape, tires screeched out in the street, an engine gunned and tires peeled out. She snapped her head to look at the other end of the long galley kitchen; Gustav was not lounging on his day bed. Heart pounding, she threw down the utensils and exploded out the front door. As she sprinted across the lawn, she heard herself half-whimpering, "Dear God, please."

His fawn and black form lay motionless in the grass on the side of the road where he had been thrown by the impact. A neighbor had come out of his house across the street and was also running toward the dog. Gustav was bloodied up but alive. With the neighbor's help, she got his 123-pound bulk into her car and sped to the animal emergency clinic while Gustav panted and whiffled in the back seat.

His "mass and size saved him" from more serious injury opined the vet after he had examined the dog gently, but thoroughly. He injected a sedative, cleaned his wounds, wrapped his lacerations and sent him home with pain meds. Time would tell how well he would recover.

That night, she sat by his bed in her room and stroked his domed forehead as he slipped into a drugged sleep. Her eyes swept across the face and form she knew so well, emotion squeezing her heart and tears coming up for the first time in a long time. *My sweet boy.*

She sat there beaming at the miracle of his spared life, the dearness of his dogness and crying at the same time. She fixed her mind on the mission. He was going to be okay. She was going to be okay. Whatever came, they were going to be okay. Strength poured into her and peace suffused the room as she glided through the big door.

She ministered to him day and night. Giving him his meds, helping him up and down, taking him on drives in the car (television for dogs, she thought) and talking to him. He accepted the gift and returned it by healing perfectly and completely. He healed on the outside. She healed on the inside.

By the time he was up and around again, he was her dog and she was his person. Even though he was a dog, the bond she felt comforted and reassured her. He had become so dear to her that the thought of losing him sunk into her like a mining shaft in a mountainside. At some point, she noticed this and acknowledged it as a sign of healing and wholeness. She thought of it as seeing color again after living in a land of fog.

When the vet confirmed that Gustav was ready to get more exercise, they resumed their walks in short increments. She was happy to see his strength returning and his reunion with his dog buddies on the various trails. His favorite dog park was one with a small river flowing through it. They always walked on the north side because that's where his buddies were. He had buddies of all shapes and sizes, but his best buddy seemed to be a gray malemute, who taught him to dig, which he began to do with great joy in the backyard. Rather than fight it, Sunny brought in sand and dedicated a big area to accommodate

Gustav's need to dig; she even hid bones for him in his sand pile. It was a fine treaty.

She wore his leash across her shoulders as a formality. He never let her out of his sight and behaved as though there was an invisible tether between them. On her occasional blue days, she felt unworthy of benefitting from someone else's work, of owning such a fine dog.

One day, they did a short, flat walk then sat on a bench to watch a couple of spring-loaded border collies catch frisbees as fast as their people could throw them. A small crowd of people gathered on both sides of the field to watch the performance.

As was his custom, Gustav positioned himself at Sunny's feet. After she sat down, he stretched out like a sphinx, his powerful haunches tucked in. As was her custom, she put her feet on either side of his barrel and tucked them into the triangular space between his ribs and elbows—contact without restriction.

She didn't notice the tall man and dog approach from her right. He leaned against the stone wall behind the bench where she sat. Gustav noticed them. He followed them with his eyes, perked his ears and worked his nose. She turned to look only when Gustav sat up. Sunny reached forward and put a hand on his shoulder, her cue to him to stay with her. She did not recognize the man or his white shepherd from the dog parks. Gustav rose to his feet and her hand fell away. It was her turn now to follow him with her eyes. He stretched and walked over to the shepherd, who sat quietly. He paused a yard in front of her and then looked up at the man, whose countenance warmed as he gazed at the dog. The shepherd leaned out to touch Gustav's nose and then did a little play bow. Sunny was riveted until the man spoke, "She isn't usually this keen to play with a stranger."

"Neither is he—I don't know what…"

"Dogs—sometimes they just know."

"Hmmm."

Sunny pushed her sunglasses up and looked to see her dog sitting before the white shepherd, his tail waving back and forth across the grass. The man reached down to rub Gustav's head and spoke in a low tone to him.

"Where did this come from? He has never acted this way with a new dog. Ever."

The man laughed, took off his cap and sunglasses, kneeled down and held out his arms. Both dogs stood on their haunches and got folded into a bear hug.

"Perhaps we should let them get to know each other."

Slack-jawed, Sunny beheld the mass of dog and man, then she looked at his crew cut and tan face with recognition slowly dawning. She felt peace all around her and took a step toward them, "I suppose that would only be fair."

| 51 |

To Exist or To Live

There is more going on in any relationship than meets the eye and this goes double for those engineered by psychopaths. If toxic individuals were easy to identify, relationship violence would cease to exist. But they are not easy to identify, so the carnage continues. The fact remains however, that interpersonal abuse of all sorts becomes identifiable and thus preventable once you learn the terrain.

What happens when a woman gets involved with a man who becomes abusive? She gets abused in more than one way and the experience affects her in more than one way. The psycho-dynamics in such a bond exert multiple negative influences over her, all of which work together to take her apart. A cruel irony is that as she becomes more beaten her down, she bonds more deeply with her abuser. She learns how to placate him. She seeks his approval and actually cooperates with his architecture of control—out of desperation and fear. This doesn't happen in every relationship, but in those where circumstances are extreme, it is not uncommon.

Even though a woman consciously recoils from mistreatment, her subconscious programming keeps pulling her into it. As things progress, she begins to dismiss or diminish the damage she is sustaining and puts her own safety and welfare on the back burner. From the point at which she becomes hooked or trapped in the relationship, she is in an intense, subconscious tug of war with herself and her abuser. She is also struggling with external circumstances that add to this burden. This *trifecta* exacerbates other destructions inherent in the experience of abuse such as sapping her will to escape and in some cases, her will to live. *What would it take to destroy your will to live?*

The intensity of abuse derives from influences on both sides of the human equation of an abusive relationship. His compulsion to entrap and abuse is enabled by her willingness to attach and tolerate. In virtually every article and book about abuse, survivors report that the attachment and intensity they felt in the beginning was unlike anything they had ever experienced before. "I thought he was my soul mate...It felt like the most important experience of my life...In the beginning, he seemed like the love of my life...It was the most intense love I'd ever felt...I didn't know it could be like that...It was like we were one person in two bodies."

How does an abuser do this? He "reads" the woman and then he "mirrors" her wants and needs back to her, which gives her the impression that he "really gets her," which she takes to mean he wants to give her the desires of her heart. His cunning is holding up the mirror to make it *irresistible*. She doesn't realize she's being set up. Some women say they feel like they have been drugged or put into a trance. The trance reaction galvanizes the abuser who gets caught up in the excitement and gratified by his apparent mastery of the game. In the heat of the moment, they each confuse these complex influences for love. He doesn't recognize it as his sick need for sensation; she doesn't recognize it as her lack of healthy boundaries. At whatever point the wheels come off, all that intensity compounds her inner work of getting perspective, facing reality and mustering her forces to get out.

In WOMEN WHO LOVE PSYCHOPATHS, Sandra Brown, MA described how women who report feeling like they'd been put into mild hypnotic states also said that this state worsened the toll the relationship took on them.

Every woman who's abused gets worn down in lots of ways: she gets worn down by not getting enough sleep, not taking good care of herself and expending enormous amounts of energy (sexually, financially, emotionally, etc.) to placate her toxic partner. Abusive relationships by definition are counterfeit, so the bond the woman imagines is not real; it is a transitory illusion emanating from the suggestive state she's in.

Sex plays a key role in pulling her deeper into the vortex of a psychopathic bond. Therapist Sandra Brown describes how sex causes myriad reactions in the body, including the release of higher levels of *oxytocin* by the brain. Oxytocin acts as yet another emotional intensifier because it is released after sex (and also after childbirth). It's known as the "bonding hormone" and the "love hormone." (Some say it's why mothers don't kill their children.)

Scientists have found that *high levels of oxytocin* are also associated with a *high willingness to trust.*

> Oxytocin evokes feelings of contentment, reductions in anxiety and feelings of calmness and security around the mate. This suggests oxytocin may be important for the inhibition of the brain regions associated with behavioral control, fear and anxiety... Oxytocin also functions to protect against stress. Meta-analyses conducted in 2003 demonstrated that oxytocin can alleviate mood and reduce stress with a good efficiency.
>
> Wikipedia

The results of sustained high doses of oxytocin have been described by many survivors as the hardest part of getting away and the biggest internal hurdle they faced. Aside from all of the practical considerations of exiting a relationship, it takes time to process the act because of the intense attachment oxytocin facilitates. It's not just in your mind, it's in your bloodstream. It's not just emotional, it's chemical.

Relationship Illiteracy

The average person knows little or nothing about the powerful dynamics at work in an abusive relationship and what it takes to exit and recover from one. The reality of being trapped or held against your will is unimaginable to them, yet it is standard operating procedure in the world of abuse.

Here's a telling statistic: the average number of escape attempts is *seven*. Think about that for a moment-- seven attempts to get away once and for all. What makes escape so problematic? For starters, the abuser does not want his woman to get away, so her plans must be hidden. The difficulties of escape run the gamut—emotional, financial, legal, physical, spiritual and social. Escape is the most arduous and dangerous effort an abused woman must mount to win her freedom. It is also undertaken when she is depleted and exhausted.

Escape from abuse is an act of uncommon courage undertaken against all odds and at great personal risk. Only when you understand this does the enormity of the choice reveal itself—to stay or to go. A woman has to know her limitations, and these are good indicators of the price she will pay for the choice she makes: *to exist or to live.*

The most pressing needs for a woman getting ready to run is having a safe place to go and the resources to get there. Lack of funds is the number one reason an abused woman stays in a dangerous relationship. For some, it is a fatal delay.

Ask Yourself

Deliberations about staying or leaving are serious business. It is critical that each woman come to her own moment of awakening and draw her own line in the sand. If she is coerced by outside forces (family or friends) before she is ready, her chances of success go down. She can become informed about relationship violence from any number of sources, but she must do her own thinking. (The exception to this is a woman who has been rendered mentally incompetent by abuse, in which case, a trusted family member acting with an appropriate professional may need to step in. Consult your local women's shelter if this applies to you or someone you love.) In other cases though, assessing a relationship is not the time sugar-coat reality.

- If your partner's treatment does not change, can you tolerate it for the long term? *no*
- If it gets worse, can you tolerate it? *no*
- Do you understand the critical distinctions between emotional problems and brain damage? *yes*
- If your partner is unable to get better, do you want to continue to invest yourself in the relationship? *no*
- If your partner says one thing, but does another, do you understand what that means? *yes.*
- Is your present relationship worth the missed opportunities it has already cost you and will cost you in the future? *no*
- What effect has the relationship had on your health? Other important relationships? Your finances? Your personal standards? Your job or career? Your spiritual life? Your other interests? Your relationship with yourself?
- Has your partner harmed your <u>children</u> or animals? *yes*
- Has your partner damaged or stolen any of your assets? *yes.*
- Do you know the two provisions God makes for leaving a bad marriage?

Staying—The Choice to Exist

For some women, the effort is too great and the price of freedom is too high, so they stay. They may have a comfortable lifestyle and choose material security over the possibilities of life without abuse. Perhaps they believe that they are too broken or do not possess the skills they would need to make a fresh start.

This is the choice that *victims* make because abuse is all they know. They grew up with it, they married it, they raised their children in it and they stay in it. They blame their abuser. They miss the opportunity to see how they plug into it, they don't generate enough desire to break free, so they never learn how to get out of the cycle of abusive relationships. This is why I call abuse a *generationally transmitted disease.* Parents give it to their children: an alcoholic raises a spousal batterer who raises a pedophile who raises a hopeless addict who raises a serial murderer and so forth. Each generation of abuse creates another until something breaks the chain.

Leaving—The Choice to Live

For some women abuse is doubly unendurable because they know what love is. Women who were not raised in abuse and do not have a history of toxic relationships will go to extraordinary lengths to win their freedom. While they got taken down just like victims, they have something inside that seeks release.

This is the choice that *targets* make because chances are they had vibrant lives before they stepped into a predator's trap. The pain of abuse and their history of healthy relationships are powerful motivators to get away no matter what. They are not just interested in temporary relief and sympathy. They are determined to escape, put their lives back together and take steps to prevent a recurrence. They do not make the mistake of blaming the abuser, they understand that something in them made them prey, and they are willing to do the work, whatever it is, to address that.

| 52 |

Absolute Exit

It is far easier to avoid an abusive relationship than it is to escape one. When a woman decides to leave, she embarks on the most dangerous rite of passage of her life. A predatory partner does not want his prey to get away. This is evidenced by the high number of attacks that occur during this period. Seventy-five percent of women who die at the hands of their abuser are killed *after* their escape. Even men who have not resorted to physical violence do so when their woman leaves.

Like many women, I left and then had to go back due to engineered circumstances—financial brokenness. Even though I did not want to go back to his home, it was the only option I had at the time. As it turned out, that gave me the chance to observe and test all that I was learning about the dynamics of abuse. Armed with information, resolve and therapeutic support, I went back to his house to put our marriage under the microscope while I worked out the details of my final escape.

What my marriage turned into when the gloves came off was not how it began—not at all. When it began to get difficult, weird and toxic, I hung in there because I did not recognize the danger, did not know what it all meant and was losing perspective. This is how the toll of abuse can affect thinking.

I kept taking the blame because I kept hoping there was some way to recover the "love" I thought we had. Now, I know this is the vicious cycle of denial and ignorance. This is how it goes for many women: they can't find a logical basis for their partner's behavior, they try to deny it and then they begin to sink in the quicksand. The simple fact is that logic does not get you anywhere when you are dealing with a pathological person.

Eight weeks was not enough time for me to get on my feet and I was forced to back to my husband's house. The night before I had to leave the shelter brought an unexpected and galvanizing revelation. My social worker did some checking in the files and learned that I was the second or third woman who had sought shelter there after a relationship with my husband. When I had to go back to his house, I did so with more than information, I did so with validation, understanding and determination to get away from him for good—all of which I drew on as I studied him and prepared for my final exit.

Being around him was both an emotional labor and an anthropological feast. Every day was swollen with events that confirmed and expanded upon the information I was immersed in. Much of this, though unpleasant, was life-affirming because as I saw his pathology, I began to find some peace, and even hope for myself. I saw and understood that his behavior was about him—not me. He was abusive because he was sick, not because there was

347

something wrong with me. For so many months I had taken his furious judgments and seething insults to heart. I remember coming to feel truly stupid and wondering how I had lived for so long without realizing it. Bit by bit, I began to get over that. Getting over it begins with recognizing the disease that underlies abuse and then dealing with the fact that "something" in you let you get sucked into it.

Getting Clear

There are lots of contingencies with serious consequences to deal with in making a successful exit. It's not unlike planning an intervention or preparing to take drugs away from an addict. Anything can happen—including the unthinkable. During the planning phase, it's a good idea to have trustworthy people aware of your situation and ready to help. If you have the opportunity to communicate with police or the county sheriff, that can afford you another layer of protection. Of course, if your abuser is a member of law enforcement or county judiciary, then this would not be a safe option. Relationship violence occurs twice as often in law enforcement and military families as it does in civilian families.

The more you can do to accomplish a complete exit the first time, the better off you'll be; *absolute exit*, a clean break, is safest. Working with your local women's shelter will increase your chances of success. They are seasoned experts in helping women understand and get out of dangerous relationships.

About Protection Orders

Many agencies that deal with domestic abuse recommend protection or restraining orders. This seems to be the usual practice when there is a history of verbal threat or physical violence. At first glance, this might seem like a good idea, but let's take a closer look to see if this practice makes sense with what has been learned over the last few decades.

The first thing to consider is that an abuser lives in a world of blame, denial, justification, minimization and refusal to be accountable. He believes he is above the law. His drive for gratification is so great he will do almost anything to quench it. Does this suggest that he will respect a court order? Here is an opinion from an internationally known threat assessment expert:

> "Since 75 percent of spousal murders happen after the woman leaves, it is estrangement not argument, that begets the worst violence...

> "So how does the system usually respond to society's most predictable murder risk? ... a temporary restraining order, because it is expected to restrain the aggressor... a protection order, expected to protect the victim. In fact ... it doesn't achieve either goal...

> "We should stop telling people that a piece of paper will automatically protect them, because ... it may do the opposite. It is dangerous to promote a specific treatment without first diagnosing the problem in the individual case...

spousal stalkers, the very type most likely to kill."

Gavin de Becker, THE GIFT OF FEAR

No Contact

If you're serious about getting out of an abusive relationship, you must understand and implement No Contact. It's something you do for yourself and it can be a matter of life and death. It's also easier said than done because of the normal emotional upheaval of exiting a relationship, even a toxic one.

Self Assessment

- Does your resolve to leave the marriage keep getting sandbagged by wishful thinking?
- Are you still making excuses for your husband's abuse?
- Do you think if you stick it out your husband will change?
- Have there been previous separations?
- If so, did your husband pursue/stalk you?
- Does your husband act better after blow-ups or discussions of separation?
- Do you keep hoping somehow things will be different?
- Are you getting mixed signals from him?

No Contact takes some fortitude because even in the worst marriages, it isn't all bad. There are non-abusive aspects, even pleasant aspects. But when abuse is present, the marriage is hopelessly toxic.

If abuse is emotionally-based, there is hope IF the abusive partner wants help to heal whatever it is that makes him abuse. If the abuse is physiologically based, there is no hope. In fact, the abuse will get worse with age because that is the nature of brain damage.

Implementation

- If you're leaving, collect your possessions and paperwork and exit.
- If he's leaving, separate your personal property from his to expedite his exit.
- Have a police stand-by (police in parked car at the curb) to deter violence.
- Advise your partner that you will be incommunicado for a while.
- Store or dispose of all memorabilia connected to him (gifts, pictures, etc.).
- Cleanse your space in whatever ways are meaningful for you (prayer, candles, sage, lemon, etc.).
- If you are married or in business with him, initiate the appropriate proceedings to sever all ties and let the attorney/paralegal/secretary handle all direct communications.
- Do not communicate with your partner in any way.
- Do not accept gifts, calls or visits from him.
- Change your accounts (phone, mobile, email, etc.), use strong passwords, which you change monthly to thwart cyber-stalking.
- Block his access to your social media accounts by doing whatever it takes to make you invisible to him from manual blocks to going offline to using a new handle.
- Do not go to the door, do not listen to his voice mail, do not read his emails or texts.

- Check around your car for a GPS device to make sure he is not tracking you.

- If you see him in public, do not make eye contact and exit the area without showing emotion.

- Alter your social and community activities for a while to avoid contact with him or friends of his.

- Tell mutual friends you don't want to hear about him and vice versa.

- If there are child custody issues, use a mediator whenever possible.

- If child custody issues necessitate contact with your former partner, observe these two guidelines:
  o always be on alert
  o always have at least one other adult with you (as protection and witness)

Tricks of the Trade

Understand that months, even years can go by, and then he will reappear. This is not because he cares about you or realizes the error of his ways (although he may say exactly that), it's because he wants to see if he can engage you again. For you, his reappearance may pluck the same heartstrings as before or he may pluck new ones. Be aware that any communication with an abuser will cost you. For him, he's just looking for his blood feast or narcissistic supply. When you refuse to provide that, he'll go elsewhere—that's what he is, nothing more, nothing less.

- If he contacts you by phone, hang up as soon as you realize it's him and change your number or block his.

- If he sends email or letters, do not read them.

- If he shows up as your door or workplace, be prepared to hear sad stories (including about his latest breakup!) or heartrending pleas for another

352

chance. Ignore them. These are just attempt to run another con on you. Do not fall for any of it. It's not your responsibility to clean up after him, take care of him, comfort him, etc. Let him "face the music" on his own.

Always remember: the worst abusers are inveterate, they can put on a big act (to include going to therapy, crying, proposing, falling on the floor, threatening suicide, proclaiming regret), but that's all it is, an act. At core, they have nothing to offer because they do not change because they are incapable of love. The lengths to which some abusers will go to re-enroll an escaped partner can be extreme to include rape and murder.

Also remember: most assaults occur during the first six to nine months after exit; this includes relationships in which neither partner has resorted to physical violence before.

Maintaining No Contact is about you taking care of yourself so you can heal and move forward. This is not about being weak or afraid or mean. If you get blow-back from family or friends, they simply don't know what they're talking about—consider the source of their criticism or advice. You now know better.

Exceptions

There are none. Do whatever you have to do to implement and maintain No Contact. This does not mean it will be easy, but it will get easier. The thing to keep front and center in your mind is that your former partner is abusive. Countless women have learned the hard way taht nothing good can come from going back. If he has abused you once, he will abuse you again and it will be worse the next time around. You have already been there. If you begin to cave and think you have made a mistake in exiting the relationship, reach out to a social worker at your local women's shelter or a therapist trained in domestic violence in your community.

Once lost, trust is rarely regained because in our subconscious, most of us know that if someone has deceived us once, they'll do it again. Anything else is just wishful thinking. This is a painful realization. Trust is one of the deepest bonds we are capable of forming, it is not won in an instant, but it can be lost that quickly.

At the first sign of someone who says one thing but does another, pick up your marbles and go home. This is a sign of incapacity. Be a friend to yourself. Implementing and maintaining No Contact with an abuser for the rest of your life is a step towards self respect and self protection.

You'll know you're starting to heal when you begin to want to work on yourself. Repairing the breaches in your self image will help you get your life back. It's your journey toward another chance.

> *Absolute Exit is your best defense against his offense—getting you to step into another trap.*

| 53 |

After Exit

A primal human need is the *need to believe;* it is essential to all endeavor. Belief serves you by carrying you through hard times, but the other side of the coin is that *when trust is misplaced*, the need to believe can hold you back. The need to believe can manifest in a pathological relationship as a "love is blind" point of view and in a partner who "can do no wrong." It can be a beautiful thing or it can be hideous. It can propel you beyond previous limits or it can fence you in. When the need to believe is ingrained in your mindset, chances are you also have an over-abundance of forbearance, patience and tolerance. When the need to believe is about a pathological person, it becomes a serious liability: we grit our teeth and bear it or we suffer for the one we love and wind up sustaining terrible wounds. Too much tolerance can lead to grave problems and grim damage. The need to believe can play havoc with your mind and keep you from seeing that something more serious than emotional baggage and more dangerous than mood swings is at hand.

Emotions and the Subconscious

Do we choose our emotions or are we programmed? Some say we choose emotional responses. Some say our emotional programming is formed during the first years of life when our brain is developing. Ironically and tragically, this "blueprint" is drawn for us by the key figures in our early life. It reveals itself in the experiences we have in life. The emotions that dominate your life are a key to the influences that went into your blueprint.

The problems of life all reflect the morality of the person(s) who created them. Most of the risks we face in day-to-day life arise from these problems that were put into our blueprints years ago. Each one of us has our own strengths and weaknesses, many of which began to take root in early childhood. As we grow, we become "more" according to the blueprint we carry deep in our subconscious. A pretty little girl with a jealous caregiver may never realize her full potential until she understands that her blueprint was infected and her development hindered by false and negative input. This is an over-simplified example of how it works.

Social problems are a manifestation of collective blueprints. Psychologists know that persons with certain mental illnesses gravitate to positions of influence. That is just the nature of the thing. Government corruption, for example shows the ongoing consequences of this just like family violence does. Both are transmitted from one generation to the next. Remember, the mental illness called *psychopathy* today was called *moral insanity* two hundred years ago and *demonic possession* two thousand years ago. The labels have changed with time, but the behaviors have not.

Consider the Source

One of the wisest counsels I ever received was: "consider the source," which means to *qualify the messenger before accepting the message*. Imagine how lives and relationships could be transformed if more people learned how to do this? Evil's gig would be up!

- Is the source credible? How so?
- Can the information be proved?
- Is there evidence to support it?
- Could the messenger have an agenda?
- What's the blowback if it's wrong?
- What's the payoff if it's right?

Much happiness and many lives have been destroyed for want of counsel that is truthful. The world is full of weasel words. How can you know if something is true? Some of us have learned that deceits are often wrapped in pretty packages to make them more desirable (and to make us lower our guard), but many have not learned this. So, how can you tell if what you are hearing is the truth? Saint Augustine put it this way,

> "The truth is like a lion. You don't have to defend it. Let it loose. It will defend itself."

In LOVING WHAT IS, Byron Katie shows readers how to end their suffering by looking at the validity of their beliefs before they turn themselves inside out trying to adhere to them. We suffer when our beliefs are not based on the truth. When we free ourselves of *misplaced trust* in false beliefs, the suffering ends because the truth has set us free. It's a simple concept and a profound work that can last a lifetime. It is especially relevant to the feelings of rejection that follow the end of a relationship.

Feeling Rejected

Rejection is a form of failure. It's no small irony that abused women feel rejected by their partners after they have left the relationship. Even women who have been hideously abused get sandbagged by these feelings once they get away. For her, a relationship has ended, hopes have been dashed, future plans have been shattered. For him, he is just "cycling" through prey items in his game. In a spent moment at the end of a violent day, my husband said to me, "I don't want to have to break in someone else."

Pathological partners are different and they're dangerous. Keeping the principle of "consider the source" in mind will help you safeguard your energy as you work through the aftermath of adversity. It will help you stay strong in your resolve to think accurately about what you have experienced. When any relationship ends, it's natural to feel sad, to grieve the unrealized potential, to miss the other person—even when they're toxic. Feelings of loss and rejection come from the shattering of the *illusion* of the relationship rather than the reality of it.

Some of the grief you feel after a relationship ends is over the loss of your hopes and dreams for it. As you go through it, if you feel yourself succumbing to thoughts of going back or wondering "what if," remind yourself of the abuse. This is a time to get clear about the reality of what you went through and resist the temptation to soften it or excuse it. In an abusive relationship, you were set up by your abusers' lies. He painted pretty word pictures about the life you were going to have with him so that you would buy his story and step into his trap. Know this, he did not tell the truth then and he will not tell the truth now, except if he thinks it would serve his interests.

Abusive individuals don't pair with other abusers for good reason; they require victims whose attributes they can *exploit*. Some of the best women in the world fall prey to some of the worst abusers for this reason. This doesn't make sense until you begin to understand how these relationships work: *predators seek prey*.

Of course, abusers are reluctant for their victims get away. Part of the aftermath experience is dealing with the abuser's reaction—he may try to romance you or he may stalk you. Understand that this is not because anything has changed with him. If he makes an attempt to romance you, this is because it's easier for him to get you back than find and break in another victim. He is looking for a *something* not a *someone*. Understand that any pursuit, whether romantic or violent, is not personal. It's not about you—it's about him—and it will always be about him. A leopard does not change his spots. A true predator does not change his behavior. Talk is cheap: he may make promises to the contrary, but his behavior will show that his life is an insatiable quest to fill his emptiness with someone else's pain. Abusers are serial con artists, they go from one victim to another to another. Despite the romances they put on, they are not capable of love.

The Primacy of Rejection

A woman who has been savaged by her intimate partner sustains many wounds, one of them is rejection. On the surface she has hurt feelings, bruises, lacerations, debt, ill health, lack of confidence, shame and hopelessness, but below the surface, she has been attacked at the core of her being. Evil found an opening and entered. The wounds that show, that she feels every day are serious and pervasive. It can take years to rebuild her body, mind and spirit even when she is determined and strong. But she often faces this task with a mountain of spiritual evil on top of practical difficulties, which hinders her ability to heal and move forward.

Hindering is the nature of evil. It wants to perpetuate the deepest wounds of self so that you cannot recover, so that you will bear the scars of what you fell for and what was done to you for the rest of your life. It wants to prevent you from fulfilling your purpose.

Toxic relationships are a prime cause of substance abuse and suicide after escape—which shows the nature of the wounds to the self. Understanding that a man's abuse is about him won't eradicate all the pain of the end of a marriage or relationship, but it will help the emotional severing you need to accomplish. Why? Because "getting it" is the lifeline that will pull you up out of the abyss: an abuser is not worth the pain of rejection. Remember that: he is not worthy.

To be on the receiving end of abuse is devastating because it assails the spirit and damages self image, it attacks who we are and derails our purpose. This is an age-old tactic employed by evil. Rejection is such a deep wound because it is so primal, it scatters life force and weakens connection to God. Rejection has a way of taking apart a woman's life with a force that few other emotions can equal. A woman who has been betrayed by her intimate partner is stung by feelings and haunted by invasive thoughts of rejection in her darkest moments. The hope for what could have been, the investment of resources (tangible and intangible) and other losses sit on her for months, even years. They may ebb if she finds shelter in knowledge or they may swamp her with huge waves of despair.

Facing reality is a powerful antidote to feelings of rejection in the aftermath of interpersonal terrorism and violence. But in order to face reality, you must consider the source so that you can think accurately.

The Effects of Rejection

Many people who have experienced abuse in childhood grow up with complex, unresolved wounds that, when not addressed, grow worse with time. Childhood abuse can transmogrify into resentment, rage, unforgiveness, envy, jealousy, materialism and so forth. These primal wounds make us prey for predatory influences, human and spiritual. Psychologists call these influences *pathologies*, theologians call them *strongholds*. You can recognize them by the sequence of events that play out when they are at work in someone's life:

- Appeal/Enticement
- Attention/Contemplation
- Engagement/Indulgence

- Persuasion/Craving

The most common channel for these influences travel is *personal debasement*. Self-ruination expresses the "inevitable harm" of being deceived. If you take a look at the typical offerings of media programming, you'll see endless examples of this phenomenon. The best way to protect yourself from pathologies and strongholds is to see them for what they are. Insights from psychologists and theologians for protection from human and spiritual evil can be expressed as:

- Acknowledgment/Confession—the power of language
- Remorse/Repentance—the power of emotion
- Therapy/Baptism—the power of knowledge

One part of the abuse experience is getting loaded down with emotional and spiritual baggage, the weight of which shows up as counter-productive inclinations. This baggage works below conscious awareness and often has to do with compliance and conformity that is *not* in your best interest.

- Vulnerability to negative people and spiritual influences
- Emotional instability, especially a tendency to keep others at bay (so as not to risk rejection again)
- Making yourself into someone you're not in order to gain acceptance (seeking approval like a child)
- Feeling starved for love and protection (being vulnerable to a sexual predator)
- An overwhelming need for continual acceptance and strong assurance
- Feeling so sorry for yourself that you are unable to let go of the past and move forward

- Discomfort in being given constructive criticism (exaggerated sense of insecurity and unworthiness)
- An overcompensating militancy about love or men (feminism or man-hating)
- Becoming overbearing to protect yourself from being controlled or dominated (such as being inappropriately opinionated)
- Collapse of self image (loss of hope about the future, loss of confidence in your abilities, feeling of extreme inadequacy and insecurity)
- Basing your sense of self more on external circumstances and feedback than on what you know (or used to know) about your self worth
- Falling into negative thinking and poor-mouthing (attracting and expressing envy, jealousy, lack and withholding)
- Tolerating abuse or exploitation for fear of confrontation (not standing up for yourself because you care too much about what others think of you)

Two common outgrowths of the deep wound of rejection are letting others' opinions supplant your own or becoming something of a bully yourself. Both are over-compensations for losing your sense of self. The first expresses emptiness, the second expresses defensiveness. Rejection can call up feelings of worthlessness that are painful to reckon with.

Another outgrowth of rejection is getting overtaken by ambition and the need for approval. This becomes counter-productive when you base your identity on things that don't matter. Becoming obsessed with physical fitness tends to implode over time because it makes your world smaller rather than larger. You are so much more than your physical body, marvelous as it is, it is just a vessel. Likewise, becoming overwrought about material concerns is equally stultifying because it is transitory stuff. Even so, it is not uncommon for a woman to exit an abusive relationship with a selfish, shallow man and then go through an equivalent, uncharacteristic phase herself.

Guard your thoughts and cultivate self awareness as protection against habits that hark back to the abuse because those thoughts and the habits that spring from them will not serve you or anyone else.

The Origin of Rejection

The wound of rejection, like abuse, delivers an extreme blow to the spirit in a message of unprovoked, unjustifiable hatred:

- "You are not worthy."
- "You are not good enough."
- "You do not deserve love."
- "You do not deserve respect."
- "You do not deserve to live."

The way the mind works: the more authoritative the messenger, the more devastating the wound to your deepest self. In this way, the origin of rejection can be seen as something of an identity crisis. When your self image becomes so tenuous that another person's assessment overrides your own self examination, you become vulnerable to pathological influences and their consequences. As Maxwell Maltz, MD wrote in PSYCHOCYBERNETICS, the best solution to personal problems is to "develop the self," to "become more," to grow beyond being controlled by what others think. This is not to say there are not times to receive feedback, even critical feedback, from people we trust—but watch out for messages that harm and hinder rather than inform and inspire. If you discern that people don't have your best interests in mind, which they demonstrate by treating you unfairly, take that as a cue to reassess your relationship with them.

It is not uncommon to find that the cast of characters in your life changes in the aftermath of an abusive relationship. The people who enter and leave your life will tell you a lot about who you were then and who you are becoming now. Over time, you will find that some of the things that define you will change—a little or a lot. Your relationships will change. Your sense of self will change. Your priorities will change. Your interests will change. Understanding and recovering from the wound of rejection hinges on your ability to remember the source of the rejection, assess the basis of your identity (or lack thereof) and take steps to heal your own self image.

If you discover that you were basing your sense of self on what your toxic partner said, then you have a lot in common with other women who have been pulled down by pathological entanglements. Until you consider the source—his criticisms, you will be vulnerable to them, even after you've left the relationship. You will know you're healing when his past condemnations become less important to you and less present in your mental habits. Giving responsibility for what you think of yourself to someone else is actually entrusting them with something that does not belong to them. Once you recognize your responsibility for this, you will begin to heal.

| 54 |

The Little Hinge

Vigilance is the little hinge that swings the big door. The success of your exit and your future safety both depend on it.

If You Leave

If you have time to plan an organized exit, here are some ideas to help you achieve the best possible outcome. The following are best practices based on advice I got from others and my own experiences.

- Confide only in key people you can trust about the true nature of your relationship and your plan to leave. Do not confide in people you cannot trust because they could jeopardize the success of your exit, or worse. "Loose lips sink ships."

- Give your trusted network a time frame so they can assist you or at least be present as witnesses to reduce the likelihood of violence.

- Give them each other's contact info to ensure seamless communication.

- Have important papers and phone numbers duplicated and mailed or taken off site for safe-keeping. Getting records out of the house well ahead of time will make the actual exit easier. Papers you want to take are your identification, asset documents (birth certificates, car title, mortgage, stock certificates, animal registrations, etc.), policies (car insurance, medical insurance, etc.), accounts (bank accounts, credit cards, utilities, etc.), contact information for key people (mailing addresses, emails and phone numbers).

- Have a place to go and a pre-planned way to exit the premises. Take an indirect route to your new location. Arrange for someone to block the driveway for a few minutes so that you can get away without being followed.

- This is not a time to do the obvious. Go someplace he does not know about or cannot access. If he knows where you are, the success of your exit is at high risk.

- Practice your escape route if it's new to you. Think it through as best you can. If you think your abuser might suspect your intentions, have as many contingent ideas and plans as possible.

- Take your animals with you or make other arrangements to get them away from your abuser before or during your exit. Do not leave them behind. Whatever you leave behind will be destroyed. An abuser will not hesitate to vent his rage on animals when he realizes he has lost control of his target.

- One exit option is to have a "police standby." This is when a police officer is present while you remove your things. They may park in your driveway or stand on the front porch while you remove your possessions.

- Another exit option is to have several people arrive in a group to escort you away from the premises. This might be the safest way to accomplish an exodus in which children, animals and personal property need to be removed. Keep in mind that abusers are cowards—this is why they do their abusing behind closed doors. You can achieve a certain amount of protection, albeit temporarily, by having a number of people at hand.

- Change all of your accounts to other providers so that he cannot access your funds, interfere with your services or use your records to cyber-stalk you.

- Delete and discontinue any social media activity, set up new email accounts as needed and do not let him know of them.

- Do not communicate with him directly. Period. You are in a weakened condition and he knows all your buttons. Have a social worker or attorney conduct any business on your behalf.

If you cannot get essential items out of the house before your actual exit, here are some thought joggers for things to copy, gather and take:

- Children and animals
- Keys and car registration
- Cash, credit cards, check books
- Clothing, shoes, outerwear
- Identification (driver's license, passport)
- Important papers (financial, legal, medical)
- Names, addresses, email and phone numbers
- Small things of value (jewelry, photographs)

Be as methodical as you can. Keep focused.

If He Leaves

If you are in a position to have your partner removed from the residence and you choose to remain there, here are some considerations for increasing your safety after his exit.

- Make sure your neighbors know that he does not live there anymore and is not allowed on the property.

- Tell them to alert you and call the police if they see him there.

- Make sure key people in your life know what's going on with you so they can lend a hand or be witnesses. Confide in friends, coworkers and authorities toward this end. Make sure they also have each other's contact information. Two heads are better than one. This also accomplishes "outing" the abuser to some extent.

- Have friends or relatives—preferably couples, so that there is a man on the premises—take turns staying at the house for as long as possible so that if your abuser is stalking you, he'll see that you're not alone. Part of his fury comes from his sense of being "falsely accused of being abusive," so having other people around may dissuade him from acting in a way that would confirm that implication.

- Change your routines and schedules as much as possible. Become less visible by becoming unpredictable. Change your habits and movements as much as possible. If you can alter your work schedule so that you're not coming and going at predictable hours, do so. As much as possible, take alternate routes and shop at alternate stores—at least for a while.

- Swap automobiles with your friends temporarily. You have a better chance of eluding him if he does not know what kind of vehicle you're in.

- Consider getting a dog or two. Dogs are great companions and security systems on four legs. However, if your abuser would not hesitate to hurt an animal, then this would not be helpful to you or fair to the dog(s).

- Change all the door locks to a single key, this way you won't ever have to fumble for the right key if something is amiss and you need to get in the house fast.

- If you have doors with large glass expanses, get dead bolts that key from both sides and keep the inside key out of line of view and further than an arms' reach away from the door.

- Keep the exterior doors locked at all times.

- Put a dead bolt on your bedroom door.

- Get a shotgun and keep it by your bed. You can put birdshot in it, which will drop an intruder but not inflict lethal wounds. If he breaks into your house, you should assume that his intent is to kill you. You must be mentally prepared and physically equipped to protect yourself, your children and animals.

- Put nails or razor wire on any outdoor window ledges that would otherwise be easy to crawl into after breaking a window.

- Keep the windows locked at all times.

- Cover all windows and keep shades down at night. Install light-filtering shades or curtains.

- Install flood lights with motion sensors around all entry areas.

- Install an alarm system and learn how to use it.

- Install real or fake surveillance cameras on the roof or in trees around your house.

- If your dwelling is not sturdy or well lit outside, place noise-making objects (like empty cans) in strategic places to alert you to prowling or stalking activity.

- Consider taking a martial arts class for self defense.

- Do not respond to any communications from your abuser except legal ones and only through your attorney or a social worker.

Be vigilant in all your activities. Remember that you are at heightened risk for six months or more after exiting an abusive relationship.

A New Mindset

Learn to think like a predator so you won't be victimized by harassment or stalking from your ex or anyone else:

1. Of course I look familiar. I was here last week cleaning your carpets, painting your shutters or delivering your new refrigerator.

2. Hey, thanks for letting me use the bathroom when I was working in your yard last week. I unlatched the window to make my return a little easier.

3. Love those flowers. That tells me you have taste, which means there are nice things inside.

4. Yes, I do look for newspapers and flyers on the front porch; I might leave one myself to see if someone's home or not

5. If it snows while you're out of town, get a neighbor to create car and foot tracks. Virgin drifts are a dead giveaway.

6. If decorative glass is part of your front entrance, don't let your alarm company install the control pad in line of sight. That makes it too easy.

7. A good security company alarms the window over the sink, windows on the second floor and the master bedroom. Motion detectors are a good idea, too.

8. If you forget to lock your door, that's understandable. But know this: I don't take a day off.

9. I always knock first. If you answer, I'll smile and ask for directions somewhere or offer to clean your gutters.

10. I always check dresser drawers, the bedside table and the medicine cabinet. But I almost never go into kids' rooms.

11. You're right: I won't have enough time to break into that safe where you keep your valuables. But if it's not bolted down, I'll take it with me.

12. A loud TV or radio is an excellent deterrent. If you don't want to leave one on, you can buy a device that simulates the flickering glow of a real television. (www.faketv.com)

13. Sometimes, I carry a clipboard. Sometimes, I dress like a lawn guy and carry a rake. I do my best to never, ever look dangerous.

14. The two things I hate most: big dogs and nosy neighbors.

15. I'll break a window to get in, even if it makes noise. Single noises rarely get a reaction. It's human nature.

16. I love looking in your windows. I'm looking for signs that you're home, and for flat screen TVs or gaming systems I'd like. I'll drive or walk through your neighborhood at night, before you close the blinds, just to pick my targets.

17. Avoid announcing your vacation on Linked In, Facebook, MySpace and Twitter. It's easier than you think to look up your address.

18. To you, leaving that window open just a crack is a way to let in a little fresh air. To me, it's an invitation.

19. If you don't answer when I knock, I try the door. Occasionally, I hit the jackpot and walk right in.

Sources: Convicted burglars in North Carolina, Oregon, California and Kentucky;
Security Consultant Chris McGoey (www.crimedoctor.com)
Richard Wright, Professor of Criminology, University of Missouri, Saint Louis.

Wasp Spray

Did you know that police recommend wasp spray over pepper spray for personal protection? Here's why:

- It sprays in a straight line for up to 20 feet
- It is more accurate than pepper spray
- Wasp spray is safe to use indoors (mace and pepper spray are not)
- It is disabling but not lethal.
- It incapacitates an attacker for several minutes so you can flee
- It costs less than mace, pepper spray or a gun
- It doesn't attract attention like mace pepper spray or a gun

If/when you have to use wasp spray against an attacker, spray them in the face and keep spraying until they are on the ground or unable to see, then run! Self defense expert Val Glinka suggests keeping a can of wasp spray in your car and in several places in your house.

Glinka says wasp spray is effective for personal defense, "This is better than anything I can teach...."

Key Fob

Keep your car keys with you at all times. If you hear a noise outside your home or someone trying to get in your house, press the panic button on your key fob. The car alarm will go off without giving away your location in the house.

Think of your key fob as a *mobile security alarm system*:

- You already have it
- It requires no installation
- The alarm will go off no matter where you are
- It will keep sounding until you turn it off
- It works no matter where you park (driveway, garage, street)
- Attention-getting stimuli are strong deterrents to criminals

Not Over

Chances are slim your former partner will let you go without a fight. Be prepared mentally and physically so you can heal in peace and keep moving forward.

| 55 |

Strength From Adversity

Adversity is a state of being in difficult and serious circumstances, which may include danger, hardship, misfortune and prolonged suffering. By definition, it describes conditions that are unalterable and intractable. Adversity comes in many shapes and sizes; it can happen suddenly or come upon you gradually. Either way, it is painful, even terrifying and you can find yourself face-to-face with circumstances that put you at great disadvantage and even threaten to destroy you.

Most man-made adversity occurs because we lack knowledge of the warning signs. As explained, relationship red flags are often counter-intuitive, so they remain unseen even if they're in plain sight and we don't see them at all or until it is too late. Most self-made adversity comes about as a result of another kind of lack: that of an adequate self image. Not to be confused with self esteem, self image is larger. It is or should be nourished from birth by adept parents. Alas, the state of relationship reveals a terrible truth about the extent of deficit parenting. The massive state of emotional hunger—a universal consequence of tragically poor parenting, is all around us. You don't have to look far to see legions of lost souls, young and old, who did not get what they needed when they needed it from their parents.

The Wound

Just about any psychologist will tell you that the universal wound is that of personal insufficiency or inadequate self image, "I'm not good enough." For some it is a death sentence, for others a life sentence—until your moment of truth comes. Emotional hunger expresses itself in all kinds of ways:

- bullying
- drug addiction
- anorexia
- binging
- bulimia
- promiscuity
- self mutilation
- adolescent smoking
- alcoholism
- juvenile delinquency
- animal torture
- pornography addiction
- overwork
- gambling
- white collar crime

Energetically, it should be understood that everything we do attracts and repels energy. This energy comes to us as unforeseen events; it also shows up as the way people respond to us. This "resonance" is part of the invisible power of life—it operates at all times regardless of our awareness of it. When we behave badly, more of the same is drawn to us. This is cause and effect in action. This expresses the momentum behind "nothing succeeds like success" and this is why a downward spiral can become an avalanche before you know it. When you hear that someone is riding the wave or spiraling downward, that's an example of those energies at work. Sometimes we do it to ourselves, sometimes we let other people do it to us.

Recovering from adversity requires accurate thinking, emotional grit and the ability to hold fast—to keep going despite what you see and feel. It is very much about mind over matter. The righteous live by faith, not by what they think or see. The strength we need has often been exhausted by the storm. Our lives have been interfered with and our thinking messed with. So, here you are, you have survived one adversity only to realize you face many more on the journey to wholeness. What is at hand here is much more than just resting up and letting time heal your wounds. This is a time in which tremendous regeneration and transformation can take place. Those intensifying energies and fortifying forces will come to your aid if you choose to work toward becoming more instead of giving up or settling for less. You may not have had many choices for a while, but this is yours and yours alone.

History is replete with examples of people who overcame crushing injustice and grinding poverty to transform themselves. In many cases, their lives left an indelible signature on their time. How did they do it? What was it that kept them going? Is there something available to us at these times that can inform us and improve as we work to get over adversity? I think there is.

The process of recovery is work, so it must begin with rest. Along the way, you will reap more reward as you learn how to:

- Manage anxiety so you can feel your feelings
- Purge physical toxins safely
- Prioritize stress so you rest, work and live better
- Purge limiting beliefs so you can make constructive choices and attract better opportunities
- Neutralize negative habits so your life force can be renewed
- Clarify your thinking so your perspectives can be empowering
- Discharge trauma so your heart can heal
- Regain confidence and hope so you can make your plans
- Begin to build momentum by using immutable laws

Adversity can make it seem like everything that's good is either out of reach or ruined. Circumstantially, that may be the case, at least as far as you can see. But I'm here to tell you that there are spiritual energies and energy technologies available to us that can do great good in our lives. These energies are summoned by request and they work with your physiology. They work whether you think they will or not because they are based on immutable spiritual laws and proven principles of brain function. Many of these principles have been known and practiced historically by the elite, who also went to great length to keep this knowledge to themselves. The greatest impediment to putting all of this to work is the depleting effect of anxiety and stress.

Fear

Fears, even the most basic ones, can totally destroy ambition and undermine resolve.

Indifference. What a tragic condition this is. "It's okay.... I'll get by... No big deal.." Indifference is a trip to nowhere and if you've been touched by interpersonal abuse, you've already been there and done that.

Indecision. This a mental burglar that robs you of a mindset that draws opportunity and creativity. It steals what you need for a second chance.

Doubt. Be mindful that doubt doesn't get its foot in the door when you apply critical thinking to daily life because it can spread itself and crowd out everything else out.

Worry. "Faith in the negative" is a phrase that describes this useless emotional expenditure. I think it also creeps in when things are unfinished.

Trepidation. A halting, timid approach to life gets little or no result. If you want to grow, trepidation must be overcome.

What Stress Does

The pain of any adversity is multiplied by its emotional consequences--the death of a loved one, a betrayal by someone you trusted or abuse at the hands of your spouse can drive the iron deep into your soul.

A woman who has survived a dangerous relationship has lived through one of the most soul-killing experiences on earth. It is well known in therapeutic circles that intractable stresses are the ones that do the most damage. It is the cyclic, escalating nature of the stress of abuse that is so pernicious. The good news is that advances in neuroscience are encouraging for anyone who is engaged in recovery. Recent discoveries in brain research reveal:

- Neurogenesis, the growth of new neurons (brain neurons once believed to be finite, are now proven to be infinite)
- Neural networks, connections between neurons are dynamic not static (this means mental habits and thought processes can be altered)
- Neural plasticity, the brain is adaptable because neural networks can be changed (this is the physiological basis of mental change)

We all have millions of neural networks in our brains and this is what you need to know about them:

- The stronger a neural network is, the more control it exerts over your thinking.
- The more awareness you develop of your thinking, the higher your consciousness and the more powerful your energetic vibration.
- This frequency is real and you can learn how to fine-tune and use it to help yourself recover.
- This is not psychology or philosophy, this is physics and physiology.

These are the major principles at work in this process:

- Repetition creates neural pathways

- Sensory data impresses neural pathways
- Emotion intensifies the formation of neural pathways
- Feeling good amplifies all brain functions
- Physical circumstances and spiritual energy respond to brain activity
- Clarity and desire accelerate results

Isn't this exciting? You can purge and remap your brain's neural pathways as you recover. As the dominant thoughts in your subconscious are corrected (healed), you will move closer to restoration and wholeness. How will you know when it's working? When you're effecting change at the subconscious level. And how will you know when you're doing that? You'll start to feel better for no reason in particular. And then, the emotions that give juice to life will begin to reappear—appreciation, gratitude, wonder, curiosity, confidence, faith, cheer, energy, willingness, determination, focus, love and hope. As you consciously cultivate feeling better, your brain will begin to *magnetize circumstances* that reflect your emotional state. This is when fortuitous events or happy accidents will begin to come your way.

Your Thoughts

Thoughts are measurable energies that influence temporal reality. Your body is vibrating energy and it is affected at all times by your thoughts and feelings, all below the level of consciousness. When you learn to harness this power, you'll be able to see things with a new perspective, in the moment *and* in retrospect.

The value of your own experiences will expand as new insights open to you. This should give you lots of "ah-ha" moments. Never underestimate the big shifts that come from little realizations. When you work in alignment with brain function, you get more results with less effort. You can embark on a journey of solving problems in new ways with new authority by calling forth what you want and need. While actions are rewarded, the gifts of the mind surpass what hands can do. Attuning yourself to your mental habits and incorporating simple practices into your daily life will empower you in ways that go beyond words. This is the realm of *creation*.

Your Feelings

You have emotions, but you are not your emotions like you have a body, but you are not your body. Emotions are "data packs" of information interpreted by your brain as navigational aids. They are chemical charges stored in memory that influence experience. They can be consciously discharged and released. For example, focusing on feeling better will build a stronger neural network and feeling better will become manifest over time. Observing a melancholy emotion and responding to it or correcting it with a cheerful emotion will help dismantle the melancholy neural network and replace it with a hopeful one, which will free you from the limitations of melancholia. This doesn't mean you won't be able to feel melancholy when that's appropriate, it means you will no longer be stuck in it. You will be vibrating at a level higher than melancholia, much of which feeds on inaction and self pity.

Accurate Thinking

When you get to the point that you're able to see through circumstances to the *basis* of an adversity, you'll begin to see through your own reactions and your own thought patterns. Making corrections to your thinking may sound simple, but it's a challenging process. It's challenging to develop the discipline you need to observe this part of yourself and to see through the beliefs that are attached to your thinking. When you're recovering, it can be a tall order, but one that will help you if you do it. It may take months to understand what happened and why, and months more to begin to process it. The magnitude of some life experiences require time to reckon, a dangerous relationship is one of them.

These are the summary statements I came up with as I worked towards accurate thinking about my marriage:

- My husband's history suggests that he is psychopathic (he does the same things in each relationship but with more intensity and he does not learn from his past).
- He is becoming a social pariah in Jackson.
- His actions show that he does not care about me at all.
- Since psychopathy is permanent, irreparable and progressive, there is nothing that can help him.
- His behavior is typical of his type of pathology and its advancement because of his age.
- His influences on me and my life have been damaging and destructive in the extreme.
- He has made numerous attempts to kill or injure me and my animals that I could not face at the time but that I now see and understand.

- Because he has no conscience, it is dangerous for me and my animals to be around him.

- Even though he hasn't harmed me physically yet, his behavior in prior relationships suggests he would (at least two backcountry accidents resulting in serious injury to women, one on horseback, one on skis).

- My appeals to fairness and reason will continue to fall on deaf ears and provoke more abuse because logic and fairness are not in his psychological repertoire.

- The marriage will continue to devolve no matter what I do.

- Staying in the marriage will accomplish nothing except my destruction. *and Billy's*

- He is not worth dying for or suffering for.

I realized my survival depended on my ability keep calm, plan carefully and leave as soon as possible.

In dangerous relationships, it is often not safe to show fear or to challenge the adversary. This emotional editing requires enormous stores of energy and further drains you. Having to be "on guard" and maintain a non-reactive stance saps the body as well as the mind—and yet—it is part of what must be done to live another day.

Your Realm of Power

No matter how terribly you have been wounded, you can get better if you want to. You have a source from which you can derive great benefit. Your realm of power is your mind. Through your mind you can access energy and information to help you overcome present suffering. As you work towards recovery and restoration, these energies will help sustain you while others are gathering. After you have won your freedom and earned your restoration, there's more. You will see that the benefits are *cumulative*. The work you've done will continue to lend clarity and force to your life. It will give you strength. It is not at all uncommon for women who are "just trying to survive" to wind up reinventing themselves in the process of recovering from abuse.

The primary requisites for recovering from adversity are that you want to, you possess the self honesty to get the lessons and you are willing to do the work. This is your domain. Other people can encourage and support you in some of it, but it is your work to do. Getting started is the most important part. Because of how the mind works, it gets easier after the three-week mark, which is how long it takes the brain to begin to adjust to new conditions. After a few weeks, you will also have momentum to help counter normal resistance or psychological reversal that may arise. Normal resistance is the temptation to quit, psychological reversal is the influence of our inner brat whose response to almost everything is "I don't want to" or "you can't make me."

Your Context

There's something to be said for "getting fed up" because it can lead to a personal tipping point where you are disturbed enough to do something. When this happens, whether you realize it or not, you are poised for success; that is, you have:

- Desire that drives you to do the work. Taking action reduces anxiety and musters your forces.
- Commitment not to settle for less and limping through life. "Oh, it's okay" is a deadly state of mind.

385

- Time for yourself to think about your life and honor your commitment to making things better.

- Vision to dream and hope again. A map of what you want that you can focus on every day will feed your soul and direct your energy toward your heart's desire.

- Courage to keep going despite inevitable frustration and setbacks. If something doesn't pan out the first time or soon enough, reassess and retry.

- Discernment to help guard your thoughts by purging negative ones immediately.

- Strength to resist the temptation to indulge in horribilizing or enrolling people to feel sorry for you. This will only keep you stuck.

- Knowledge that frustration and indignation often signal breakthroughs and can give you power to keep at it. Your purposes will give you power.

| 56 |

Personal and Social Solutions

To avert or mitigate interpersonal abuse, knowledge of predatory and parasitical models must be offered. For those who get it and take up the charge, they will become more equipped every day to handle an encounter with a predator. Dave Grossman puts it this way in his article "Sheep, Wolves and Sheepdogs":

> "This business of being a sheep or a sheepdog is not a yes-no dichotomy. It is not an all-or-nothing, either-or choice. It is a matter of degrees, a continuum. On one end is an abject, head-in-the-sand-sheep and on the other end is the ultimate warrior. Few people exist completely on one end or the other. Most of us live somewhere in between. Since 9-11 almost everyone in America took a step up that continuum, away from denial. The sheep took a few steps toward accepting and appreciating their warriors, and the warriors started taking their job more seriously. The degree to which you move up that continuum, away from sheep-hood and denial, is the degree to which you and your loved ones will survive, physically and psychologically at your moment of truth."

One of the biggest needs in the aftermath of abuse is to find some peace so your mind can be quiet and your heart can heal. Relief from stress should be a priority because its disorders can be so profound and long lasting:

- PTSD
- a-social behaviors
- heart health issues
- acid reflux and ulcers
- hormone imbalance
- adrenal fatigue
- endocrine collapse
- auto-immune diseases

Healing is complicated by these stressors *and* by the fact that most Pathologicals do not want their victims to get away. The woman's exit is often followed by various forms of monitoring and stalking. The abuser may try to romance his former partner, but he quickly resorts to assaultive behaviors if she does not respond to the romantic overtures. Law enforcement and the court system are behind the ball in learning how to work with the high-conflict cases that pathological partners create.

Trauma is stored in cellular memory and so must be cleared/discharged at the cellular level. The brain can get overloaded and change body chemistry over time if protection from abuse and relief is not available. The woman who has escaped years of emotional, mental, physical, financial, sexual, spiritual and verbal savagery needs a safe, supportive environment in which to rest and recover. She needs this so she can heal adequately and function fully in the world again. The deeper her wounds, the more time she may need. Because of what we know about brain function, her prospects for recovery are good. She won't heal overnight, but she will heal *if she wants to heal.*

Those around her with understanding will watch as she comes back to life one molecule at a time—and they will be amazed by what they witness.

To Heal

Crisis housing, such as that supplied by women's shelters, typically provides six to eight weeks of room and board. The safe harbor they offer is critically important, but shelters are only a first step. This is not enough time to catch up on your sleep, let alone get a good start on rebuilding a life. For women without family or money, a next step into a more efficient situation would be more productive in accelerating their return to independence.

Private Safe Houses

One solution would be private safe houses. Through a private arrangement, a family, couple or woman would open their home to a woman who has exited abuse and is a good prospect for mentoring. Both parties could be vetted by an appropriate third party to ensure mutual safety and terms of agreement. Each arrangement could include things like:

- Room and board provided in exchange for cooking, errand running, office assistance or personal shopping.

- Mentoring provided for child care, animal care or home improvement projects.
- Networking or skills development provided for gardening or housekeeping.

This would be a safe solution for a woman who has perhaps lost everything to earn her way by providing services at which she is adept while rebuilding her self confidence. It could also be a rewarding experience for the person(s) providing the home base. Private solutions such as this would foreshorten the abused woman's financial recovery by allowing her to work without the full burdens of housing costs for a while.

The enormous difference such an arrangement could make to the rest of her life cannot be overstated.

- It could make every difference between her being able to afford decent housing for herself in the near future or not.
- It could accelerate the restoration of a healthy self image and all the opportunities that makes possible.
- It could empower and accelerate her re-entry to work and her community outside the home.

Done in the private sector without bureaucratic interference, private safe houses could be an effective and elegant solution tailored to both parties for their mutual benefit.

Transitional Housing

In over 70 percent of households where women and children are abused, the animals are also abused, oftentimes even more cruelly. With millions of toxic households, the amount of torture being visited upon the animal targets of pathological violence is unimaginable.

Another solution for abused women would be transitional housing for those with animals. There are many resources for women with children, but few for women with animals. I was forced to give my cats and dogs to foster homes in order to enter the women's shelter. Like me, many women stay in dangerous relationships longer than they want to because they have no place to go with their animals and they refuse to leave them behind because they know they will be harmed. Even if women don't know the statistics, they know that their tormentor would not hesitate to lash out against their animals.

The woman who turns to a shelter does so because she is desperate. She has had enough and she may also feel that her abuse is about to turn lethal. She is either without funds or unable to get to her friends or family. When she comes to a shelter, she has been dispossessed of everything she owns except her animals. She has been robbed of what would comfort and help her as she begins to recover and works to get back on her feet. To be in this situation and then be forced to part with your beloved animals is like being stabbed in the heart. It begets years of guilt, and all things considered, it is perhaps the cruelest cut of all. Transitional housing for women with animals remains a great need.

To Halt

By and large, abusers are made by genetics and environment. In the most simplistic terms, much of it is due to tragically poor parenting. But another reason abusers exist is because the law allows it. Until abusers commit what the legal system considers a crime, there are no legal remedies for stopping them. My former husband, for example, is an internet predator. He is in the advanced stages of psychopathy and has become a master of his preferred methods of entrapment and abuse: financial destruction, social isolation and back-country "accidents." He is known by some in his small community as a serial abuser of women. But even though he has left a trail of destruction, he has not been caught breaking any laws and so, he carries on his predations to this day.

There are a lot of ways to try to destroy a woman without putting an axe through her skull or ruining her career. In the present legal system in the US, a woman has to be visibly wounded before legal remedies with any teeth in them are available to her. Even then, the financial hurdles are such that most victims cannot obtain them— the system by default protects the predator and fails society. In this way, the legal system has devolved into its own counterfeit: it is nothing more than a conveyor belt to fill the coffers and the prisons for the profit of their corporate owners. The dysfunction of these systems is a big reason why abuse persists.

Two of the most pervasive feelings in the daily life of an abused woman are shame and fright. These cause her to keep her situation unspoken, even denied. The regular ruin of formerly productive women by the schemes of charismatic con artists is epidemic. Complexity implies deep meaning and too many in our once-great society act as if they are afraid of meaning. The losses here are great, as is the waste.

If abusers were to commit their fraud in any other realm, it would be actionable. The most sophisticated abusers are cognizant of their legal leeway and use it to full advantage. It's time to return to a much simpler and more effective means of delivering justice to the abuser and giving protection to his target: **ostracism**.

Social ostracism has been an extremely effective way of exposing and expelling human wickedness for centuries. It won't redeem the abuser, but exposing him for his deeds will inhibit further predations on his home turf and maybe even run him out of town. Ostracism works because it threatens the abuser with the thing he most fears: accountability. Being confronted and forced to account for his behavior is antithetical to the personality dynamics of a predator. Abusers run on delusion, denial, blame, justification, minimization and lying.

There are at least three online databases in operation at this time for this purpose. Kudos to their founders:

- www.domesticviolencedatabase.org
- www.theweakervessel.org
- www.womansavers.com

Ostracism is one principle behind registering sex offenders. It gives notice to the community and it exposes the perpetrator. It is by no means justice for the victim(s), but it's a start at stopping or at least interrupting the abuse.

A Wish

The principle behind ancient laws is to reprove or remove wrongdoers, that is, restitution or execution. Personally, I would like to see the Golden Rule applied to the property and the person of every human predator in a manner consistent with and to the extent of his abuse of his victim(s). If he is alive after this, remove him from society, distribute his assets to his victim(s) not the courts and put him to work so that he is no longer a danger and not a burden to society.

| 57 |

With Fresh Eyes

The material for this book came to me unexpectedly. As I contemplated my final escape from my husband, the beginnings of our relationship rolled through my mind. Thoughts and images came to me in the wee hours as I lay alone in a tiny guest room in his house. During the four weeks I was confined there, I sought insight about the moment when darkness found me and where it had taken me. Night after night, dozens of details from our courtship and marriage meandered across my mind's eye. Random, unconnected memories drifted across the sleepless hours. And then one morning, hindsight was upon me. With fresh eyes, I *saw*. I saw, heard and felt the warning signs I'd failed to apprehend years before.

The warning signs had been there. One by one they rose up before me—red flags everywhere. I had not known enough to discern them before. How had I missed such a multitude? I'd missed them because I wasn't looking for them. I'd missed them because they didn't look like warning signs. I'd also missed them because nothing in my life had trained me to look for signs of abuse. It's like training yourself to be in a car crash. You simply cannot. It's an unexpected, overwhelming experience that occurs at blinding speed. Until you've been in one, felt the impact, seen the carnage, studied the wreckage, interviewed the survivors and autopsied the victims—or—someone has shown you what to watch out for, you simply can't know.

My journey through relationship violence occurred over a period of years rather than decades, but its severity has changed me forever. I was tempered by earlier experiences that helped me survive. But many women were not tempered and do not survive. I grieve for them. I also grieve for all the baby boys who are damaged to such an extent that they grow up to be monsters.

The Burning Question

In between my first and second exit attempts, I found a seasoned therapist who specialized in abusive relationships. By the time I got in to see her, I had a huge question burning in me—something I needed to know, but also dreaded to know. It wasn't until our third or fourth session that I was able to ask: "What is wrong with me that I have attracted this sick man into my life?"

She leaned forward and looked me in the eye. I held my breath and braced myself. Sunlight streamed in the window behind her. She told me that this is the first big question every woman asks. She said nothing was wrong with me. She held my gaze and told me I had been *conned*. She went on to say that she considers domestic abuse a hideous con. She also said it happens to all kinds of women—including those you wouldn't think it could happen to.

After 18 months of withering criticism from my husband, her words ran over me like water on a thirsting plant. It was a shock at first, but it created the soil in which everything else I was learning could take root and hold. It was as if she had pulled back the curtains and opened a window. Light.

Pathologies exert enormous power over the afflicted and their victims. The uninitiated simply have no idea of the reality of this situation. Because abusers act like Jekyll and Hyde, their victims have twice as much to process because they have, in effect, been involved with two people. Pathological relationships can take twice as long and twice as much work to get over. Aftermath symptoms are twice as complicated as those from normal relationships:

- intrusive thoughts (good and bad)
- flooding memories (good and bad)
- cognitive dissonance (good and bad)

Truth, when we recognize it, is often strange and often a surprise. Most people prefer what is comfortable, undemanding and pat; the realities of abuse are anything but.

Withdrawing Consent

As you get your arms around this information, you will start to think and feel differently about some things. The ultimate response is that you begin to withdraw your consent to be abused. Withdrawing consent to the relationship means much more than a superficial rendering of this phrase suggests. It is a process that begins inside and must gain firm footing before being expressed or acted upon outside.

Withdrawing consent is the beginning of the end of abuse and as such is a far-reaching mental re-set. To withdraw your consent means you are no longer loyal to your partner because you now see him as fundamentally cruel, dishonest and disrespectful. It means acknowledging that your partner's behavior will result in continual injustice, pain and damage
to you. Therefore, by withdrawing your consent you are no longer willing to deny or excuse his actions because you understand them to be toxic, hostile and dangerous.

It means no longer participating in the unnatural rituals of daily life with a psychopath because you have seen through them and him. It means a psychological divorce from feeling hopeful or positive about the relationship or your abuser. It means working toward your freedom in whatever ways you can. It means no longer thinking of yourself as his woman or his wife and being obligated to the regular sacrifices of your dignity to the altar of his ego or insanity. Instead it means believing that you are good enough and deserve to love and be loved.

This mental re-set has the opposite effects of PTSD and Stockholm Syndrome, which extend your sentence in the mental prison your abuser has built for you. It is important to know that withdrawing consent can be done without hatred as that emotion reinforces the warped roles of abuser and abused. (This is not to say that force may not be necessary to escape, because it may.)

By your own self activity to learn and discern, you acquire the power to deconstruct the toxic relationship, deny its premise and affirm your value as a person. This is a choice that you make every day by the way you perceive yourself and interact with the world around you.

The Big Picture

Before my final exit from my marriage and despite the misery of daily life, misplaced compassion and hope lived in my broken heart for a long time. This is a common part of the journey. It takes some rigor and time to grasp the realities of abuse intellectually, it takes even more to accept them emotionally. This is due to the extreme emotional exhaustion inherent in abuse. When love dies, even from abuse, there is despair, sorrow and torpor.

Even though I understood more and more of what I was dealing with, it took some time for my head and my heart to get on the same page. Even though I understood that it was a hopeless situation, it took time for my resolve to become firm. Flashes of insight continued to break through that helped drive home the reality that I was imprisoned and my marriage was hopeless. With every realization of what my husband's behavior amounted to, I was able to move closer to seeing the big picture, to looking at it without blinking and to winning my release.

The struggle to free one's self from abuse is not unlike the struggle to get out of quicksand. One must do it with great care. Abuse is disabling and some ways are better than others for getting out of both. Before I was able to get out of the quicksand and see the big picture, I faced personal stumbling blocks in deciding to leave. I cringe as I write this now, but it's the truth of what I went through as I processed two years of marital terror. I know now that this is not an uncommon part of the journey. Abuse does a lot of bad things to your psyche—it makes you doubt yourself and it undermines your confidence to the point that you need extraordinary amounts of encouragement and evidence to move forward. These are also symptoms of the need to bolster self image.

The first stumbling block—the shame of breaking my vows and failing at my marriage—was cleared by prayer and counsel. The spirit of a marriage covenant is based on love, respect, protection, tenderness, trust and dependence that are shared.

A woman married to an abusive man does not receive these considerations of marriage. After a while, the abuse renders her unable to fulfill her duties as her heart, mind and body begin to recoil. Walking on eggshells and enduring attack have no place in a real marriage. It cannot be said enough that toxic relationships are *counterfeit*, they look authentic from the outside, but behind closed doors, they are the opposite of what they appear to be.

> "The biggest coward is a man who awakens a woman's love with no intention of loving her."
>
> Bob Marley

The second stumbling block—wondering if there was "something" that could restore our marriage—was demolished by the work of internationally known child development expert Bruce Perry, MD, PhD. Dr Perry's work on the effects of trauma on brain development, showed me that the biological reason for pathological relationship violence, such as I had experienced, was organic brain damage. By definition, this type of brain damage, known as psychopathy, is permanent and progressive. The anti-social behaviors it leads to become worse with time. This explained my observation that my husband seemed to be getting more pathological as time went by.

The organic nature of the brain damage behind psychopathy also explains why their rate of recidivism is close to 100 percent (like that of certain addicts, pedophiles, spousal batterers and serial murderers). Individuals afflicted with damage to the frontal (and sometimes the temporal) lobe(s) do not respond to treatment because the physiological capacity for normalcy does not exist.

To date, nearly half a trillion dollars has been spent in treatment facilities around the world in search of ways to help psychopaths recover or mitigate their behaviors so that they do not inflict harm—all to no avail. This is the plain fact of organic brain damage and its enormous implications for society.

Connecting the Dots

All of this swirled around in my mind for months and gave me new insights for dealing with the realities of daily life. For months I saw the concepts and principles of abuse I'd been learning being acted out in front of me. So much so, I began to be able to predict some of his behaviors. As I realized that his conduct had already broken our marriage vows and that his condition was irredeemable, I began to think and feel differently. The implications were life altering. I began to feel some hope that someday soon I would no longer be trapped. At some point, I realized my marriage was a sort of laboratory and my husband, a rather large lab rat. I also realized it was a tremendous opportunity to observe, qualify and learn.

Learning something and being able to put it into action may not occur at once. The time between learning about abuse and getting away from it was excruciating and surreal. I now recognized what he was doing as I experienced him doing it to me. While I was still in my husband's house, I treated him with consideration, but my feelings were burnt out.

One evening in the kitchen, I watched with something akin to detachment as my husband worked himself into a rage over what he liked to call my "latest idiocy." In this case, he objected to the asking price I'd put on one of my horses. As I fixed dinner, he paced back and forth along the counter, yelling and gesturing. From the other side of the room, he picked up a chef's knife and waved it around as he continued his verbal skewering. He sliced and stabbed the air with it to punctuate his sentences. And then he turned toward me.

I had learned not to ignore threatening gestures, so I turned to face him. He could see he had my full attention. He came close and held the knife up to my face, gesturing furiously, almost spasmodically with it—for a moment, I thought I saw the ruined little boy—holding the knife an inch or two from my right eye, I knew what he wanted to do. His face flushed and contorted with fury, spittle flying, the knife shook in his hands as he stabbed the air with it and raked me over the coals of the wrath that burned in him. I stood still, looked him in the eye and held his empty, black stare. I saw and I understood what I saw.

Still agitated, but spent, he continued to yell as his rage subsided. Glaring at me, he stepped backed, slammed the knife down, hurled a few final insults, turned on his heel and stormed out of the room. I exhaled. Inside me, it was over. And I wanted it to be over outside me as well. I hungered for complete release from him and return to a life worth living. It wasn't until hours later that my heart pounded and my palms sweated.

Sometimes it takes these kinds of moments to clarify the mind and fortify the heart. Later that evening, when I was alone, I realized something had broken free inside me and I wondered if my husband had sensed it, too.

The worm had begun to turn. It was my first glimmer of coming back.

Coming Back

As prey, we have been hounded, torn and violated. We have been used, twisted and held down. We have been poisoned with lies about what we are and what we will never be, do or have. We have had so much life force sucked out of us we can barely move. We have been clawed at and fed on, but somehow not quite unto death.

Then, someone came along and opened a window. We filled our lungs with fresh air and remembered. We gathered ourselves to ourselves and escaped. Knowing there would be more danger after leaving, we left anyway. We got out. We walked out alone to face a stark world not knowing where to go or what do.

Had we survived all that only to contend with circumstances over which we still had no control and face obstacles we no longer had the means to surmount?

Starting over is exhilarating, but it is also terrifying. We have been robbed of our love, our vigor, our confidence, our funds. Our purposes and careers and friendships have been profoundly interfered with. We have left our homes, our work, our everything. Our former resources, which we need now, are gone. It shows in our faces, it shows in our bank accounts.

Society at large does not know or care about what we have endured. We have lived through a personal tragedy. Now we must interact with the world to begin to rebuild our lives. And to do that, we must be actresses, for were we to disclose the depth of our woundedness, we might not secure that job or client, that car loan, that house lease and so forth.

Coming back is a labor of body, mind and spirit. The beginning is the most important part and it is the hardest part. The healing begins once you get away. It begins with purging and needs not to be rushed.

When your body begins to let down, you will be stunned at how much more of the trauma it held than you knew. You will sleep hard and long or not at all. You will come off the mattress through the night as the stress leaves your body. You will jump when someone touches your arm. You will gasp when anything moves close to you. You will drop things. You will walk into walls. You will stumble or fall down. You will laugh or cry too quickly. You will be quiet or need to talk. You will be hungry or have no appetite. You will feel feverish or chilled. You will feel weak or excited. You will be calm or nervous. You will be numb or hurt all over. You will feel fearful or fierce.

Whatever emotions run through will pass as you are able to feel safe.

In the fragile season of starting over, you will stop feeling afraid. Your heart will slow down and your hands will be still.

No one is in the next room about to go off on you. No one is going to lock you in or lock you out. No one is going to lie to you or sneer at you or rush you or rape you or hurt your children or your animals. No one is going to knock you around or mock you or yell at you or tell you what to do, feel or think.

Deep is calling unto deep.

Your self is coming back to you. You are becoming more, not less. You may pick up where you left off or you may change direction. Whatever follows, it will be bigger, because you are bigger.

One day it will dawn on you that you are coming back to life. Your hopes and dreams will reappear. Your purposes will renew and return to you. Your heart will be calm. Your mind will be clear. Your eyes will see and your ears will hear—and woe to anyone who tangles with you.

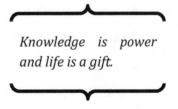

Knowledge is power and life is a gift.

Appendix A

Psychological Perspectives

Abusive individuals in general and psychopaths in particular put others at risk—a little or a lot. These highly aggressive social predators subject those around them to inevitable harm because they are:

- driven
- egotistical
- impersonal
- emotionally immature
- unempathic
- self centered
- without conscience
- progressively worse over time

They develop as one or more of the following:

- Abusers (animals, children, elders, spouses)
- Addicts (alcohol, drugs, food, gambling, sex)

- Pedophiles (hetero or homosexual)
- Serial sexual deviants (sadism, rape, bestiality)
- Serial torturers or murderers (animal, human)

Like addicts, abusers seek their fix. They have certain parameters about their drink or drug of choice. They're intent on getting their fix, but the source is not important; that is, it's not personal. Like pedophiles, abusers seek something they can use to gratify themselves. They have preferences about the object of their gratification, such as hair color or body build, but otherwise it's not personal. Like serial murderers, abusers seek something they can stalk, capture, play with and destroy. Again, they use physical or relational preferences to home in on their prey, but it's not personal.

The impersonal nature of the psychopath, regardless of the mask he wears, cannot be overemphasized. No matter how many long faces and (alligator) tears he gives you, the reality is that underneath all those attempts to play on your emotions is a cold-blooded, self-obsessed creature totally lacking in conscience and a danger to anyone in close proximity to him.

The psychopath seeks something—not someone—to use.

The Psychopathy Checklist

The following list is excerpted from Dr Robert Hare's massive 35-year study of the personality dynamics and operative indicators of psychopathic individuals. It was assembled from his observations and interactions with psychopaths in clinical settings, namely the Canadian prison system.

- Charm: The use of personality to be smooth, charming, slick. Not quiet or retiring. Not inclined to observe social conventions or use good manners.
- Delusions of grandeur: A grossly inflated view of personal ability and worth. Extremely self-assured and opinionated. An arrogant braggart.
- High need for stimulation: An enormous need for stimulation including risk-taking. Poor follow through, low self-discipline, bored quickly.
- Pathological lying: Moderate lying is shrewd, crafty, cunning and clever. Extreme lying is underhanded, unscrupulous, manipulative and dishonest.
- Conning, manipulativeness: The use of deceit to defraud for personal gain (as distinguished from ruthless deceit).
- Lack of guilt, remorselessness: A lack of feelings for the loss, pain and suffering of victims; unempathic, disdainful of and disgusted by victims.
- Shallowness: A limited emotional landscape, undeveloped interpersonal abilities, social coldness in spite of open gregariousness.
- Callousness, lack of empathy: A lack of feelings towards others in general, an attitude of coldness, contempt, lack of consideration and the absence of tact.
- Parasitic lifestyle: An intentional, manipulative, selfish and exploitative financial dependence. Lack of motivation, low self discipline and the inability to begin or complete responsibilities.
- Poor behavioral controls: Expressions of irritability, annoyance, threats, aggression and verbal abuse; inadequate control of temper; hasty reactions.
- Promiscuity: Brief, numerous, simultaneous, superficial sexual involvements. An indiscriminate

selection of partners; a history of sexual coercion or pride at discussing sexual exploits.

- Lack of realistic, long-term goals: An inability or persistent failure to develop and execute long-term plans; a nomadic existence; lacking direction and goals in life.

- Impulsiveness: Behaviors that lack planning; the inability to resist temptation, frustration and urges; a failure to deliberate about ideas and consider consequences; foolhardy, rash, unpredictable, erratic and reckless.

- Irresponsibility: Repeated failure to fulfill obligations such as paying bills; failure to honor contractual agreements such as doing competent work; failure to keep personal promises such as attending a birthday party.

- Lack of accountability: A low conscientiousness, an absence of dutifulness, antagonistic manipulation, denial and manipulation through lack of accountability and responsibility.

- Brief relationships: A lack of commitment to a long-term relationship reflected in inconsistent, undependable and unreliable commitments in life, including marital relationships.

- Juvenile delinquency: Behavior problems between the ages of 13-18; mostly behaviors that are crimes or clearly involve aspects of antagonism, exploitation, aggression, manipulation or a callous, ruthless tough-mindedness.

- Criminal versatility: A diversity of types of criminal offenses (regardless if arrested or convicted); taking great pride at getting away with crimes.

Not all abusers are substantially psychopathic or full-blown psychopaths, but the most dangerous are.

Psychopaths in Society

At this point in time, we have more than 200 years of serious, structured inquiry into psychopathy, yet the public seem to be either oblivious or resistant to looking at it. Why? My observation so far is that it is due to a sort of *hive-mind thought paralysis*—the unwillingness to consider new information with frightening implications. In the hive, one never thinks independently or changes one's mind. This happens for various reasons: some people are influenced by social engineering, some are heavily invested in being right, some are surface thinkers.

The moral insanity for which psychopaths are known is broadcast every night on the news, sensationalized in entertainment to the point that it is no longer shocking. Unless there is something that affects so many people it cannot be buried or spun, it doesn't register that millions of people are being damaged by human evil every day.

Why are so many people checked out? There's a physiological basis to it, but I think there's also a psychological and spiritual basis. Each of us has our belief system that we've patched together as we've lived. Some of us have questioned whether our beliefs are based on truth, but many have not. When something contradicts our view, the result is what psychologists call *cognitive dissonance,* a "disconnect" or non-sequitor between what we think we know and what we see. This is threatening on many levels. This shift in personal security is part of the experience of being victimized by a psychopath. It facilitates confusion and vulnerability, fear, insecurity and anxiety.

The reality of having psychopaths in society challenges fundamental questions about daily life. One response to this is that our psychological defenses kick in, ostensibly to protect us from the emotions we'd otherwise be feeling when we recognize the threat. This is where denial comes in. Denial is our most primitive psychological defense and it is part of the cause and effect interplay in pathological relationships. Denial plays a major role in the psychology of the abuser and denial is a natural reaction in the abused.

When we get overwhelmed, we shut down, like a computer that gets overloaded. This happens to the individual and to the group. What some of us do is deny what we're experiencing so we can stick to our story. This is a natural attempt to regain and maintain equilibrium so we can function. It is easier to deny than it is to face human evil. But, when it happens to you, the retreat into denial may not hold up against the hammering reality of living with a monster. Once denial crumbles, there is shut-down, fight or flight.

At some point, we decide to look at the conflicting evidence, the disparity between what we thought we were participating in and what we are actually doing. This takes enormous courage. And then, most of us get deeper into the quicksand of the psychopathic bond because we resort to our experience, logic, intuition, intelligence to try to find our way out. We don't yet realize that we are in a counter-intuitive realm. This is when a lot of people seek counsel from well-meaning but uninformed confidants and wind up getting advice that puts them in even more danger.

Many of us would do just about anything to defend our view. We don't want to be messed with. We're comfortable with how things are in our heads and we don't want to be burdened with having to consider something that could upset us or interfere with our way of going. And then it touches you—it happens to you or someone you love, you read an article or watch a movie and a door opens in your mind.

Some people respond to the truth about psychopathy with fear, which is understandable. Some react viscerally, like they've been punched in the stomach, some people back off and turn away. We each process information in our own way.

Whatever the reaction, the fact is that learning about psychopathy is like opening Pandora's Box. It's going to rattle some cages and rock some fundamental beliefs about the world we live in and the lives we can lead in it. We may have to face inconvenience, mocking, being misunderstood, feeling vulnerable, being helpless, even been shunned.

Psychopaths lash out for the most trivial reason or for no reason at all. Another hallmark is their predatory nature and high drive for gratification. Being in a position of authority or influence is helpful because it gives them access and influence. And this is why a high percentage of individuals in those positions turn out to be psychopathic.

Another hallmark of this form of brain damage is *delusion*. The psychopath that wears a white lab coat, a black robe, a uniform, a pin-striped suit, a badge, a stethoscope, etc., thinks he is successfully hiding his true nature from his victims. And for a while, he is. But his is a progressive disease and eventually he outs himself by losing control and going too far:

- The police maims a detainee
- The judge takes a bribe
- The doctor kills a patient
- The financial advisor ruins a client

Some experts say that abuse correlates to an inability to handle anxiety and stress. The dynamics of a police officer and a detainee are similar to that of an abusive husband and his wife. The detainee and the wife are not supposed to defend themselves or fight back, even when they are being brutalized while overpowered and restrained. For the detainee, this is the law; for the wife, this is the unspoken rule. Of course, police are not supposed to assault detainees and husbands are not supposed to assault their wives, but some do.

The Local Psychopath

Those at the beginning of their psychopathic "career" or at the low end of the socio-economic scale function in the world of brutality, carnality and petty crimes. Many of them operate on the fringe of society, not working or earning an adequate salary, living as parasites off family, friends and government.

If they have jobs, you'll find them in blood and guts factories (mortuaries, rest homes, clinics, hospitals, animal research labs, factory farms, training stables), child care, pornography, casinos, counseling, sanctuaries, classrooms, law offices and so forth where they can indulge themselves in the course of their normal duties, or after hours. A good number of these bullies and punks get caught or get taken out by the risks of their activities. Their victim count can be quite high. In a community, they may be recognized or not, despite their heinous activities. Their reach does not extend far.

The Global Psychopath

Those at the height of their powers who have ascended or been born into the upper socio-economic strata feed their derangement through atrocities and crimes of epic proportions. You'll find them in media, politics, education, multi-national business, global charities, entertainment, technology and finance.

Their big drivers are sex, money, power and the ability to unleash hell. The well-heeled psychopath may have vast resources of all kinds at his or her disposal. That coupled with the demonic energy also present in the insane megalomaniac gives them incredible scope—for a while. But as their derangement overtakes them, their activities are curtailed by exposure. Their victims can number in the millions and billions.

The remorselessness of psychopathic predation could be compared to the crocodile that patrols the shadows along rivers where migratory animals cross. He is a killing machine, there to fill his belly (gratify himself). He waits out of sight until he's in position to strike. The crocodile uses the camouflages of nature to hide his presence like the psychopath uses masks of social acceptability to gain access to his prey.

Unlike other mammalian predators that raise their young to thrive, the psychopath transmits to his offspring the life sentence of his disease. It is very much a family affair, whether the generational transmission is genetic, environmental or both.

The nature of their brain damage renders them incapable of higher emotions like love, empathy, compassion, altruism, loyalty, kindness, generosity, patience. They are equally incapable of deep feelings like contrition, broken heartedness, longing, guilt, shame, meekness, humility, embarrassment, mortification. They cannot create although they insinuate and install themselves into creative positions where other people do their work while they take the bows. They do not learn from their mistakes because their inner lives are not informed by access to the divine.

The psychopath is incapable of belief in or worship of anything other than himself. As such, he is cut off from contact with the Creator. He is his own god and the center of his own universe. He is wholly consumed with getting and taking. He does not play fair and he does not share. Nevertheless, he deigns to attend church and charitable events, coach little league or lead scouts because it gets him leverage. He enjoys playing the part and getting the goodies all the while sharpening his acting skills.

Over time, this quality is seen in how the psychopath talks about his life. The more sophisticated are adept at acting humble by saying things like, "You know, I really don't like to talk about myself" or "I was just lucky" when in fact, he likes nothing more than to talk about himself and take credit for everything. During the campaign/entrapment/positioning phase, he acts magnanimous, even giving credit to or sharing the spotlight with someone else. Mark this rare event because it won't last. It will vanish from view as soon as possible or be rewritten as needed for the next con. This is the story behind "gas-lighting" and "crazy-making" the psychopath uses to confuse those around him.

You can also observe his lack of access to higher nature and the self obsession it leads to by his egregious double standards and hypocrisy. Remember, he is better than everyone else, he is the people's champion or God's gift to women. He is entitled and above the law. He may routinely rape his woman, abuse his office and sneer at the damage he causes, but when he scratches his leg or is misquoted, he will carry on as if the world has ended. *Yes!* That's how small the inner landscape of the psychopath really is.

His spiritual emptiness and gross immorality are revealed over time as your discernment increases. If you have ever looked into the eyes of a psychopath up close, you have beheld the soulless.

So, how do we protect ourselves from them and maybe even rout them? Know this: the thing the psychopath fears most is being exposed. As long as no one knows what he is and how he operates, he has the upper hand. He is so inscrutable that people will never, ever figure him out, which enables him to keep doing what he lives to do: hunt, capture, torment and destroy.

That is why Bob told no one That we were separated... 5 yrs later he has yet to tell some people

416

His nature gets by undetected because it is "other" like colors and sounds that are beyond the normal range of sensory perception. The difference however, is that discerning them can be learned and honed, although that is the exception to people's typical response to an encounter with a predator. If they escape with their lives or fortunes, most people run and never look back. Once they're out of danger, they don't take the time to reflect and learn, and so they remain unwitting prey for another predator another day. This is why certain women have the misfortune of falling prey for a predator more than once.

It takes guts to look at this issue because it is straight out of the pits of hell. It takes guts to acquire the specialized knowledge that trumps this evil because it is counter-intuitive. It is a new way of thinking, but it conveys enormous personal power that can revolutionize relationships and revitalize lives.

Exposure leads to accountability, thwarting, justice, reprisal, loss of access, less gratification. Like any true predator, he knows this. When exposure looms, he removes himself. This can be seen in the mass resignations of international bankers and other charlatans of late.

The psychopath knows how to fake his way through nearly every interpersonal encounter. He knows how to channel his drive, impulsivity and parasitism so that it looks like ambition, passion and success to the undiscerning. He is all style and no substance. He can't stand up to honest inquiry or information he doesn't control. This is a key to sending him packing.

A monster in the throes of advanced psychopathy always gives himself away. The extent to which the demon betrays them will lead them to relocate, retire, retract or some such.

As more and more people waken to the reality of what psychopaths are, more and more psychopaths will be apprehended. They will be plucked off the streets and jerked out of office. If we're serious and have the courage of our convictions, they will also be removed from the planet. They are not just without conscience they are without the capacity to be benign or safe—they bring inevitable harm to every environment and relationship they enter.

It is possible to get these things out by *exposing* them. It is also possible to take steps to wrest a victim out of their maw. Once you're on to them, their game is over. The first step requires wide awareness. The next step happens automatically.

At core, the psychopath is a coward, so the more who are on to them, the better. There is strength in numbers and the numbers are on our side. The most constructive way to deal with trauma, personally and socially, is to address the difficulty and search for solutions.

We need the truth in order to heal.

Appendix B

Spiritual Perspectives

Deuteronomy 18 contains the proscription of practices; the basis of which was everyday knowledge to the ancients, but virtually unknown today: certain practices open the portal to demons and evil spirits.

Note: The word "abomination" is the strongest word of condemnation used in the entire Bible. It comes from the Hebrew word "Tow`ebah" (Strong's #08441, pronounced "to-ay-baw"). It means disgusting, unclean and wicked in the extreme.

> "There shall not be found among you any one that maketh his son or his daughter to pass through the fire, or that useth divination, or an observer of times, or an enchanter, or a witch, or a charmer, or a consulter with familiar spirits, or a wizard, or a necromancer."

Language changes over time, so some of these terms may not have clear meanings today:

7

- "pass through the fire"—Human-organ trafficking, medical procedures (especially cancer "treatments"), ritual murder, snuff films, abortion
- "useth divination"–Acquisition of useful knowledge with guidance from the spirit world
- "observer of times"–Modern astrology (Aries to Pisces) expresses the stars' influence over humanity is a counterfeit of Divine Cosmology (Virgo to Leo, Psalm 19) which shows God's influence

Essential Oils!

- "enchanter"–Supernatural spells delivered through organic material to manipulate actions and emotion (love potions)
- "witch"–Spell casting by gathering, magnifying and focusing psychic power to effect an outcome, earth worship
- "charmer"–Manipulation of inanimate objects or overtaking of animals and/or people through demonic influence
- "consulter with familiar spirits"–The gleaning of "knowledge" from spirits (demonic contact)
- "wizard"–The study and practice of magical arts for various purposes
- "necromancer"–Making contact with demonic spirits in the name of a dead person

Scriptural References to Demonics

Psalm 106:37

"They sacrificed their sons and their daughters to the **demons**."

James 4:7

"Submit yourselves therefore to God. Resist the **devil**, and he will flee from you."

Mark 5:1-20

"And when Jesus had stepped out of the boat, immediately there met him out of the tombs a man with an **unclean spirit**. He lived among the tombs. And no one could bind him anymore, not even with a chain, for he had often been bound with shackles and chains, but he wrenched the chains apart, and he broke the shackles in pieces. No one had the strength to subdue him. Night and day among the tombs and on the mountains he was always crying out and cutting himself with stones."

1 Peter 5:8

"Your adversary the **devil** prowls around like a roaring lion, seeking someone to devour."

Matthew 8:16

"That evening they brought to him many who were oppressed by **demons,** and he cast out the spirits with a word and healed all who were sick."

James 2:19

"You believe that God is one; you do well. Even the **demons** believe—and shudder!"

Luke 13:11

"And there was a woman who had had a **disabling spirit** for eighteen years. She was bent over and could not fully straighten herself."

Matthew 10:8

"Heal the sick, raise the dead, cleanse lepers, cast out **demons**."

Luke 11:24

"When the **unclean spirit** has gone out of a person, it passes through waterless places seeking rest, and finding none it says, 'I will return to my house from which I came.'"

Luke 9:1

"And he called the twelve together and gave them power and authority over all **demons** and to cure diseases."

Luke 8:2

"And also some women who had been healed of **evil spirits** and infirmities: Mary, called Magdalene, from whom seven **demons** had gone out."

Luke 4:33-36

"And in the synagogue there was a man who had the spirit of an unclean **demon**, and he cried out with a loud voice, "Ha! What have you to do with us, Jesus of Nazareth? Have you come to destroy us? I know who you are—the Holy One of God." But Jesus rebuked him, saying, "Be silent and come out of him!" And when the **demon** had thrown him down in their midst, he came out of him, having done him no harm. And they were all amazed and said to one another, "What is this word? For with authority and power he commands the **unclean spirits**, and they come out!"

Matthew 17:20

"And Jesus rebuked the **demon**, and it came out of him, and the boy was healed instantly."

Matthew 12:43-45

"When the **unclean spirit** has gone out of a person, it passes through waterless places seeking rest, but finds none. Then it says, 'I will return to my house from which I came.' And when it comes, it finds the house empty, swept, and put in order. Then it goes and brings with it **seven other spirits more evil** than itself, and they enter and dwell there, and the last state of that person is worse than the first. So also will it be with this evil generation."

Matthew 12:22

"Then a **demon**-oppressed man who was blind and mute was brought to him, and he healed him, so that the man spoke and saw."

Matthew 4:24

"So, his fame spread throughout all Syria, and they brought him all the sick, those afflicted with various diseases and pains, those oppressed by **demons**, epileptics, and paralytics, and He healed them."

Leviticus 17:7

"So they shall no more sacrifice their sacrifices to goat **demons**, after whom they whore."

Ephesians 6:10-18

"Put on the whole armor of God, that you may be able to stand against the schemes of the **devil**. For we do not wrestle against flesh and blood, but against the rulers, against the authorities, against the cosmic powers over this present darkness, against the **spiritual forces of evil** in the heavenly places."

Acts 19:13-16

"Then some of the itinerant Jewish exorcists undertook to invoke the name of the Lord Jesus over those who had **evil spirits**, saying, "I adjure you by the Jesus whom Paul proclaims." Seven sons of a Jewish high priest named Sceva were doing this. But the **evil spirit** answered them, "Jesus I know, and Paul I recognize, but who are you?" And the man in whom was the **evil spirit** leaped on them, mastered all of them and overpowered them, so that they fled out of that house naked and wounded."

Spiritual Abuse

Over 40 percent of women stay in toxic marriages because they meant their vows, don't adequately interpret scripture and/or don't understand what a covenant agreement means. Follwoing are three of the most widely misconstrued verses, their most common misinterpretation and their correct meaning in the context of the entire Bible using the principle of double witnesses. Most misinterpretations occur because scripture is taken out of context and/or applied in the lowest or narrowest sense.

Malachi 2:14-16

"Yet you say, 'For what reason?' Because the Lord has been a witness between you and the wife of your youth, against whom you have dealt treacherously, though she is your companion and your wife by covenant. But not one has done so who has a remnant of the Spirit. And what did that one do while he was seeking a godly offspring? Take heed then to your spirit, and let no one deal treacherously against the wife of your youth. For I hate divorce," says the Lord, the God of Israel, "and him who covers his garment with wrong," says the Lord of hosts. "So take heed to your spirit, that you do not deal treacherously."

MISINTERPRETATION

The abuser blames the woman for leaving or withdrawing (which she does because of the abuse) which allows him to deny his behavior and avoid accountability.

CORRECTION

The man is to treat his wife at least as well as he treats himself. When abuse is committed, whether before or after the marriage ceremony, it breaks the union by destroying the sanctity (sanctuary) of marriage. A covenant must be upheld by both parties fulfilling their respective responsibilities—it is not valid as a one-sided agreement.

Genesis 2:18, 21-22

"And the LORD God said, 'It is not good that the man should be alone; I will make an helpmeet for him. And the LORD God caused a deep sleep to fall upon Adam, and he slept: and He took one of his ribs, and closed up the flesh instead thereof; And the rib, which the LORD God had taken from man, made He a woman, and brought her unto the man."

MISINTERPRETATION

The woman is made for and belongs to the man in the poorest sense. All benefits of the marriage accrue to the man and to the man only. The man possesses the privileges of ownership without any of the responsibilities. The woman is chattel only and may be treated as her owner sees fit. Her happiness and welfare do not matter to the man who feels entitled to use her in any way he pleases as long as he can get away with it.

CORRECTION

Man and woman were made to fit together in the highest and most profound sense. They have the capacity to complete each other and bring fullness to each other. Man is to acknowledge the woman's needs and feelings and treat her as a created being, a final creation and worth of love, respect and protection.

Ephesians 5:21-33

"Submitting yourselves one to another in the fear of God. Wives, submit yourselves unto your own husbands, as unto the Lord. For the husband is the head of the wife, even as Christ is the head of the church: and He is the saviour of the body. Therefore as the church is subject unto Christ, so let the wives be to their own husbands in every thing. Husbands, love your wives, even as Christ also loved the church, and gave Himself for it; That He might sanctify and cleanse it with the washing of water by the word, That He might present it to himself a glorious church, not having spot, or wrinkle, or any such thing; but that it should be holy and without blemish. So ought men to love their wives as their own bodies. He that loveth his wife loveth himself. For no man ever yet hated his own flesh; but nourisheth and cherisheth it, even as the Lord the church: For we are members of His body, of His flesh, and of His bones. For this cause shall a man leave his father and mother, and shall be joined unto his wife, and they two shall be one flesh."

MISINTERPRETATION

Woman is the property of and subordinate to man; he is therefore free to do with her as he pleases without limitation and with God's blessing.

CORRECTION

Man is to love his wife; woman is to respect her husband, sacrificially if circumstances warrant. The man's and the woman's actions should be such that they seed the emotions their spouse is to feel and nourish them consistently. The love with which Christ treated the church is the model for the husband's love of his wife. The man is to express love for his wife in thought, word and deed. The woman is to show respect for her husband by ongoing consideration of him.

Some of the foregoing material was drawn from a workshop for clergy "Ending Silence in Our Congregations" prepared and presented by Cheyenne Regional Medical Center in Wyoming and Shalom Bayit in California.

Appendix C

Identifying Abuse

Does your partner:

1. Accept it when you say "no"? no
2. Keep his promises and stay true to his word? no
3. Take responsibility for his behavior? no
4. Have good friends or just acquaintances?
5. Have authentic relationships with his parents and children? no
6. Control your access to funds, and if so, to what extent? yes!.
7. Exhibit callousness towards the suffering of others?
8. Attack what you hold most dear?
9. Try to isolate you from your family and friends? yes
10. Seem a little too good to be true at first?

11. Speak ill of others behind their backs? *[handwritten]*

12. Interfere with your work or social life? *[handwritten]*

13. Criticize your character instead of your behavior?

14. Blame you for deficiencies in the relationship? *[handwritten]*

15. Force you to have sex?

16. Try to pick out your clothes?

17. **Tell you how to be and act?**

18. Operate with double standards yet deny it? *[handwritten]*

19. Manipulate situations to gain the upper hand? *[handwritten]*

20. Blow up for little or no cause? *[handwritten]*

21. Act fake or overly friendly in social situations? *[handwritten: acts differently]*

22. Threaten to abandon you?

23. Restrict your access to communication with the outside world (computer, phone, vehicle)? *[handwritten: yes]*

24. Endanger you and others with his driving? *[handwritten: yes]*

25. Seem amused by seeing others hurt or demeaned?

26. Rewrite history to justify his behavior? *[handwritten: yes]*

27. Withhold important information from you? *[handwritten: yes]*

You are with a toxic partner if you answered "no" to any of the first five questions and "yes" to any of the remaining 22.

A Checklist for Change

Once you see that your partner's "caring" is doing damage to you and your life, you have an opportunity to consider if this is what you want to live with. Once you understand that one or more behaviors have crossed the line and become toxic, the next questions might be:

- Are you willing to settle for the relationship in its present form? *no*

- Are you aware that it may get worse over time? *yes*

- Do you want to work on the relationship?
  not *~~~~~~~~~~~~~~~*

- Does he want to work on his unhealthy behaviors? *no*

- Can he relate without being controlling and abusive? *no*

Before you answer any of these, remember that this is where the rubber meets the road. This is where the all-important distinction between the two broad categories of unhealthy partners comes into play. If your goal is to be in a healthy relationship, you need to determine if your partner's behavioral patterns are expressions of an emotional disturbance or brain damage.

Keep in mind the cyclical nature of abusive relationships (the escalation cycle) as well as the possibility of brain damage as you review the following list. These guidelines are sourced from THE VERBALLY ABUSIVE MAN—CAN HE CHANGE? by Patricia Evans, PhD.

The perpetrator of relationship violence will not change if he:

•   has little or no financial investment in the relationship (he has nothing to lose if/when the relationship ends). *A man that is saving for financial reason to not living in the hotel.*

•   engages in behaviors that keep him from being alone and having to face himself (alcohol, drugs, gambling). *works a lot, School*

•   has a history of damaging, deceptive, parasitical behavior (anger, lying, withholding, stalking, immorality, stealing, betraying).

•   has no friends or emotional connections despite giving the appearance of being gregarious (he may act too friendly with acquaintances).

•   shows indifference or malice towards animals or children (he is cruel, neglectful or disrespectful towards subordinates).

•   was verbally abusive before marriage (lost his temper, used foul language, blamed others, exhibited lack of loyalty and respect).

The more of these characteristics and behaviors your partner possesses or engages in, the less likely it is that he has the capacity or the willingness to change.

These two checklists are for informational purposes only and not intended to be interpreted as the final word on any relationship.

A Counseling Caveat

It's important to get guidance only from individuals who have been trained and have experience in abuse.. Do not risk your life or waste your time and money with an advisor who does not grasp the principles of toxic interpersonal relationships. Many lives have been lost or further harmed by well-intentioned but wrong advice from well-meaning, but uninformed family, friends, co-workers, teachers, ministers, etc.

The best place to get referrals to therapists, attorneys, physicians for help with relationship violence is your local women's shelter. Most shelters also offer free or sliding-scale counseling. If after reading this book, you do not know if what you're contending with is abuse, they can help you understand the distinctions between difficult and dangerous. If your town does not have a shelter, contact the national hotline for help locating the resources you need. You can reach them online at www.thehotline.org and by phone at 800-799-7233.

Recognizing the Abused

Once you understand the agenda at work in toxic relationships, you will be better able to recognize the signs of abuse when you see or experience them, and when you have some foreknowledge of the affected person, all the more so. These are typical signs that someone is in trouble.

- Isolation by financial, geographic, social means
- Age-inappropriate behavior such as role reversal (an adult acting like a child and vice versa)
- Peculiar acts of doting by abuser in public
- Defensive wounds to hands and arms
- Assaultive wounds to face, neck, torso, genitals
- Nervousness, over-reaction to surprise stimuli
- Persistent digestive upsets, headaches
- Uncharacteristic change in overall health
- Onset of binging, purging, anorexia
- Significant change of appearance and/or hygiene
- Signs of exhaustion/fatigue/lack of sleep *- me*
- Attempts to be unattractive
- Unusual revulsion of anything related to sexuality
- Radical mood swings
- Not wanting to be home or go home
- Nightmares, insomnia, sleepwalking and other sleep disturbances
- Pressure to excel or over achieve at home and work
- Depression, crying episodes, etc.
- Substance abuse/addiction
- Sense of doom and futility
- Trance-like demeanor
- Feelings of being damaged and damned
- Anxiety around and fear of partner
- Overly accommodating or compliant behavior

- Intense desire for encouragement
- Suicidal thinking, which could lead to attempts
- Self-loathing
- Memory loss or confused memory
- Loss of sense of direction
- Fear of the unknown
- Difficulty concentrating and following through
- Appearing spaced out or in another world
- Excessively worried or withdrawn
- Lack of enthusiasm, interest

Consequences of Abuse

Relationship violence leads to all kinds of outcomes, most adverse. The following list shows the most common; some are the direct result of physical violence, some demonstrate the impact of chronic stress on mind and body:

- Premature aging
- Gynecological disorders
- Fertility issues
- Pregnancy problems (low birth weight, peri-natal death)
- Central nervous system disorders
- Gastrointestinal disorders
- Heart or circulatory conditions
- Depression and anxiety
- A-social behavior (wanting to be alone)
- Suicidal thinking and behaviors

- Lack of confidence and purpose
- Unwillingness to trust
- Fear of intimacy
- Emotional detachment
- Sleep disturbances
- Flashbacks (PTSD)

The leading cause of substance abuse in women is the attempt to self medicate while in the relationship and/or after escape. Partner abuse is associated with several unhealthy behaviors that demonstrate inadequate self image and other psychological wounds of abuse.

- Unprotected sex (irresponsibility, self sabotage)
- Indiscriminate sex (emptiness, self harm)
- Smoking (low self esteem)
- Substance abuse (despair, loneliness)
- Driving under the influence (frustration, death wish)
- Poor food choices (lack of discipline, malnutrition)
- Under/over eating (anorexia, bulimia)

References

Breiding MJ, Black MC, Ryan GW. 2008. CHRONIC DISEASE AND HEALTH RISK BEHAVIORS ASSOCIATED WITH INTIMATE PARTNER VIOLENCE—18 U.S. states/territories, 2005. Ann Epidemiol 18:538–544.

Coker AL, Davis KE, Arias I, Desai S, Sanderson M, Brandt HM, et al. 2002. PHYSICAL AND MENTAL HEALTH EFFECTS OF INTIMATE PARTNER VIOLENCE FOR MEN AND WOMEN. Am J Prev Med 23(4):260–268.

Crofford LJ. VIOLENCE, STRESS AND SOMATIC SYNDROMES. 2007. Trauma Violence Abuse 8:299–313.

Department of Justice. INTIMATE PARTNER VIOLENCE. http://bjs.ojp.usdoj.gov/index.cfm?ty=tp&tid=971#summary

Heise L, Garcia-Moreno C. 2002. VIOLENCE BY INTIMATE PARTNERS. In: Krug E, Dahlberg LL, Mercy JA, et al., editors. World Report On Violence And Health. Geneva (Switzerland): World Health Organization. p. 87–121.

Leserman J, Drossman DA. 2007. RELATIONSHIP OF ABUSE HISTORY TO FUNCTIONAL GASTROINTESTINAL DISORDERS AND SYMPTOMS. Trauma Violence Abuse 8:331–343.

Plichta SB. 2004. INTIMATE PARTNER VIOLENCE AND PHYSICAL HEALTH CONSEQUENCES: POLICY AND PRACTICE IMPLICATIONS. J Interpers Violence 19(11):1296–1323.

Roberts TA, Auinger P, Klein JD. 2005. INTIMATE PARTNER ABUSE AND THE REPRODUCTIVE HEALTH OF SEXUALLY ACTIVE FEMALE ADOLESCENTS. J Adolesc Health 36(5):380–385.

Silverman JG, Raj A, Mucci L, Hathaway J. 2001. DATING VIOLENCE AGAINST ADOLESCENT GIRLS AND ASSOCIATED SUBSTANCE USE, UNHEALTHY WEIGHT CONTROL, SEXUAL RISK BEHAVIOR, PREGNANCY, AND SUICIDALITY. JAMA 286(5):572–579.

Tjaden P, Thoennes N. EXTENT, NATURE AND CONSEQUENCES OF INTIMATE PARTNER VIOLENCE: Findings From The National Violence Against Women Survey. Washington (DC): Department of Justice (US); 2000. Publication No. NCJ 181867. http://ojp.usdoj.gov/nij/pubs-sum/181867.htm

Appendix D

Books

VERBAL ABUSE—HOW TO RECOGNIZE IT AND RESPOND
THE VERBALLY ABUSIVE MAN—CAN HE CHANGE?
by Patricia Evans, PhD

WHY DOES HE DO THAT? INSIDE THE MINDS OF ANGRY
AND CONTROLLING MEN
by Lundy Bancroft

NO VISIBLE WOUNDS—IDENTIFYING THE NON-PHYSICAL
ABUSE OF WOMEN BY THEIR MEN
by Mary Susan Miller, PhD

THE GIFT OF FEAR—SURVIVAL SIGNALS THAT PROTECT
US FROM VIOLENCE
by Gavin de Becker

MEN WHO HATE WOMEN AND THE WOMEN WHO LOVE
THEM
EMOTIONAL BLACKMAIL
by Susan Forward, PhD

I CAN'T GET OVER IT—A HANDBOOK FOR TRAUMA
SURVIVORS
TRUST AFTER TRAUMA—A GUIDE TO RELATIONSHIPS

by Aphrodite Matsakis, PhD

WOMEN WHO LOVE PSYCHOPATHS, INSIDE
RELATIONSHIPS OF INEVITABLE HARM
HOW TO SPOT A DANGEROUS MAN BEFORE YOU GET
INVOLVED
by Sandra Brown, MA

THE SOCIOPATH NEXT DOOR
THE MYTH OF SANITY: DIVIDED CONSCIOUSNESS AND
THE PROMISE OF AWARENESS
by Martha Stout, PhD

WITHOUT CONSCIENCE—THE DISTURBING WORLD OF
PSYCHOPATHS AMONG US
SNAKES IN SUITS—WHEN PSYCHOPATHS GO TO WORK
by Paul Babiak, PhD and Robert Hare, PhD

MALTREATED CHILDREN—EXPERIENCE, BRAIN
DEVELOPMENT AND THE NEXT GENERATION
THE NEUROSEQUENTIAL MODEL OF THERAPEUTICS
SELF REGULATION—THINK BEFORE YOU ACT
by Bruce Perry, MD, PhD

WHEN LOVE GOES WRONG
by Ann Jones and Susan Schechter

TRAUMA AND RECOVERY—THE AFTERMATH OF
VIOLENCE FROM DOMESTIC ABUSE TO POLITICAL
TERROR
by Judith Herman

LIFE CODES
by Philip C McGraw, PhD

BUT HE'LL CHANGE—THE THINKING THAT KEEPS YOU
IN AN ABUSIVE RELATIONSHIP
by Joanna V Hunter

DARK SOULS
by Sarah Strudwick

NOT TO PEOPLE LIKE US
by Sarah Weitzman

DANGEROUS LIAISONS
by Claudia Moscovici

LOVEFRAUD
by Donna Andersen

A DANCE WITH THE DEVIL—Marriage to a Psychopath
by Barbara Bentley

IT'S MY LIFE NOW—Starting Over After An Abusive
Relationship
by Meg Kennedy Dugan and Roger Hock

IN LOVE AND DANGER—A Teen's Guide to Breaking Free
of Abusive Relationships
by Barrie Levy

Appendix E

From a Social Worker

I have worked for a Domestic Violence program for 14 years. I have talked to hundreds of women and heard thousands of stories of abuse and over the years I've seen three things common to every case. The first is the horrible experience they have lived through. The second is the controlling agenda their men seek to impose on them. The third is the body of red flags they didn't see early on. Abuse victims get conned, manipulated and tricked by men who are very good at what they do. These men act very charming in the beginning—*and then they change.*

It's only been in the last 30 years that this subject has been researched and studied seriously. Many people still do not know much about it even though it now affects over 30 percent of the population.

What happens in abuse is the opposite of what a woman expects when she enters a relationship. Instead of love, respect and trust, she becomes trapped in a world of deceit and cruelty. In nearly every case, the woman is bewildered because logic and intuition do not help her understand what her partner is doing to her. When she tries to communicate with him, her appeals to fairness and reason fall on deaf ears, leaving her to think she is crazy. I cannot count how many times I've heard a woman say "He exhibited so many red flags in the first several weeks that, if I had known what I was looking at, I would have run far, far away."

Some women are able to extricate themselves quickly, some not so quickly, some never. I have hope. I could not have continued doing this work for so long if I did not. I have heard many of my clients say "Now that I have this knowledge, I will never let this happen to me again and I will never let this happen to my daughters."

Education is prevention. Women need this information. Young girls need it too, so they can learn to recognize red flags, and use that discernment to seek happy, healthy relationships. I don't see any other way to cure this plague in our society. The reality is that if society continues to ignore this problem, it will escalate because that is the nature of the thing. Education is the key to real change. This book is an excellent resource and I am glad to have been a part of Anna's journey.

Stephanie Capps, MSW
Jackson Hole

Acknowledgments

Many people upheld me and safeguarded my animals in the aftermath of my marriage. I thank them with all my heart:

Mary, Suzanne, Joyce and Tom, Don, Shelley and Jerry, Tammy and John, Doris, Nancy, Aimee, Joan, Stephanie, Jane, Denise, Kay, Frank, Coralie, Norma C and Pat.

I thank the Community Safety Network of Jackson Hole, and I thank God for delivering me from evil.

Questions for Discussion

1. What is the "other cancer" and why is it called that?

2. What are the characteristics of the two broad categories of perpetrators?

3. What are the characteristics of the two broad categories of recipients?

4. Why is domestic violence the fastest growing social plague on earth?

5. In what households does family violence (spousal battery, child abuse, animal torture) occur twice as often? Why?

6. Why does it get so little meaningful media attention?

7. What is the difference between an argument and verbal abuse?

8. Why is it important to see how a man handles frustration?

9. How does a predator select his prey?

10. Why does a predator camouflage his presence and his true nature?

11. What roles do surveillance and monitoring play in pathological relationships?

12. How can you tell if you might be vulnerable to a predator?

13. What is self image?

14. What role does it play in abusive relationships?

15. What is love hunger?

16. What role does it play in society?

17. How do you tell the difference between difficult and dangerous?

18. What are the first three warning signs of entrapment?

19. What role do hormones play in entrapment?

20. How do perpetrators use money in an abusive relationship?

21. What is a white-out pre-nup?

22. What role does sex play in a dysfunctional relationship?

23. What is neuroplasticity and how does it work?

24. What is the connection between substance abuse and domestic violence?

25. What is the "generationally-transmitted disease"?

26. What affect does violence in the home have on children?

27. What does bed-wetting indicate?

28. How many children see their mother abused each year?

29. In what percentage of homes are animals routinely neglected, abused, killed?

30. Why is animal torture a significant hallmark?

31. What did 99 percent of murderers and serial murderers do as children? Why?

32. What does bestiality signal?

33. What is the first mistake women make when getting to know a new man?

34. Do restraining orders work? Why or why not?

35. What is the difference between emotional baggage and brain damage?

36. What is psychopathy?

37. How does it differ from possession?

38. Why is the psychopath "other"?

39. What is the root cause of psychopathy?

40. What five ways does psychopathy express itself?

41. Why is psychopathy progressive?

42. What is chemical psychopathy?

43. Where are you most likely to find psychopaths in society?

44. Why does abuse increase exponentially?

45. What does it mean to have psychopaths loose in society?

46. How do the media and social engineers facilitate the spread of domestic violence?

47. What does pornography and media violence do to the brain?

48. Where is the best place to go for legal, medical and psychological referrals?

49. What is a police stand-by?

50. What do perpetrators most want to avoid?

Fill-in-the-Blanks

51. In the name of love, he steps in to _____ you with this or that. And this is how he begins to get _____ over your life—your lifestyle, routines, thoughts and emotions. First, he _____ you.

52. He tells you what you can _____ and cannot _____.

53. And always, an incomprehensible _____ lurks under the surface threatening to attack if you don't surrender.

54. He _____ you for principles you hold he does not support.

55. In time, you find that, like a _____, he _____ you for his own behavior.

56. What he can't accomplish through _____ and deceit, he gets done through the wearing-down process of unrelenting and precisely targeted _____.

57. You exist to please and _____ him. In his eyes, the _____ you no longer exists or matters. You have been _____. He is only reminded of the real you when you try to _____ yourself.

58. What he doesn't see doesn't matter; and he doesn't see anything about himself that doesn't _____ him. He can and will do anything to get what he wants and justify it later.

59. _____ gives him freedom to do as he pleases with you; no one to hear, no one to _____.

60. He _____ for all kinds of reasons, but mostly he _____ to control you.

61. _____ is an insidious behavior that, like denying and lying, works cumulatively to _____ you and empower him. It chips away at your _____ by making light of your experiences and disrespecting your _____.

62. He feeds on _____ and his appetite for entertainment is _____.

63. He openly operates with ____ _____ because he utterly fails to recognize them as such.

64. Directly or indirectly, he may seek to control your access to _____ or anything else that could help or empower you.

65. He _____ himself at your expense in private and in public. _____ is his hobby.

66. _____ vulnerability is a situation he knows how to exploit and leverage powerfully. He looks for it.

67. One of the wages of his lifelong use and abuse of women is his inability to give and receive _____.

68. On top of your emotional, mental and spiritual exhaustion, the steady buildup of ____ deprivation ages and exhausts you physically.

69. He is in a huge _____ to get the relationship nailed down. You mistake this for love.

70. He knows precisely how to _____ information so that you draw the conclusion that serves him. He does this because he knows you'll give him the _____ of the doubt.

71. His first reaction to the slightest infraction is ____, fury, rage. It's a shock to witness. His ____ is out of all proportion to the present reality.

72. At first, his _____ may appear as extraordinary disciplines or high passions. Later, they reveal themselves to be weapons of coercion that he uses against you.

73. He is self centered, but not self ____.

74. Whatever he may have promised you, he is quick to take away. In this way, his _____ can be cruelly employed.

75. He is a ____ in an adult's body. His devices and maladjustments are the adult manipulations of a child's _____.

76. He is uninterested in other people's _____ and personhood. He shows no _____ or empathy for others because he feels none.

77. He is an accomplished ____ and an expert deceiver. If you don't look for the dichotomy between his ____ side and his _____ side, you won't see his true colors until it is too late.

78. One pitfall you face in dealing with alcohol is getting distracted by his _____ rather than deciding what to do to protect yourself. Another pitfall is using alcohol yourself as a means of ____ and self medicating.

79. He leverages your affection for your _____ every way he can to weaken you. He is indifferent to the physical abuse he visits on them and the mental abuse he visits on you. You and your _____ will suffer in ways that violate the dignity of life.

80. Later, he may abuse or neglect your _____. He may mistreat them in front of you, but more likely he will do it when you're not around. He likely uses techniques that do not leave a mark, like _____ or suffocation.

81. He greets people the ___ way, usually with a hearty handshake and a show of ___-friendliness. He may even use the exact ___ gestures and words with every person.

82. You realize it is really a sense of _____ born of selfishness. And you see it is out of all _____ to reason and reality.

83. Abuse gets ___ qualitatively and quantitatively over time. You learn to walk on _____.

84. A broken bone heals far quicker than a broken ____.

85. What you find is once he has you, he won't take "___" for an answer. This should tell you two things: he cares only about getting what he ___ and he does not see you as something that matters.

86. This type of man has the uncanny ability to find and attract women who fall under his ___. He is especially adept at dispelling the ____ that the kind of woman he seeks is sure to have.

87. It is the 21st century and your ___ have been removed. Once your _____ were gone, he took you over like a warlord.

88. People sometimes do in traffic what they would never do face-to-face. ___ ___ is a dangerous and extremely hostile set of learned behaviors.

89. ___ have been slowly introduced, one subtle change after another over time—like a political takeover—requested with reason and a smile, urged with propaganda and finally delivered with a threat.

"Listen to the whispers so you won't have to hear the screams."

Cherokee Saying

About the Red Flags Books

These books are offered in the knowledge that specialized understanding is crucial in crisis, but only available when acquired in advance. They are each designed to help:

- Train your mind for the most complex challenge you'll ever face: the charismatic con of a social predator
- Impart understanding of the predator's mindset and the dangerous deceits he brings to the game
- Decode the dynamics of the con of a pathological relationship from beginning to end
- Describe how the extreme stress of an intimate con affects your mind and body
- Show how to focus awareness and preparation to protect yourself and control your response
- Reveal the day-to-day realities of being trapped in a psychopathic bond and how to survive it until escape
- Explain how natural, intuitive but uninformed responses can increase danger
- Examine what can happen after escape, including the escalation of threat from the ex-partner

... so you can live your life in peace and share your gifts with a world that needs them.

The Red Flags Books (2008-2015)

The Relationship Literacy Series:

1. RELATIONSHIP RED FLAGS
2. THE RED FLAGS WORKBOOK
3. PREVAILING

The Red Flags Series:

1. READ HIM
2. YOUR PAIN, HIS GAIN
3. TOO GOOD TO BE TRUE
4. PSYCHO OR POSSESSED
5. YOUR MOMENT

THE MONSTER OF JACKSON HOLE

One Last Thing

If this book has helped you, please consider posting a review on Amazon or otherwise letting some people know about it. If it turns out to make a difference in their lives, they'll be forever grateful to you, as will I.

"For all your days prepare and meet them ever alike: when you are the anvil, bear and when you are the hammer, *strike!*"

Edwin Markham

About The Author

Author Anna Moss draws on several disciplines to write about relationship. She lives in the mountains of the great American west with her surviving animals. Connect with her at http://relationshipredflags.com and http://facebook.com/relationshipredflags

3/26/18

My sleep is being interrupted again.
Last night I woke up around 2:00
I heard what sounded like an
alarm. Then my calf throbbed
and pulsed w/ a slight pain.
The night before I woke up to
the beep. I fell back asleep
after resting a long while.

Last week I spoke to Patricia
Jones at Doe counseling — Phone
Consult. She said 'Bob is a
psychopath'. 'You're dealing with a
psychopath'. I also saw two
attorneys about divorce. I ordered
two books on abuse. This book
is one of them. The other book
cost $70.00 (out of print.)
The week before I had an appointment
w/ an attorney about divorce and
have spoken to many attorneys in
the last two weeks.

CPSIA information can be obtained
at www.ICGtesting.com
Printed in the USA
BVHW03s1808150318
510688BV00001B/147/P